The Ultimate

No Grid Survival
Projects Bible

Everything You Need to Thrive Off the Grid

TALON WAVERLY

Table of Contents

Introduction - Welcome to Self-Reliance

Imagine a world where you're no longer dependent on the conveniences of modern society—electricity at the flip of a switch, clean water from the tap, and food readily available at the nearest grocery store. Now, picture that same world, but instead of feeling vulnerable, you're prepared, capable, and fully self-reliant. This is the world of no-grid or off-grid living, a lifestyle choice that provides not only independence but also resilience in the face of uncertainty.

In today's rapidly changing environment, the importance of preparedness cannot be overstated. Whether you're driven by a desire to reduce your environmental impact, escape the stress of urban life, or be ready for whatever the future holds, more and more people are turning to off-grid living as a viable solution. The appeal of being self-reliant is growing, and with it, the realization that this way of life is not only possible but immensely rewarding.

But self-reliance isn't a new concept; it's a practice deeply embedded in human history, especially during times of crisis. Throughout history, communities and individuals have had to rely on their ingenuity, resourcefulness, and determination to survive and thrive in the face of adversity. By examining real-life examples, we can better understand the vital importance of self-reliance and the lessons it holds for us today.

Learning from History: The Power of Self-Reliance

Case Study 1: The Great Depression (1929-1939)

One of the most poignant examples of self-reliance in recent history occurred during the Great Depression. As the economic collapse spread across the United States and beyond, millions of people found themselves out of work, out of money, and struggling to provide for their families. With the safety nets of modern welfare and social services either nonexistent or severely limited, many had to turn back to the land and their own abilities to survive.

During this period, urban dwellers transformed vacant lots into "victory gardens", growing vegetables to supplement their meager food supplies. Rural families, already familiar with self-sufficient practices, increased their efforts to can, preserve, and store food for the winter months. Bartering became a common practice, with people exchanging skills and goods in lieu of cash. This era also saw a resurgence in home-based skills like sewing, mending, and making do with what was available.

The Great Depression taught a generation the importance of self-reliance, not just as a means of survival but as a way of reclaiming dignity and independence in the face of hardship. The lessons learned during this time laid the groundwork for the homesteading movement that would reemerge in later decades.

Case Study 2: The Cuban "Special Period" (1991-2000)

A more recent example comes from Cuba during the "Special Period" in the early 1990s. Following the collapse of the Soviet Union, Cuba lost its primary source of economic support, leading to severe shortages in food, fuel, and other essential goods. Faced with an economic crisis, the Cuban people had to innovate quickly to survive.

Urban agriculture became a necessity, with citizens converting rooftops, vacant lots, and even public parks into gardens. The government encouraged this shift by providing education on organic farming methods and distributing seeds and tools. Despite the hardships, Cuba became a model for sustainable, localized agriculture, with urban farms providing a significant portion of the food supply in cities like Havana.

This period also forced Cubans to rethink their energy consumption. With oil imports drastically reduced, they turned to alternative energy sources, such as solar power and biofuels. The Cuban experience during the Special Period highlights the importance of adaptability and resourcefulness, showing that even in the face of severe constraints, a community can pull together to create a more sustainable, self-reliant way of life.

Case Study 3: The Israeli Kibbutz Movement

The Israeli Kibbutz movement offers another fascinating example of self-reliance in action. Starting in the early 20th century, groups of Jewish settlers established collective communities, or kibbutzim, based on principles of communal living, agriculture, and self-sufficiency. In the harsh, arid lands of pre-state Israel, these communities had to innovate to survive, developing advanced irrigation techniques, including drip irrigation, which is now used worldwide.

The kibbutzim were entirely self-reliant, producing their own food, generating power, and even manufacturing goods for trade. Over time, they became economic powerhouses, contributing significantly to the development of Israel. While many kibbutzim have since modernized and integrated into the broader economy, their legacy of self-reliance, cooperation, and resilience remains a powerful example of what can be achieved when a community works together with a shared purpose.

Case Study 4: The COVID-19 Pandemic (2020-Present)

In more recent history, the COVID-19 pandemic has reminded us of the vulnerabilities inherent in modern society. The sudden, widespread impact of the virus led to global disruptions in supply chains, food shortages, and overwhelmed healthcare systems. The pandemic underscored the importance of being prepared for emergencies and the value of self-sufficiency. From home gardening to off-grid power solutions, many rediscovered the importance of sustainability and resilience, with off-grid living emerging as a viable long-term option.

These historical examples illustrate that self-reliance is not just a concept but a proven survival strategy that has enabled people to thrive in adversity. Drawing inspiration from these real-life cases, we can better understand the importance of preparedness and self-sufficiency in our lives.

How to Use This Book

This book includes several DIY projects, but before diving into them it's important to understand how this book is structured and how to get the most out of it. Every chapter focuses on a specific aspect of off-grid living, from setting up your base camp to ensuring you have reliable power, water, and security. The projects within each chapter are designed to be straightforward, with step-by-step instructions guiding you from start to finish.

Understanding the $ and ★ Rating System

To help you assess the feasibility of each project, I've implemented a simple rating system:

- **Cost Rating ($):** Projects are rated on a scale from $ to $$$$$, where $ represents low-cost projects that require minimal investment, and $$$$$ indicates more expensive endeavors. This allows you to prioritize projects based on your budget.
- **Difficulty Rating (★):** Projects in this book are rated on a scale from ★ to ★★★★★ to help you assess the level of effort and skill required before starting. A ★ rating indicates a project that is easy and suitable for beginners, while a ★★★★★ rating is reserved for more complex projects that may require advanced skills or additional tools.

It's important to note that difficulty is a relative parameter — what might be challenging for one person could be straightforward for another, depending on their experience and skill level. However, as a general guideline, projects rated ★★★ and above typically require more specialized skills, a greater time commitment or the support of another person. For instance, digging a well or installing a comprehensive solar power system might necessitate technical knowledge, physical endurance, or teamwork.

Understanding this can help you better plan your approach, ensuring that you're prepared with the necessary skills or assistance to successfully complete each project.

Tips for Planning and Prioritizing Projects

As you explore the various projects, consider your personal needs and circumstances. Not all projects have to be completed at once. Some may be essential for your off-grid setup, while others can be tackled later as you expand your capabilities. Start with the basics then move on to more complex systems like power generation and food production.

Safety Considerations and Necessary Tools

Off-grid projects often involve the use of tools and materials that can be hazardous if not handled properly. Before beginning any project, it's essential to familiarize yourself with basic safety protocols. Always wear appropriate protective gear, such as goggles, gloves and reliable footwear. Make sure you understand how to use each tool correctly, and never rush through a task—taking your time can prevent accidents.

Throughout the book, you'll find a list of tools required for each project. While some projects only need basic hand tools, others might require more specialized equipment. Where possible, I've kept the tool requirements simple and affordable, so you won't need to invest in expensive machinery to get started. If you do need a specialized tool, consider renting or borrowing it rather than purchasing outright, especially if it's something you won't use frequently.

Understanding the Book Structure

This book is thoughtfully organized to guide you through the journey of no-grid living, starting with the essentials and building up to more advanced concepts.

In **Chapter 1**, we begin with the basics, helping you set up an off-grid base camp. You'll learn how to choose the perfect location, secure vital resources like water, and build a portable shelter that suits your needs.

As you move into **Chapter 2**, we focus on making your off-grid shelter not just livable, but comfortable and sustainable. You'll explore techniques for insulation and heating, including the creation of efficient heating systems like the rocket stove, which will keep your home warm even in harsh conditions.

From there, **Chapter 3** delves into water systems—perhaps the most critical aspect of off-grid living. You'll discover how to procure, store, and purify water through practical DIY projects, such as setting up a rainwater harvesting system and building your own water filtration unit.

Building on these essentials, **Chapter 4** takes you into the world of off-grid food production, preservation, and cooking. You'll learn how to grow your own food, raise livestock, preserve your harvest, and cook efficiently without modern conveniences. This chapter is about ensuring you have a steady, sustainable food supply year-round.

Next, **Chapter 5** addresses waste management, showing you how to handle waste responsibly with composting toilets, recycling strategies, and methods to reduce household waste—essential for maintaining a clean and sustainable environment off the grid.

Chapter 6 continues with the theme of sustainability, focusing on maintaining hygiene in an off-grid setting. You'll master the art of making homemade soap, toothpaste, and even set up an outdoor shower, ensuring you stay clean and healthy while living self-sufficiently.

In **Chapter 7**, we shift gears to explore off-grid power solutions, guiding you through the process of harnessing renewable energy. Whether it's solar, wind, or backup systems, this chapter equips you with the knowledge to power your off-grid life confidently.

Security becomes the focus in **Chapter 8**, where you'll learn how to protect your off-grid home. We'll cover everything from establishing a secure perimeter to building a safe room, ensuring your sanctuary remains safe from potential threats.

Communication is another crucial aspect, and **Chapter 9** covers how to stay connected while off the grid. This chapter explores various communication and networking options, ensuring you can maintain contact with the outside world, no matter how remote your location.

Chapter 10 serves as a special hands-on guide, revisiting key survival skills and techniques introduced in earlier chapters. Here, you'll dive deeper into essential survival strategies like wilderness shelter building, fire-starting, and navigation—offering a practical, quick-reference tool to ensure you're always prepared.

Finally, **Chapter 11** prepares you for those unexpected moments when you might be forced into off-grid living due to emergencies. This chapter is another vital 'add-on', providing a rapid-consult guide that not only reinforces concepts from earlier chapters but also equips you with strategies for quickly securing your home, creating a comprehensive bug-out bag, and ensuring long-term survival in a crisis.

To wrap it all up, the book concludes with a handy Appendix, where you can easily find and reference all the DIY projects covered. This resource is designed to make your off-grid journey as seamless and successful as possible, offering you both the knowledge and the tools to thrive.

Get Your Exclusive Bonuses

As you begin your journey into off-grid living, I want to remind you that your learning and growth don't stop with this book. To support you further, I've prepared a collection of (at least) **8 exclusive bonuses that are always accessible**, along with free, forever updates to help you expand your skills and knowledge over time.

Here's what you can expect:

- **Emergency Preparedness Plans**: Templates for creating family or community emergency plans and disaster scenario checklists, ensuring you're ready for any situation.
- **Skill Evaluations**: Comprehensive assessments to test your knowledge across critical areas like survival techniques, basic chemistry, electrical work, and food preservation.
- **Seasonal Planting and Harvesting Calendars**: Detailed guides tailored to various regions, helping you maximize your garden's productivity year-round.
- **Book 1: Food Security and Self-Sufficiency**: Strategies to ensure year-round food security and self-sufficiency through innovative growing techniques and sustainable ecosystem design.

- **Book 2: Expert Gardening Techniques for Off-Grid Living**: Advanced methods for soil health, companion planting, crop rotation, and seed saving.
- **Book 3: Off-Grid Health and Wellness**: A guide to maintaining health and wellness in an off-grid environment, focusing on herbal medicine, mental well-being, and nutrition.
- **Book 4: Sustainable Building Techniques**: Eco-friendly construction methods, including earthbag construction, straw bale homes, and cob and adobe building.
- **Book 5: Urban Off-Grid Living**: Practical techniques for achieving off-grid living in an urban setting, focusing on energy systems and space optimization.
- **Forever Updates**: Stay connected with future projects, new resources, and valuable updates—always free and accessible.

These bonuses are designed to complement the content of this book and help you continue your journey toward complete self-reliance.

Curious? Jump to the Bonus Section at the end of the book!

Share Your Experience

Before you dive into the book, I have a heartfelt request: I would greatly appreciate it if you could **take a moment to share your thoughts on this book**. Your feedback is invaluable and helps others who are exploring self-reliance find the guidance they need.

Writing a review is a powerful way to support me as an author, and I truly thank you for your support!

Ready, Set, Go!

With this foundation in place, you're ready to embark on your off-grid journey. Each chapter will guide you through essential projects that will bring you closer to complete self-reliance. Whether you're building a solar power system, constructing a rainwater harvesting setup, or learning to grow your own food, you'll find the information you need right here.

So, let's get started — **your path to off-grid living begins now**.

Chapter 1 - Setting Up an Off-Grid Base Camp

Setting up an off-grid base camp is the foundation of your self-reliance journey. Whether you're choosing this path for the freedom it offers, or because external circumstances have made it a necessity, creating a sustainable and secure living environment away from modern infrastructure is a critical step. In this chapter, we'll cover the essential steps you need to take to establish a base camp that will support you and your family, no matter what life throws at you. From understanding what "off-grid" truly means to choosing the right location and securing critical resources like water, this chapter is your guide to laying down the roots of your off-grid lifestyle.

Understanding the Basics of Off-Grid Living

What Does "Off-Grid" Mean?

Living "off-grid" refers to a lifestyle where you are not connected to the public utilities that most people depend on—electricity, water, and sewage systems. Instead, you generate your own power, collect and purify your own water, and manage your own waste. This can be achieved through a combination of renewable energy sources (such as solar or wind power), sustainable water collection methods (like rainwater harvesting), and eco-friendly waste management systems (such as composting toilets).

But going off-grid is more than just disconnecting from utilities; it's about embracing a lifestyle of self-sufficiency and independence. It means taking control of your basic needs and meeting them through your own efforts and resources, often in a way that minimizes your environmental impact. For many, this lifestyle is a choice—a way to live more freely, closer to nature, and with less reliance on modern conveniences.

However, it's important to recognize that going off-grid might not always be a choice. External factors, like natural disasters, economic collapse, or other crises, can force you into a situation where self-reliance is no longer just an option, but a necessity. Imagine a powerful tornado tearing through your town, cutting off access to electricity, water, and food supplies. In such a scenario, your ability to survive and thrive will depend on your preparation and your willingness to embrace off-grid living. This chapter is about preparing you for both the voluntary and involuntary aspects of off-grid life.

Benefits and Challenges of Off-Grid Living

The benefits of off-grid living are numerous, but so are the challenges. Understanding both sides of the equation is crucial to making informed decisions as you embark on this journey, whether you're doing so by choice or by necessity.

Benefits:

1. **Independence:** One of the most significant advantages of off-grid living is the freedom it offers. You're no longer tied to utility companies or reliant on public services. This independence gives you control over your resources and how you use them. In a crisis, this independence can be the difference between survival and hardship.

2. **Sustainability:** Off-grid living often goes together with sustainable practices. By generating your own energy, managing your own waste, and producing your own food, you can significantly reduce your environmental footprint. In times of disaster or economic instability, sustainability becomes a lifeline, ensuring you have what you need to continue living comfortably.

3. **Resilience:** In times of crisis, such as natural disasters or economic downturns, off-grid systems are often more resilient and less susceptible to disruption. Without dependence on external utilities, off-grid households can continue to function even when others cannot. For those who find themselves suddenly off-grid due to unforeseen events, having a resilient system already in place can make all the difference.

4. **Cost Savings:** While the initial investment can be high, over time, you can save money by eliminating utility bills and reducing your consumption of resources. By generating your own energy and growing your own food, you also become less vulnerable to fluctuations in prices and availability of these essentials—an important consideration in uncertain times.

Challenges:

1. **Initial Costs:** Setting up an off-grid system may need a considerable initial investment in infrastructure and equipment. Solar panels, batteries, water purification systems, and building materials are just a few of the costs you'll need to consider. However, when a disaster strikes and traditional systems fail, the initial investment in off-grid systems can pay off many times over.
2. **Technical Skills:** Off-grid living demands a broad range of technical skills, from carpentry and plumbing to electrical work and agriculture. If you're not already skilled in these areas, you'll need to be willing to learn or be prepared to hire help. The more self-sufficient you aim to be, the more skills you'll need to develop, especially when external help might not be available during emergencies.
3. **Maintenance:** Off-grid systems require continual repair and upkeep. Solar panels must be cleaned, batteries monitored and water systems checked on a regular basis to guarantee proper operation. This means you must be prepared to troubleshoot and fix issues as they arise, often without immediate access to professional help—an essential capability if you find yourself unexpectedly off-grid.
4. **Isolation:** Depending on your location, living off-grid can be isolating. This may be a challenge for those accustomed to social interaction and easy access to services. While some

people thrive in isolation, others may find it difficult. In a crisis, isolation can become a serious concern, making it vital to have a plan for communication and social interaction, even if you're cut off from the rest of the world.

By acknowledging both the voluntary and involuntary paths to off-grid living, we can better prepare ourselves for whatever the future holds. Whether you're choosing this lifestyle out of a desire for freedom or preparing for a situation where it may become a necessity, the principles in this chapter will equip you with the knowledge and skills to create a stable, sustainable off-grid base camp. Remember, the goal is not just to survive—but to thrive, no matter what challenges you may face.

Case Study: Successful Off-Grid Communities

To better understand the practical realities of off-grid living, let's look at some successful off-grid communities. These examples provide valuable insights into how others have navigated the challenges of living off the grid and the benefits they've gained from this lifestyle.

Earthship Biotecture, New Mexico, USA

Earthship Biotecture is a community in Taos, New Mexico, known for its innovative, self-sustaining homes. These "Earthships" are constructed using recycled materials like tires, bottles, and cans and are designed to be entirely off-grid. They generate their own electricity through solar and wind power, collect and treat their own water, and grow food in indoor gardens. The community has become a model for sustainable, off-grid living, attracting visitors from around the world.

The Earthship design is particularly noteworthy for its focus on passive solar heating and cooling, natural ventilation, and rainwater harvesting. The homes are built into the earth, with thick walls that provide insulation and thermal mass, helping to maintain a stable indoor temperature year-round. Water is collected from the roof, filtered, and used in multiple ways—first for drinking and cooking, then for plants, and finally for flushing toilets.

The success of Earthship Biotecture highlights the importance of innovative design and sustainable practices in off-grid living. By utilizing natural and recycled materials, the community reduces its environmental impact while creating comfortable, energy-efficient homes.

Tinkers Bubble, Somerset, UK

Tinkers Bubble is a small off-grid community in the UK that has been thriving since the 1990s. The residents live without electricity from the grid, using wood-fired steam engines for power and practicing organic farming. The community is built on principles of low-impact living, with all buildings constructed from local materials and energy derived from renewable sources.

One of the unique aspects of Tinkers Bubble is its reliance on manual and horse-drawn farming techniques, which reduce the need for fossil fuels. The community produces much of its own food, from vegetables and fruit to meat and dairy, and sells surplus produce to support the community financially. Buildings are constructed from locally sourced timber, straw bales, and clay, emphasizing sustainability and low environmental impact.

Tinkers Bubble demonstrates that a simple, off-grid lifestyle is not only possible but can be highly rewarding. The community's commitment to low-impact living, combined with their strong sense of cooperation and shared values, has allowed them to create a resilient and sustainable way of life.

Choosing the Right Location

Selecting the right location for your off-grid base camp is perhaps the most critical decision you'll make. Your choice will affect every aspect of your off-grid life, from the availability of resources to the type of shelter you can build. The ideal location will provide access to necessary resources like water, food, and energy, while also offering the security and privacy you need to live independently. Here, we'll explore the key factors you need to consider when choosing your site.

Climate

The climate of your chosen location will dictate many aspects of your off-grid setup, including the type of shelter you need, the crops you can grow, and the amount of energy required for heating and cooling. Understanding the climate is essential for planning your energy needs, food production, and overall comfort.

- **Hot, Arid Climates:** In desert-like conditions, you'll need to focus on water conservation and cooling strategies. Structures should be designed to maximize shade and insulation. Consider using materials like adobe or earthbags that provide excellent thermal mass, helping to keep the interior cool during the day and warm at night. You'll also need to plan for efficient water use, possibly incorporating greywater systems and drought-resistant crops.
- **Cold, Temperate Climates:** In colder areas, the priority will be on insulation, heating, and ensuring a steady food supply through long winters. Your shelter should be well-insulated with materials like straw bales, wool, or modern insulative materials. You might also consider passive solar design to capture and retain heat during the day. Greenhouses can extend your growing season, and root cellars can help preserve food through the winter.
- **Tropical Climates:** In tropical regions, you'll need to account for high humidity, heavy rainfall, and potential storms. Focus on durable, weather-resistant structures that can withstand high winds and heavy rain. Ventilation is crucial to managing humidity and preventing mold growth. Raised foundations may be necessary to avoid flooding, and you should plan for a reliable water collection system to manage the heavy rainfall.

Water Sources

Access to a reliable and clean water source is non-negotiable for off-grid living. Water is essential for drinking, cooking, sanitation, and growing food. Your options include:

- **Natural Water Sources:** Rivers, lakes, and streams can provide a continuous water supply but will require filtration and purification systems to ensure the water is safe to drink. When relying on surface water, consider the risk of contamination from upstream activities and the seasonal availability of water.
- **Groundwater:** Wells can be drilled to access groundwater, providing a reliable source of water year-round. However, this may require a significant investment in equipment. The depth and quality of groundwater can vary, so it's essential to conduct a thorough survey before drilling. Regular testing is also necessary to monitor for contaminants.
- **Rainwater Harvesting:** In areas with adequate rainfall, collecting and storing rainwater can be an effective solution. This method is sustainable and relatively easy to implement, though it requires proper storage and filtration to ensure the water remains potable. You'll need to calculate the amount of rainfall you can collect based on your roof area and local precipitation patterns.

Natural Resources

Consider the availability of natural resources like wood, stone, and soil, which can be used for building, heating, and growing food. Proximity to forests, quarries, or fertile land can reduce your reliance on purchased materials and enhance your self-sufficiency.

- **Wood:** Wood is a versatile resource that can be used for building, heating, and crafting. If you're in a forested area, sustainable logging practices can provide a renewable supply of timber for construction and fuel. Be sure to plan for reforestation or responsible forest management to ensure the long-term availability of this resource.
- **Stone:** Stone can be an excellent building material, particularly in areas prone to extreme weather. It's durable, fire-resistant, and provides good thermal mass. Look for local quarries or natural deposits that you can use to reduce costs and transportation needs.
- **Soil:** Fertile soil is crucial for growing food, particularly if you plan to establish a garden or farm. Test the soil for nutrients, pH levels, and contaminants before committing to a location. In some areas, you may need to amend the soil with organic matter or other nutrients to support healthy plant growth.

Legal Considerations and Zoning Laws

Before you commit to a location, it's crucial to research local laws and regulations. Some areas have strict zoning laws that may limit your ability to build off-grid or live sustainably. Permits may be required for certain types of construction, and there may be restrictions on water use, waste disposal, and renewable energy systems.

- **Zoning Laws:** Zoning laws determine how land can be used in different areas. They can dictate whether you're allowed to build a residence, farm, or business on your property. Some rural areas have fewer restrictions, making them ideal for off-grid living, while others may have specific requirements for building codes, minimum lot sizes, or environmental protection.

- **Building Codes:** Even in rural areas, building codes may apply. These codes set standards for construction safety, which can include everything from structural integrity to plumbing and electrical systems. Off-grid homes may need to comply with these codes, even if they don't rely on conventional utilities.
- **Water Rights:** In some regions, water rights are a significant legal issue. You may need to secure rights to collect or use water from natural sources, and there could be restrictions on the amount of water you can divert or store. Research local water laws to avoid conflicts or legal challenges.

Accessibility

While isolation is often a goal of off-grid living, complete isolation can be problematic. Consider your need for occasional access to nearby towns for supplies, medical care, and social interaction. Ensure that your location is accessible enough to allow for the transportation of materials and emergency evacuations if necessary.

- **Road Access:** Evaluate the road conditions leading to your property. Seasonal weather can significantly impact access, especially in remote areas where roads may become impassable due to snow, mud, or flooding. You may need a four-wheel-drive vehicle or even consider investing in road improvements.
- **Proximity to Services:** While the goal of off-grid living is to be self-reliant, proximity to essential services like medical care, emergency services, and supplies is still important. Consider how far you're willing to travel for these services and whether the location you choose provides reasonable access.
- **Community Connections:** Even if you live off-grid, maintaining some level of connection with a nearby community can be beneficial. Neighbors can provide support in emergencies, trade goods or services, and offer social interaction, which can be important for mental well-being.

By expanding on these core elements of setting up an off-grid base camp, we aim to provide you with a comprehensive understanding of the decisions and challenges involved. Each factor plays a critical role in the success of your off-grid lifestyle, from the practicalities of resource management to the legal and social considerations of living independently. As you move forward, keep these principles in mind to create a base camp that is not only sustainable and functional but also aligned with your personal values and goals for self-reliance.

DIY Project 1: Portable Shelter Construction

Once you've chosen your location, the next step is to establish a temporary or permanent shelter. This section will guide you through the process of constructing a portable shelter that can be easily assembled, disassembled, and moved as needed. This type of shelter is ideal for the initial stages of your off-grid journey, offering protection from the elements while you build a more permanent home.

Cost	$$	Difficulty	★★

Materials:

- **Tarps**: Heavy-duty, weather-resistant tarps to provide protection from rain, wind, and sun.
- **Ropes**: Strong, durable ropes to secure the tarps and structure.
- **PVC Pipes**: Lightweight and easy-to-assemble pipes for the frame.
- **Ground Stakes**: To anchor the shelter securely to the ground.
- **Zip Ties**: For securing the tarp to the frame.

Tools

- **Hammer:** For driving in stakes.
- **Saw:** For cutting PVC pipes to the desired length.
- **Utility Knife:** For trimming tarps and ropes.
- **Measuring Tape:** To ensure accurate cuts and measurements.
- **Marker:** For marking measurements on pipes and tarps.

1	**Site Preparation** • Choose a flat, well-drained area for your shelter. Clear away any debris, rocks, or vegetation that could interfere with the structure or cause discomfort. • Measure the area where you plan to set up the shelter, ensuring that it is large enough to accommodate the frame.
2	**Building the Frame** • Cut the PVC pipes to the desired length using the saw. For a simple rectangular shelter, you'll need four pipes for the base and four for the vertical supports. • Assemble the base of the frame by connecting the pipes using PVC elbows. This will form a sturdy rectangle. • Insert the vertical supports into the corners of the base and secure them with PVC elbows to form the corners of the frame. • If needed, add cross-bracing along the top of the frame for additional stability.
3	**Securing the Frame**

	• Place the frame on the prepared site and anchor it to the ground using the stakes. Drive the stakes into the ground at each corner and secure them to the frame with ropes.
4	**Attaching the Tarp** • Drape the tarp over the frame, ensuring it covers all sides evenly. • Use zip ties to secure the tarp to the frame, tightening them as needed to eliminate slack. Pay special attention to securing the corners and edges. • If you have multiple tarps, overlap them to ensure full coverage and protection from the elements.
5	**Final Adjustments** • Check the shelter for any gaps or loose areas. Adjust the tarp and ropes as necessary to create a snug, weatherproof structure. • Add additional tarps or insulation inside the shelter if you're in a colder climate or need extra protection.

Your portable shelter is now complete! This structure will provide you with a comfortable, protected space while you work on more permanent solutions. It's designed to be easily modified or moved, offering flexibility as you develop your off-grid base camp.

Conclusion

Establishing your off-grid base camp is the first and arguably most crucial step in your journey toward self-reliance and independence. This chapter has provided you with the foundational knowledge and practical steps necessary to begin this transformation—whether you're motivated by the allure of freedom, the desire to live more sustainably, or the need to prepare for unexpected circumstances. By choosing the right location, understanding the essential components of off-grid living, and constructing your initial shelter, you're setting the stage for a lifestyle that offers both resilience and peace of mind.

However, it's important to recognize that this is just the beginning. Building a sustainable off-grid lifestyle involves much more than simply setting up a shelter and securing water and energy sources. The challenges you'll face will evolve over time, requiring ongoing learning, adaptation, and problem-solving. Insulating your shelter for year-round comfort, heating your home without relying on traditional fuels, producing and preserving your own food, and generating reliable energy are just a few of the areas you'll need to explore as you continue this journey.

Living off-grid is about more than survival; it's about thriving in harmony with your environment and developing the skills to meet your needs independently. As you progress, you'll find that each new challenge is an opportunity to deepen your connection with nature, enhance your self-sufficiency, and build a life that reflects your values and aspirations.

This chapter has laid the groundwork for your off-grid base camp, but the journey ahead is filled with even more exciting and rewarding steps. From mastering insulation and heating to developing sustainable food production systems and preserving your harvest, each new chapter will guide you through the intricacies of off-grid living. By the time you've completed this book, you'll have the knowledge and confidence to build a truly independent lifestyle—one that is resilient, resourceful, and ready for whatever the future may hold.

Remember, the goal is not just to create a functional living space, but to cultivate a lifestyle that allows you to flourish, no matter what challenges come your way. Whether you're driven by the desire to live freely, reduce your environmental impact, or ensure your family's safety in uncertain times, your off-grid base camp is the cornerstone of a sustainable, self-reliant future. Embrace the journey ahead with curiosity, determination, and the understanding that every step you take brings you closer to the life you've envisioned.

Chapter 2 - Off-Grid Shelter and Heating

When you think of off-grid living, the first things that likely come to mind are food and water. But have you considered how essential a well-insulated and efficiently heated shelter is to your survival? Without a warm, comfortable place to retreat to, your off-grid experience can quickly become a struggle against the elements. Shelter is more than just a roof over your head; it's your sanctuary, your protection against nature's extremes, and a critical component in your journey toward self-sufficiency. This chapter focuses on building and maintaining a sustainable, off-grid shelter that not only protects you from the weather but also maximizes energy efficiency using natural resources and innovative designs. Whether you're preparing for the long winter months or trying to keep cool in the heat of summer, the strategies discussed here will help you create a haven that's both comfortable and eco-friendly.

Insulating Your Shelter

Have you ever spent a night in a poorly insulated cabin? If so, you know how miserable it can be. The walls are cold to the touch, the floor feels like ice, and no matter how much you stoke the fire, you just can't get warm. Now imagine that same situation off-grid, where you can't simply turn up the thermostat or plug in an electric heater. Insulation is the key to keeping your home cozy in the winter and cool in the summer, and it's even more critical when you're living off the grid. Without the convenience of central heating or air conditioning, your shelter's ability to maintain a stable internal temperature relies heavily on the quality of its insulation.

But why is insulation so important? Think of your shelter as a thermos. Just as a thermos keeps your coffee hot or your water cold by minimizing heat transfer, insulation works by reducing the exchange of heat between the inside and outside of your home. In wintertime, it keeps heat inside to keep you warm. In summertime it keeps heat out, making sure your living area remains cool. Proper insulation reduces the need for additional heating and cooling, saving you energy and resources—both of which are precious commodities in off-grid living.

The Impact of Insulation on Energy Efficiency

When you're living off-grid, energy efficiency isn't just a nice-to-have; it's a necessity. The less energy you need to expend on heating and cooling, the more sustainable your lifestyle becomes. Effective insulation can reduce the amount of firewood you need to chop or the frequency with which you need to refuel your wood stove. It can also mean the difference between needing a large, expensive solar array or getting by with a smaller, more affordable system. In essence, good insulation directly contributes to your self-reliance by minimizing your dependence on external resources.

DIY Project 2: *Natural Insulation Solutions*

For those living off the grid, using natural, locally sourced materials for insulation is not only cost-effective but also sustainable. Here's a guide to insulating your shelter using straw, clay, and wood—materials that have been used for centuries to create warm, livable homes.

Cost	$$	Difficulty	★★

Materials:

- **Straw:** An excellent insulator, straw is renewable, affordable, and readily available in many rural areas. It's often used in combination with clay or mud to create what's known as "straw-clay" insulation.
- **Clay:** Clay is a natural material that, when mixed with straw, can form a durable and highly effective insulation. It's also a good thermal mass, meaning it can store and slowly release heat, helping to stabilize indoor temperatures.
- **Wood:** Wood is a versatile building material that can be used both structurally and as part of an insulation system. It's a good thermal insulator on its own, especially when used in the form of wood chips or sawdust.

Tools:

- **Saw:** For cutting wood to size.
- **Hammer:** For assembling wooden frames or walls.
- **Shovel:** For mixing and applying straw-clay insulation.

1	**Preparing the Structure** Before you begin insulating, ensure that your shelter's structure is solid and weatherproof. Check for any gaps, cracks, or holes in the walls, roof, and floor. These should be sealed to prevent drafts and moisture from compromising your insulation. If you're building a new structure, consider constructing it with thick walls that can accommodate a substantial layer of insulation. Do you remember those cold drafts seeping through the cracks in your childhood home? That experience should serve as a reminder of the importance of sealing every gap. In off-grid living, those drafts could mean the difference between a cozy evening and a night spent shivering under layers of blankets.
2	**Creating Straw-Clay Insulation** Mix straw with clay in a large container, such as a wheelbarrow or a tarp spread on the ground. The ideal mixture should be damp but not overly wet—think of the consistency of sticky dough. The straw should be fully coated with clay, which

	acts as a binder, holding the fibers together and helping the insulation stick to the walls. This process might seem labor-intensive but think about the long-term benefits. Every hour you spend now mixing straw and clay will pay off in years of warmth and comfort. Plus, you're using materials that are often readily available and inexpensive, making this method both practical and sustainable.
3	**Applying the Insulation** Apply the straw-clay mixture to the interior walls of your shelter. You can either pack it between wooden studs (similar to how you would install fiberglass insulation) or apply it as a thick layer directly onto the surface of the walls. Use your hands or a trowel to smooth the mixture, ensuring it's evenly distributed. As the clay dries, it will harden, creating a sturdy, insulated wall. Imagine how rewarding it will feel, knowing that the walls surrounding you are a direct product of your labor—built with your own hands, using materials that are in harmony with nature.
4	**Finishing the Walls** Once the straw-clay insulation is dry, you can apply a finish to protect it and improve the appearance of your walls. Options include a plaster made from lime or clay, which will create a smooth, durable surface. This finish layer also adds an extra level of insulation and helps to seal the walls against air leaks. Think about the aesthetics here as well—your shelter doesn't have to look like a rustic cabin unless that's the style you're going for. The final finish can be customized to reflect your personal taste while also serving as a functional barrier against the elements.

Straw bale construction dates back to the late 19th century, with some of the earliest examples found in the Sandhills of Nebraska. Pioneers in this region, faced with a lack of traditional building materials, began using tightly packed straw bales to construct their homes. These straw bale homes were incredibly durable and well-insulated, providing protection against the harsh weather conditions of the Great Plains. Many of these structures are still standing today, a testament to the effectiveness of straw as an insulation material.

This technique wasn't just about survival; it was about thriving in a challenging environment. These early pioneers didn't have access to modern materials or conveniences, yet they managed to build homes that stood the test of time. This serves as a powerful reminder that sometimes the simplest solutions are the most effective.

Additional Tips:

- **Use Recycled Materials:** If you have access to recycled wood or leftover building materials, incorporate them into your insulation project. This reduces waste and can lower your costs.
- **Insulate the Roof:** Don't forget that heat rises, so insulating your roof is just as important as insulating your walls. Use a similar straw-clay mixture or wood chips to insulate your roof and prevent heat loss during cold weather.
- **Consider Passive Solar Design:** If you're building from scratch, think about the orientation of your shelter and the placement of windows. A passive solar design can maximize natural heat from the sun during the winter while minimizing heat gain during the summer.

Advanced Insulation Technique for Extreme Climates

For those living in particularly harsh climates—whether it's the freezing winters of the far north or the scorching summers of the desert—standard insulation methods might not be enough. In these cases, more advanced techniques and materials can be employed to ensure your shelter remains a comfortable haven regardless of the weather outside.

Superinsulation

Superinsulation is a concept that goes beyond standard insulation methods by focusing on minimizing heat loss (or gain) to an extreme degree. This technique often involves using multiple layers of high-performance insulation materials, such as rigid foam boards, in conjunction with meticulous air-sealing practices.

Materials:

- **Rigid Foam Insulation:** Polyisocyanurate or extruded polystyrene (XPS) boards provide high R-values and excellent moisture resistance.
- **Airtight Membranes:** To prevent air infiltration, which can significantly reduce the effectiveness of insulation.
- **Triple-Glazed Windows:** To minimize heat loss through windows, which are typically one of the weakest points in a building's thermal envelope.

Techniques:

- **Double-Wall Construction:** Building a double wall with an insulated gap between the inner and outer walls can drastically reduce heat transfer. This method is particularly effective in cold climates.

- **Earth Berming:** Partially burying your home in the earth can provide natural insulation, leveraging the constant temperature of the ground to help maintain a stable indoor climate.

Case Study: The Passive House Movement

Originating in Germany, the Passive House (Passivhaus) standard represents the pinnacle of energy-efficient building design. Homes built to this standard are so well insulated and airtight that they require little to no conventional heating or cooling systems. Instead, they rely on the heat generated by occupants, appliances, and the sun. While the Passive House approach is typically associated with grid-connected homes, its principles can be adapted for off-grid living, particularly in climates where temperature extremes are the norm.

Considerations and Final Thoughts

While these advanced techniques offer superior insulation, they also come with increased complexity and cost. It's important to weigh the benefits against your specific needs and resources. For many off-grid homesteaders, a balance between natural, low-tech solutions and selective use of high-performance materials provides the best combination of sustainability, cost-effectiveness, and comfort.

Insulating your shelter is about more than just staying warm; it's about creating a space where you can live comfortably and sustainably, no matter what the weather throws at you. By using a mix of traditional methods and modern innovations, you can build a shelter that's both a refuge and a testament to your ingenuity and self-reliance.

Building a Rocket Stove: The Heart of Off-Grid Heating

When you're living off the grid, every resource counts. Heating your home efficiently, especially during the harsh winter months, can be a challenge. But what if I told you there's a way to heat your home that's incredibly efficient, burns a fraction of the wood required by a traditional fireplace, and can even be built with scavenged materials? Sounds too good to be true, right? Enter the rocket stove—a simple yet revolutionary heating system that has been gaining popularity among off-grid enthusiasts and eco-conscious builders alike.

Why Choose a Rocket Stove?

The rocket stove works on the principle of efficient combustion, where the fuel is burned at high temperatures, ensuring that nearly all of the energy is converted into heat. This not only makes the rocket stove incredibly fuel-efficient but also drastically reduces smoke and other emissions. In an off-grid setting, where resources are limited and sustainability is key, the rocket stove can be a game-changer.

Let's put this into perspective: Traditional wood stoves or open fireplaces are notorious for their inefficiency. They consume a lot of wood and, while they provide warmth, a significant amount of energy escapes through the chimney as unburned gases and smoke. In contrast, a rocket stove is designed to burn all the gases produced by the wood, turning more of the fuel into heat. This means you need less wood to achieve the same—or better—heating results.

But how does it do that? The secret lies in the design. The rocket stove's insulated combustion chamber and heat riser create a highly efficient burn that reaches much higher temperatures than conventional stoves. This leads to more complete combustion, less creosote buildup, and minimal smoke—just what you need for an off-grid lifestyle.

The Rocket Mass Heater: Taking It to the Next Level

While a basic rocket stove is excellent for cooking and small heating tasks, a **rocket mass heater** takes the concept further, making it ideal for heating an entire home or shelter. A rocket mass heater combines the efficient burn of a rocket stove with a thermal mass—such as a cob bench or stone wall—that absorbs and slowly releases heat over time. This system not only keeps your home warm for hours after the fire has gone out but also uses the heat more effectively, ensuring that no energy is wasted.

Imagine this scenario: It's the dead of winter, and the temperature outside is well below freezing. You've just finished burning a small load of wood in your rocket mass heater, and now you can feel the warmth radiating from the cob bench you're sitting on. That heat will continue to keep your shelter cozy for hours, all without needing to constantly feed a fire. This is the kind of efficiency and comfort that a rocket mass heater can provide.

Historical Anecdote: the rocket stove concept was originally developed in the 1980s by Dr. Larry Winiarski as part of an effort to create more efficient cooking stoves for developing countries. Traditional open fires are highly inefficient, requiring large amounts of wood and producing significant smoke, which can cause respiratory problems. Rocket stoves, with their efficient combustion, use much less wood and produce far less smoke. They have been widely adopted in rural areas across Africa, Asia, and Latin America, where they have improved health outcomes and reduced deforestation.

Why does this matter? The same principles that make rocket stoves valuable in developing countries apply to off-grid living. The reduced wood consumption means less time spent gathering fuel and less environmental impact. The lower smoke output makes for a healthier living environment—important in a closed-off, off-grid shelter where ventilation might be limited.

DIY Project 3: Building Your Rocket Mass Heater

Now, let's get into the details of how you can build your own rocket mass heater. This project is more involved than a basic rocket stove, but with the right materials and some dedication, you can create a heating system that will serve you for years.

Cost	$$	Difficulty	★★★

Materials:

- **Steel Barrels:** You'll need two barrels—one for the combustion chamber and one for the heat riser. These can often be sourced second-hand, which keeps costs down.
- **Fire Bricks:** High-temperature bricks are essential for lining the combustion chamber and heat riser. These bricks can withstand the intense heat generated by the stove.
- **Clay:** For building the thermal mass. Clay is readily available and, when mixed with sand and straw, forms a durable and heat-retentive mass.
- **Cob (a mix of clay, sand, and straw):** Used to create the thermal mass that stores heat. Cob is a traditional building material that's easy to work with and highly effective.

Tools:

- **Welding Machine:** For cutting and assembling the steel barrels. If you don't have welding skills, you might consider hiring a professional to assist with this part.
- **Trowel:** For applying clay and cob.
- **Saw:** For cutting wood to size.

1	**Building the Combustion Chamber** The heart of the rocket mass heater is the combustion chamber, where the fuel (usually small pieces of wood) is burned. Start by cutting the bottom out of one of the steel barrels. This barrel will serve as the outer shell of the combustion chamber. Inside this shell, create a smaller chamber using fire bricks, arranged in a U-shape. The vertical section of the U will be the feed tube where you load the wood. Why this design? The U-shape and the vertical feed tube ensure that the wood burns efficiently as it is drawn into the combustion chamber. Gravity helps to feed the wood into the hottest part of the fire, ensuring complete combustion.
2	**Constructing the Heat Riser** The heat riser is a vertical, insulated chamber that forces the hot gases to rise rapidly, creating a strong draft and ensuring complete combustion of the fuel. This can be made from a second steel barrel lined with fire bricks. Position the heat riser inside the first barrel, leaving enough space around it to allow the gases to circulate before exiting through the chimney.

	This is the engine of your rocket mass heater: the heat riser not only ensures that all the wood gases are burned but also pushes the hot air and gases through the rest of the system, driving the heat into the thermal mass.
3	**Building the Thermal Mass** The thermal mass is what makes the rocket mass heater so efficient. As the hot gases exit the heat riser, they travel through a horizontal channel embedded in a thermal mass made from cob or stone. This mass absorbs and stores the heat, releasing it slowly over several hours. Shape the thermal mass into a bench, wall, or other structure that can radiate heat into your living space. Think of this as your heat battery: the thermal mass stores the heat energy and releases it slowly, providing warmth long after the fire has gone out. This is especially useful in off-grid settings where efficiency is key, and it's one of the reasons rocket mass heaters are so popular among those who value self-sufficiency.
4	**Finishing Touches** Once the main components are in place, seal any gaps with clay or cob to prevent air leaks. Install a chimney to vent the remaining gases outside. The chimney should be tall enough to create a good draft, helping to pull air through the combustion chamber and heat riser. Finally, test your rocket mass heater by lighting a small fire and monitoring the draft and heat output. **Safety First:** Ensure your chimney is properly vented and that there's no risk of carbon monoxide buildup. A good draft is crucial, not just for efficiency but also for safety.

Expanding the Concept: Rocket Stoves for More Than Just Heating

While we've focused on rocket stoves as a heating solution, their applications extend far beyond that. In off-grid living, versatility is key, and rocket stoves can be adapted for various uses, from cooking to hot water heating.

- **Cooking:** Rocket stoves are often used in place of traditional cooking methods, especially in off-grid settings. The efficiency of the burn means you use less wood to cook meals, and the high temperatures achieved can significantly reduce cooking times. If you're building a rocket mass heater, consider incorporating a cooking surface into the design. A simple metal plate on top of the combustion chamber can serve as a highly effective stovetop.

- **Water Heating:** With some modifications, a rocket stove can also be used to heat water. By running copper tubing through the thermal mass or around the heat riser, you can create a system that heats water as it circulates through the stove. This can be a fantastic way to provide hot water for showers, washing dishes, or even radiant floor heating.

- **Greenhouses:** Extending the growing season or providing year-round food production is often a goal for off-grid homesteaders. A rocket mass heater can be used to heat a greenhouse, ensuring that your plants stay warm even during cold nights. The thermal mass can help maintain a stable temperature, preventing the swings that can be harmful to sensitive plants.

Additional Tips:

- **Use Local Materials:** Whenever possible, use locally sourced materials for the thermal mass. Cob, a mixture of clay, sand, and straw, is easy to make and provides excellent heat storage.
- **Optimize Fuel Use:** Only use dry, well-seasoned wood in your rocket stove. Green or wet wood will produce more smoke and less heat, reducing the efficiency of your heater.
- **Safety First:** Ensure that your rocket mass heater is installed on a stable, non-combustible surface. Keep flammable materials away from the combustion chamber and chimney.
- **Ventilation:** Good ventilation is crucial, especially in a small, off-grid shelter. Make sure that fresh air can enter the space to replace the oxygen used by the fire, and that smoke and gases are properly vented outside.

The Rocket Stove—A Cornerstone of Off-Grid Heating

The rocket stove, and its more advanced cousin, the rocket mass heater, are powerful tools in the off-grid arsenal. By maximizing fuel efficiency and minimizing emissions, these stoves offer a sustainable, low-cost heating solution that's perfectly suited to life away from the grid. They embody the principles of self-reliance, making use of simple, locally available materials to create a system that's both practical and effective.

Building a rocket stove is more than just a project; it's an investment in your off-grid lifestyle. It's about taking control of your heating needs in a way that aligns with your values—whether those are sustainability, efficiency, or simply the satisfaction of building something with your own hands. With a rocket stove, you're not just heating your home; you're heating it smarter, with less impact on the environment and more benefit to your self-sufficient way of life.

Creating a Sustainable and Comfortable Off-Grid Shelter

In off-grid living, your shelter is more than just a place to sleep—it's the heart of your survival and comfort. As this chapter has illustrated, the choices you make in building and heating your shelter are crucial for ensuring that you can live sustainably, comfortably, and independently, regardless of the weather or season.

Effective insulation is a cornerstone of any off-grid shelter, playing a pivotal role in maintaining a stable, comfortable indoor temperature while minimizing the need for external energy sources. By utilizing natural materials like straw, clay, and wood, you not only create a warm and inviting living space but also contribute to the sustainability and resilience of your homestead. These materials, often readily available and affordable, allow you to insulate your shelter in a way that aligns with the principles of off-grid living—using what you have at hand, reducing waste, and lowering your environmental impact.

Heating, too, is a critical consideration, especially in climates where temperatures can drop dramatically. The rocket stove and rocket mass heater projects discussed in this chapter offer efficient, innovative solutions that are perfectly suited to off-grid life. By focusing on complete combustion and maximizing the use of available resources, these systems not only provide reliable warmth but also reduce wood consumption and emissions. Whether you're building a rocket stove for cooking or a rocket mass heater to keep your entire shelter warm, these projects embody the ingenuity and resourcefulness that are at the core of off-grid living.

As you continue to develop your off-grid base camp, remember that the principles of insulation and efficient heating are not just about immediate comfort—they are long-term investments in your self-sufficiency and sustainability. A well-insulated, efficiently heated shelter reduces your reliance on external resources, allowing you to live more independently and securely. Moreover, by incorporating the techniques and materials discussed in this chapter, you're building a home that's not only practical but also deeply connected to the environment around you.

Looking ahead, your journey in off-grid living will involve expanding these concepts to other areas of your life—energy production, food preservation, water management, and more. Each step you take will build on the foundation you've laid in creating a shelter that is both a refuge and a testament to your commitment to a self-reliant lifestyle. As you explore new projects and challenges, keep in mind the importance of balancing practicality with sustainability, comfort with resilience, and tradition with innovation.

This chapter has provided you with the knowledge and tools to create a shelter that meets your needs in an off-grid environment. The journey continues as you apply these principles to other aspects of your life, deepening your connection to the land and your ability to thrive independently. By embracing the challenges and rewards of off-grid living, you're not just building a home—you're crafting a way of life that will sustain you for years to come.

Chapter 3 - Off-Grid Water Systems

Water is the lifeblood of any off-grid living setup. Without a reliable and clean water source, all other aspects of self-sufficiency—food production, hygiene, and even basic survival—become impossible. In this chapter, we'll explore essential off-grid water systems, focusing on water assessment, storage, filtration and purification, building your own well, and recycling greywater for sustainable living. Each section will include detailed DIY projects, so you can confidently build and maintain your water systems.

Water Procurement and Storage

Water is life, especially when living off the grid. Ensuring a reliable and clean water supply is one of the most crucial aspects. Without water, survival becomes impossible within a matter of days, and long-term sustainability is out of the question. In this section, we'll dive deep into how to assess natural water sources, explore various water purification methods, and guide you through the construction of a simple rainwater harvesting system. This information will equip you with the knowledge to secure a water supply that can sustain you in both emergency situations and long-term off-grid living.

Assessing Natural Water Sources

Before settling on a location, it's vital to assess the availability of natural water sources. This could include rivers, lakes, springs, or groundwater. Each source has its own set of advantages and challenges, which we'll explore in detail.

Surface Water

Surface water includes rivers, streams, lakes, and ponds. These sources are often accessible and can provide large amounts of water, but they come with certain risks and require careful management.

Rivers and Streams: These are generally reliable sources of water, especially if they are fed by glaciers, springs, or high-altitude snowmelt, which can provide a consistent flow throughout the year. However, they require careful monitoring for contamination from upstream sources, such as agricultural runoff, industrial pollutants, or natural events like heavy rainfall, which can stir up sediments and pollutants. Seasonal changes can also affect the flow and quality of water, making it crucial to have a year-round monitoring plan.

- **Purification Required:** Even in seemingly pristine environments, surface water can harbor pathogens such as Giardia, Cryptosporidium, and bacteria like E. coli. You'll need a robust purification system to ensure the water is safe to drink. This might include a combination of filtration, chemical treatment, and boiling, depending on the specific risks present.
- **Equipment and Resources:** High-quality water testing kits are essential for regularly checking the water for contaminants. These can be purchased from suppliers like LaMotte or Hach. For ongoing monitoring, consider setting up a basic water testing station with pH

meters, turbidity tubes, and dissolved oxygen sensors, which are available from scientific equipment suppliers.

Lakes and Ponds: While these can provide a steady water supply, especially if they are large and deep, stagnant water bodies are more likely to harbor bacteria, algae, and other contaminants. Algal blooms, which can be toxic, are particularly problematic in warmer months or in nutrient-rich waters. Regular testing and treatment are necessary to ensure the water remains safe for consumption.

- **Purification Required:** Besides the standard pathogens, lakes and ponds may also contain harmful chemicals from agricultural runoff, such as pesticides or herbicides. A multi-stage purification system, including activated carbon filters, is recommended to remove organic chemicals, in addition to physical filtration and boiling.
- **Equipment and Resources:** Aeration systems can help reduce stagnation and algae growth in ponds. These can be powered by solar or wind energy, which are sustainable options for off-grid setups. Companies like Kasco Marine offer solar-powered aeration systems that can be an excellent investment for maintaining water quality.

Groundwater

Groundwater is another reliable source of water and often requires less purification than surface water. However, accessing it requires significant effort and resources.

Wells: Drilling a well can give you access to clean, stable groundwater, which is often protected from surface contaminants by layers of soil and rock. However, this requires an upfront investment in drilling equipment or hiring professionals. The depth of the well, the type of soil, and the underlying geology will determine the ease and cost of drilling. Once operational, wells provide a consistent water supply with minimal maintenance, but they should be regularly tested for contaminants like nitrates, heavy metals, and pathogens.

- **Purification Required:** Groundwater can still be contaminated by natural minerals (like arsenic, which is common in certain areas) or by human activities such as industrial waste or agricultural chemicals. Regular testing and possibly installing a reverse osmosis system or other specialized filtration systems might be necessary.
- **Equipment and Resources:** Well drilling rigs can be rented or purchased from suppliers like Water Well Solutions or SIMCO Drilling Equipment. For deeper wells, you may need a submersible pump, which is available from manufacturers like Grundfos or Franklin Electric. Testing equipment for groundwater should include kits for testing nitrates, heavy metals, and basic bacterial contamination, which can be found through agricultural or environmental testing suppliers.

Springs: Natural springs are an excellent water source if available. They often require minimal treatment since the water has been naturally filtered through layers of rock and soil. However, the flow from a spring can be seasonal, so it's important to assess the reliability of the spring throughout the year.

- **Purification Required:** While generally cleaner than surface water, springs can still be contaminated by surface runoff or nearby agricultural or industrial activities. It's advisable to conduct regular testing, especially after heavy rains or changes in land use nearby.
- **Equipment and Resources:** Capturing and storing spring water can be enhanced with proper collection and storage systems. This includes installing a collection basin and a storage tank. Tanks can be sourced from suppliers who provide a variety of sizes suitable for different needs. Spring boxes, which help protect and maintain the flow of water, can be custom-built or purchased from suppliers specializing in off-grid water systems.

Rainwater Harvesting

Collecting rainwater is a sustainable and effective way to secure a water supply, especially in areas with adequate rainfall. Rainwater is relatively clean when it falls, but it must be stored properly and filtered before use to ensure it is safe for drinking.

- **Collection Methods:** Rainwater is typically collected from rooftops using gutters and downspouts. The type of roofing material can affect the quality of the water collected— metal roofs, for example, tend to be better than asphalt shingles for collecting water. The water is then directed into storage tanks or cisterns.
- **Storage Considerations:** The storage system should be opaque to prevent algae growth and must be sealed to avoid contamination by insects, dust, or other debris. Storage tanks should be large enough to hold water from heavy rains, which might only occur seasonally. Calculating your storage needs requires understanding your local rainfall patterns and the size of your collection area.
- **Purification Required:** Even though rainwater is generally clean, it can pick up contaminants from the roof or gutter system, such as bird droppings, leaves, or other debris. A first-flush diverter, which discards the initial runoff from a rainstorm, can help improve the quality of the collected water. Filtration and UV treatment are recommended to ensure the water is safe for drinking.
- **Equipment and Resources:** Rainwater collection systems can be assembled with components available at most hardware stores. Specialized rainwater harvesting systems, including first-flush diverters and UV purifiers, can be purchased from several suppliers. If you're planning a large-scale system, it might be worth consulting with a rainwater harvesting specialist to design an efficient setup.

DIY Project 4: Rainwater Harvesting System

Rainwater harvesting is one of the most sustainable and accessible methods to secure a water supply in an off-grid environment. This project will guide you through setting up a basic rainwater collection system that can be expanded as needed.

Cost	$$	Difficulty	★★★

Materials:

- **Gutters:** To collect rainwater from the roof of your shelter.
- **Downspouts:** To direct water from gutters to the storage barrels.
- **Barrels or Tanks:** For storing the collected water. Food-grade plastic barrels are recommended.
- **First-Flush Diverter:** To remove the initial flow of water, which may contain debris.
- **Mesh Screens:** To prevent leaves and other debris from entering the system.
- **Filtration System:** A basic filter to purify the water before storage or use.
- **Piping:** To connect the barrels to your shelter and the filtration system.

Tools:

- **Drill:** For creating holes in the gutters and barrels.
- **Level:** To ensure the gutters are properly aligned.
- **Wrench:** For securing the connections.
- **Saw:** For cutting the gutters and downspouts to the required length.
- **Screwdriver:** For attaching the gutters and screens.

1	**Installing the Gutters** • Measure the perimeter of your shelter's roof to determine the length of gutters required. • Cut the gutters to the appropriate length using the saw. • Attach the gutters to the edge of the roof, ensuring they slope slightly towards the downspouts for effective water flow. Use the level to check the slope. • Secure the gutters with brackets and screws.
2	**Attaching the Downspouts** • Connect the downspouts to the gutters at the lowest points. Ensure they are firmly attached and direct the water flow towards your storage barrels. • Cut the downspouts to the necessary length, ensuring they reach the barrels without excessive bending.
3	**Setting Up the First-Flush Diverter** • Install the first-flush diverter at the top of the downspout. This device captures the initial flow of rainwater, which may contain dust, leaves, and other debris from the roof. The diverter allows this water to be discarded before clean water flows into the barrels.

	• Secure the diverter in place and connect it to the downspout leading to the storage barrels.
4	**Positioning the Barrels** • Place the barrels or tanks on a sturdy, level surface near the downspouts. Elevating the barrels on cinder blocks or a wooden platform can help improve water pressure for gravity-fed systems. • Drill a hole near the top of each barrel and install an overflow valve to prevent water from spilling over during heavy rains.
5	**Connecting the Barrels** • Connect the downspouts to the barrels using PVC piping or flexible tubing. Ensure the connections are watertight. • If using multiple barrels, connect them in series or parallel using additional piping to ensure even distribution of water.
6	**Adding Filtration** • Install a basic filtration system at the entry point of the barrels to remove any remaining debris. A mesh screen or a simple sand and gravel filter can be effective. • For drinking water, consider adding a more advanced filtration system, such as a ceramic filter, to ensure the water is safe for consumption.
7	**Maintenance and Testing** • Regularly inspect the gutters, downspouts, and barrels for debris, leaks, or blockages. Clean the filters and diverter as needed to maintain optimal performance. • Test the water quality periodically to ensure it meets safety standards, especially if used for drinking.

Your rainwater harvesting system is now operational! This setup will provide you with a reliable source of water, reducing your dependence on external sources and enhancing your self-reliance. With proper maintenance, this system can serve you for many years to come.

Water Filtration and Purification

Clean water is non-negotiable. Whether you're collecting rainwater, using surface water from a stream, or tapping into groundwater, it's crucial to ensure that the water is safe to drink. Contaminated water can carry pathogens such as bacteria, viruses, and parasites, which can lead to serious illness. In this section, we'll explore various methods of water filtration and purification, from basic DIY filters to more advanced purification techniques.

The Necessity of Clean Water

Imagine you're deep into your off-grid journey, and you've built a comfortable, self-sufficient life. But without clean water, everything could fall apart in an instant. Waterborne diseases like cholera, dysentery, and giardia have historically caused more fatalities than any other natural disaster. Even today, in areas without proper water treatment, these diseases remain a serious threat. For instance, during natural disasters like hurricanes and floods, the water supply can become contaminated, leading to outbreaks of disease. By establishing a robust water filtration and purification system, you safeguard your health and the health of your family.

Water Purification Methods

Once you have identified your water source, it's crucial to ensure that the water is safe for consumption. Contaminated water can lead to serious health issues, including gastrointestinal diseases, which can be particularly dangerous in an off-grid situation where medical help may be distant. Here are some common and effective water purification methods and in the next pages you will find some DIY solutions for almost of these methods.

Filtration

Filtration is the process of removing suspended particles, bacteria, and other contaminants from water by passing it through a porous material. Different filtration methods offer varying levels of effectiveness depending on the size and type of contaminants.

- **Sand and Gravel Filters:** These are simple to build and effective at removing large particles and some pathogens. They work by passing water through layers of sand and gravel, trapping contaminants in the process. Slow sand filters are very effective and can even remove some bacteria and viruses. These filters can be constructed from barrels or large tanks and require regular cleaning to maintain efficiency.

  Construction and Maintenance: To construct a sand and gravel filter, you will need a container (such as a 55-gallon drum), layers of fine sand, coarse sand, and gravel, and an outlet pipe. The sand needs to be washed and sterilized before use. Maintenance involves periodically removing the top layer of sand, which accumulates the most contaminants, and replacing it with fresh material.

Where to Get It: Sand and gravel can be sourced locally from construction supply companies. If you're near a river or coast, you might be able to collect your own, but it must be cleaned thoroughly. Containers for the filter can be purchased from industrial suppliers or even repurposed from old food-grade barrels.

- **Ceramic Filters:** These are more advanced and can remove bacteria and protozoa. Ceramic filters work by forcing water through a porous ceramic material that traps pathogens. They are often used in portable water filters and are ideal for off-grid use. These filters need to be regularly cleaned and replaced as they can become clogged over time.

  Usage: Ceramic filters are typically housed in a plastic or metal casing. Water is poured into the top, passes through the ceramic filter, and is collected in a clean container. Additionally, some systems incorporate a carbon filter to eliminate chemicals and improve flavor.

  Where to Get It: High-quality ceramic filters are available from specialized companies. These are available online or specialty outdoor and survival stores.

Boiling

Boiling water is one of the oldest and most reliable methods to kill viruses, bacteria and parasites. However, it requires a heat source and can be time-consuming if large quantities of water need to be purified.

- **Method:** Bring the water to a rolling boil for at least one minute (or three minutes at altitudes above 6,500 feet) to ensure that all pathogens are killed. After boiling, allow the water to cool naturally before using it. While boiling is effective at killing biological contaminants, it does not remove chemical contaminants or sediments, so it is best used in conjunction with filtration.

  Fuel Considerations: If you're living off-grid, your fuel supply for boiling water might be limited. Consider using a wood-burning stove or a rocket stove, both of which are efficient and can be built or purchased for off-grid use. Solar cookers are another option, using the sun's energy to heat water, which can be especially useful in sunny climates.

  Where to Get It: Rocket stoves and solar cookers can be purchased from outdoor supply stores or from specialized off-grid living suppliers.

Boiling has been used for centuries as a method to purify water: during the Middle Ages, people often boiled water to make it safe to drink, especially when dealing with outbreaks of waterborne diseases like cholera. Boiling was also a key practice in naval history; sailors would often boil their water to ensure it was free from harmful bacteria and parasites, which were common in stored water supplies.

While it doesn't remove chemical contaminants, it ensures that the water is biologically safe to drink, and this method is especially useful in emergency situations when you don't have access to other purification methods.

Distillation

Distillation involves heating water to produce steam, which is subsequently condensed back into liquid form, leaving most contaminants behind. This approach is particularly successful at removing pollutants like heavy metals, salts, and most microorganisms. Distillation can produce extremely pure water, but it requires significant energy, making it more suitable for specific situations or as a backup method.

- **Process:** To distill water, you'll need a heat source, a boiling chamber, a condenser, and a collection vessel. Water is heated until it vaporizes, leaving behind impurities like salts and heavy metals. The steam is then condensed back into water in a separate container.

  Considerations: While distillation is highly effective, it's energy-intensive and slow. It's also not practical for producing large quantities of water unless you have a robust and sustainable energy source. Distillation can also strip water of beneficial minerals, so it's generally best used as a supplemental method rather than your primary water source.

Where to Get It: Distillation kits can be purchased online from retailers specializing in emergency preparedness or homesteading supplies. For larger-scale operations, you might consider purchasing a solar distillation unit, which uses the sun's energy to evaporate and condense water. These units are available from suppliers like Survival Still or Prepper's Peak.

By understanding and implementing these water procurement and purification methods, you can ensure a reliable and safe water supply for your off-grid base camp. Whether you're sourcing water from a nearby river, drilling a well, or collecting rainwater, the key is to have multiple methods of purification at your disposal, ensuring you're prepared for any situation. Each method has its own strengths and limitations, so combining several techniques will give you the best chance of maintaining a healthy and sustainable water supply in the long term.

Chemical Treatment

Chemical treatments involve adding substances to water that kill or inactivate pathogens. This method is effective, especially as a backup or when other purification options are not available.

- **Chlorine:** Chlorine is widely used in municipal water systems and is effective at killing bacteria, viruses, and protozoa. Liquid chlorine bleach (sodium hypochlorite) can be used in small quantities to purify water. The typical dosage is 8 drops per gallon of water if the water is clear, or 16 drops per gallon if the water is cloudy. After adding chlorine, stir the water and let it sit for at least 30 minutes before drinking.

Considerations: Chlorine can leave an unpleasant taste in the water, and over time, its effectiveness can diminish as it reacts with organic matter in the water. It's also less effective against some protozoa, like Cryptosporidium.

Where to Get It: Household bleach is readily available at any grocery or hardware store. Use unscented bleach without other cleansers or additions. Sodium hypochlorite tablets, designed specifically for water purification, are also available from outdoor and camping stores.

- **Iodine:** Iodine is another chemical used for water purification, particularly in portable water purification tablets. It's effective against bacteria, viruses, and many protozoa. However, it is less effective than chlorine against Cryptosporidium and can be toxic if used over long periods.

Usage: Add iodine tablets according to the manufacturer's instructions, typically one tablet per liter of water. Let the water sit for 30 minutes to allow the iodine to work. Iodine-treated water may have a noticeable taste, which can be reduced by adding a vitamin C tablet after the purification process is complete.

Where to Get It: Iodine tablets can be purchased at most outdoor supply stores or online.

- **UV Light Purification:** Portable UV purifiers use ultraviolet light to destroy germs by breaking their DNA. These devices are effective against germs, viruses and protozoa and are easy for people to use. However, they require a power source, such as batteries or solar charging, and do not remove chemical contaminants or sediments.

Usage: Simply immerse the UV purifier in a container of clear water and activate it and stire the water to ensure even exposure to the UV light. The process typically takes about 60 to 90 seconds per liter of water.

Where to Get It: UV purifiers are available from outdoor equipment suppliers and can be purchased through major online retailers.

DIY Project 5: Building a DIY Water Filtration System

A DIY water filtration system can be an effective way to ensure that your water is clean and safe. This system uses natural materials like sand, charcoal, and gravel to remove sediments, bacteria, and other contaminants from your water.

The concept of using sand and charcoal for water filtration is not new. Ancient Egyptians used similar methods as far back as 2000 B.C. They filtered water through sand and charcoal before boiling it to ensure it was safe to drink. This method has stood the test of time and is still one of the most effective ways to purify water today.

Cost	$	Difficulty	★

Materials:

- Sand: Acts as a fine filter to trap small particles.
- Charcoal: Removes impurities, improves taste, and eliminates odors.
- Gravel: Catches larger particles and provides initial filtration.
- Containers: To hold the filtration materials and collect the filtered water

Tools:

- **Utility Knife:** For cutting containers.
- **Buckets:** To hold water and filtration materials.
- **Drill:** To make holes for water flow.

1	**Gather Materials**	Collect fine sand, activated charcoal (from a pet store or hardware store), and gravel. You'll also need two or more large buckets or containers, depending on the size of your system
2	**Prepare the Containers**	Drill a hole at the bottom of the first container to allow water to drain out. The hole should be small enough to prevent the filtration materials from escaping but large enough to allow water to flow through
3	**Layer the Materials**	In the first container, layer the gravel at the bottom, followed by the sand, and then the charcoal. The gravel should be the thickest layer (about 3-4 inches), followed by sand (2-3 inches), and finally a thinner layer of charcoal (1-2 inches).
4	**Assemble the System**	Place the container with the filtration materials over a clean container that will collect the filtered water. Pour the water into the top of the filter and allow it to pass through the layers.
5	**Test the Water**	Collect the filtered water in the bottom container. It's recommended to test the water using a water testing kit to ensure that it is free from harmful bacteria and safe to drink.

Additional Tips:

- **Boil After Filtering:** While this system removes many contaminants, it's a good practice to boil the water after filtration to kill any remaining pathogens.
- **Maintenance:** Over time, the sand and charcoal layers will become clogged with impurities. Replace the materials regularly to maintain the filter's effectiveness.

DIY Project 6: Solar Water Disinfection (SODIS)

If you're looking for a low-cost, low-tech method to purify water, Solar Water Disinfection (SODIS) might be the perfect solution. This method harnesses the power of the sun to kill pathogens, making water safe to drink. It's particularly useful in areas where chemical treatments are not available or practical.

SODIS uses UV radiation from sunlight to inactivate harmful bacteria, viruses, and protozoa in water. The process requires clear plastic or glass bottles and direct sunlight. This method is most effective in regions close to the equator where sunlight is intense.

The idea of using the sun to purify water isn't new. Ancient Greek and Egyptian civilizations recognized the sun's power to purify water. While they didn't understand the scientific principles behind it, they knew that water stored in clear containers and exposed to the sun was safer to drink. Today, this method is still widely used in developing countries and emergency situations as a simple, cost-effective way to ensure water safety.

Cost	$	Difficulty	★
Materials:			
• **Clear Plastic or Glass Bottles**: Bottles should be clean and transparent, with a capacity of no more than 2 liters. • **Sunlight**: A strong source of UV radiation			
Tools: none			
1	**Clean the Bottles** Start by thoroughly cleaning your plastic or glass bottles. Any dirt or residue inside the bottles can reduce the effectiveness of the disinfection process.		
2	**Fill with Water** Fill the bottles with the water you want to purify. Ensure the water is relatively clear; if it's muddy or cloudy, filter it first using a cloth or sand filter		
3	**Place in Sunlight** Lay the bottles horizontally on a reflective surface, such as a metal sheet or even on a roof. This position maximizes the exposure to sunlight. Leave the bottles in direct sunlight for at least 6 hours on a sunny day or 2 days if the weather is cloudy.		

4	**Drink or Store** After exposure, the water should be safe to drink. If you don't need it immediately, store the purified water in the same bottles or transfer it to a clean container.

Additional Tips:

- **Bottle Material:** Only use PET plastic bottles or glass bottles. PVC and other plastics can release harmful chemicals when exposed to sunlight.
- **Water Clarity:** SODIS is most effective with clear water. If your water is turbid, pre-filter it before using SODIS.
- **Suggested in case of emergency:** SODIS is a low-cost, simple, and environmentally friendly method that uses natural sunlight (UV-A rays) and it is particularly useful in rural and low-income areas where access to clean water and advanced purification technologies are limited. However I suggest to use it only in extreme cases and if you don't have any additional device (like UV Light purifiers).

UV Light Purification: High-Tech Water Treatment

UV light technology was first discovered in the early 20th century, but it wasn't until the 1950s that it began to be used for water treatment on a larger scale. Initially employed in municipal water systems, UV purification has since become a popular method for treating water in hospitals, laboratories, and remote locations. Today, portable UV purifiers are a staple for adventurers, hikers, and those living off the grid and the core working principle is the same of SODIS.

UV light purifiers typically come in the form of handheld devices, water bottles with built-in UV purifiers, or larger systems for purifying water in larger quantities. They use artificial UV-C light (which has a shorter wavelength and more energy than UV-A light) to disinfect water. UV-C light is very effective at destroying the DNA of microorganisms, rendering them unable to reproduce and cause illness. UV systems are quite effective, but they do not eliminate chemical pollutants or particles, thus they are frequently used in tandem with filtration systems.

However, the main differences with SODIS are crystal clear:

- UV light purifiers are highly effective at killing a wide range of pathogens quickly (typically within seconds or minutes).
- They are less dependent on environmental conditions compared to SODIS and can be used effectively even in water with some turbidity, although pre-filtration is recommended for very cloudy water.
- UV light purifiers are more expensive than the SODIS method, requiring an initial investment in the purifier device and ongoing costs for batteries or electricity. These devices are often

battery-operated or require electricity, making them more suitable for settings where power is available or in contexts where reliable access to clean water is critical.

DIY Project 7 - Distillation: Removing Contaminants and Pathogens

Distillation is a highly effective method for purifying water that involves heating water to create steam, which is then condensed back into liquid form. This process removes not only biological contaminants but also chemical pollutants, heavy metals, and salts. While distillation requires more energy and time, it provides some of the purest water possible.

When water is heated to its boiling point, it turns into steam, leaving behind any dissolved solids, contaminants, and microorganisms. The steam is then captured and cooled in a condenser, where it returns to a liquid state. The result is clean, distilled water.

Distillation has been used for centuries, particularly in maritime settings where fresh water was scarce. Sailors would use rudimentary stills to desalinate seawater during long voyages, ensuring they had a supply of fresh drinking water. This process was vital for survival on the open seas, where access to clean water was limited. Today, distillation remains a critical method for producing pure water, especially in areas where other water sources are heavily contaminated.

Cost	$$	Difficulty	★★★
Materials:			
• Heat Source: Stove, solar still, or any method of heating water. • Pot with Lid: To boil the water. • Condensing Coil or Tubing: To capture and cool the steam. • Collection Container: To store the distilled water.			
Tools: none			
1	**Set Up the Distillation System** Place a pot of water on your heat source. If you're using a stove or fire, ensure the pot is stable. Attach a condensing coil or tubing to the pot's lid. The coil should slope downward toward a collection container.		
2	**Boil the Water** Heat the water until it reaches a rolling boil. The water will begin to evaporate, turning into steam. The steam will travel through the condensing coil or tubing.		
3	**Condense the Steam** As the steam passes through the coil or tubing, it cools and returns to a liquid state. Collect the distilled water in a clean container.		

	Store the Distilled Water
4	Once the distillation process is complete, store the distilled water in a clean, covered container. It's now ready for drinking or use in any application requiring pure water

Additional Tips:

- **Energy Use:** Distillation is energy-intensive, so it's best used when fuel or heat sources are abundant.
- **Multi-Purpose Use:** Distilled water is excellent for use in medical applications, batteries, and other equipment that requires pure water free from minerals and contaminants.

Ensuring Water Security Through Filtration and Purification

In off-grid living, ensuring a reliable source of clean, safe water is one of your most critical tasks. By mastering these water filtration and purification techniques, you can protect yourself and your family from waterborne diseases and make the most of your natural water sources. Whether you choose a low-tech solution like Solar Water Disinfection (SODIS), the reliable simplicity of boiling, the high-tech convenience of UV purification, or the thoroughness of distillation, these methods equip you to handle whatever challenges come your way.

Water is life, and in the off-grid world, your ability to secure and purify water directly impacts your survival and well-being. With these techniques, you're not just making water safe—you're taking control of your essential resources and ensuring your off-grid journey is sustainable, healthy, and secure.

Building a Well

Establishing a reliable and sustainable water source is a cornerstone of off-grid living. While there are various methods to secure water, building a well offers one of the most dependable ways to tap into groundwater, ensuring a consistent supply of fresh water for your homestead.

Wells have been essential to human civilization for thousands of years, providing reliable water sources long before modern plumbing and infrastructure. In ancient Mesopotamia, one of the cradles of civilization, wells were hand-dug to provide water for irrigation and daily use, enabling the growth of agriculture and the rise of cities. The wells in ancient cities like Ur and Babylon were often community projects, dug with primitive tools but with immense significance for survival. Similarly, in ancient India, step wells (known as "baolis" or "vavs") were constructed as architectural marvels that not only provided water but also served as places of social gathering.

One of the most famous ancient wells is the Great Bath of Mohenjo-Daro, an advanced civilization in the Indus Valley dating back to around 2500 B.C. This well, along with others in the city, supplied water to public baths and homes, showcasing the importance of wells in urban planning and public health.

Although modern well drilling often involves sophisticated machinery, many off-grid enthusiasts turn to hand-dug wells as a cost-effective and accessible alternative. However, it's crucial to approach this task with careful planning, respect for safety protocols, and an understanding of the environmental factors involved.

Understanding Groundwater: The Hidden Resource

Before breaking ground on a well, it's essential to understand the nature of groundwater—this invisible resource flowing beneath your feet. Groundwater is stored in aquifers, which are layers of permeable rock, sand, or gravel that hold and transmit water. These underground reservoirs are replenished by rain and snowmelt that seep into the ground, making them a sustainable source of water when properly managed.

Assessing Groundwater Availability

The first step in building a well is determining whether groundwater is accessible at your location. Groundwater levels can vary significantly based on geographic location, local climate, and seasonal changes. In some regions, groundwater may be just a few feet below the surface, while in others, it could be hundreds of feet down. Here are a few methods to assess the potential for groundwater on your property:

- **Local Knowledge:** Speak with local farmers, well drillers, or neighbors who have experience with wells in your area. They can provide valuable insights into the depth and quality of the groundwater and any challenges they've faced.
- **Topographical Clues:** Surface features like nearby rivers, lakes, and low-lying areas can indicate where groundwater may be closer to the surface. Vegetation that thrives in wetter conditions, such as willows or certain types of grasses, can also be a sign of accessible groundwater.
- **Water Dowsing:** Also known as divining, water dowsing is an ancient practice where dowsers use rods or pendulums to locate underground water. Although this method is not scientifically proven, some people find it useful or interesting as a traditional approach to locating water. Whether you believe in its effectiveness or not, it can be an engaging way to explore old-world techniques.

In addition, many regions have geological surveys or water resource agencies that publish maps and data on groundwater levels. These resources can provide a broader understanding of the aquifers in your area, helping you to plan your well with greater accuracy.

DIY Project 8: Hand-Dug Well

Building a hand-dug well is a physically demanding but potentially rewarding project. Unlike drilled wells, which require specialized equipment, a hand-dug well relies on manual labor and simple tools. However, the process is labor-intensive and can be hazardous if not done correctly. Here's a detailed guide to help you through the process.

Cost	$$$$	Difficulty	★★★★★

Materials:

- Shovel and Pickaxe: Essential tools for digging and breaking through hard soil or rock layers.
- Buckets: Used for removing the excavated soil and transporting it away from the digging site.
- Well Casing (Concrete Rings or Well Tiles): These are used to line the well shaft, preventing the sides from collapsing and ensuring the structural integrity of the well.
- Rope and Pulley System: To lift buckets of soil out of the well as you dig deeper. This system reduces the physical strain and increases efficiency.
- Ladder: Necessary for entering and exiting the well safely as the depth increases

Tools:

- **Shovel:** Your primary tool for digging and moving earth.
- **Pickaxe:** For breaking through tougher soil or rock layers that are too hard for a shovel alone.
- **Level:** Ensures that the well casing is installed vertically and remains stable throughout the digging process.

1	**Select the Location** Choosing the right location for your well is crucial for both water quality and safety. The well should be located uphill from any potential sources of contamination, such as livestock pens, septic systems or chemical storage areas. A minimum distance of 50 feet is recommended to reduce the risk of contaminants leaching into the groundwater. Additionally, consider the proximity to your home or garden to minimize the effort required to transport water.
2	**Start Digging** Begin by marking out a circle approximately 4-6 feet in diameter. This size allows enough space for digging and for the installation of well casing as you go deeper. The initial digging is usually straightforward, especially if the ground is soft or sandy. As you dig, remove the soil using buckets, making sure to keep the area

	around the well clear to prevent tripping hazards or soil erosion. If you encounter hard layers of soil or rock, use a pickaxe to break through.
3	**Install Casing** As you dig deeper, the sides of the well become prone to collapse, especially in loose or sandy soils. To prevent this, you'll need to install well casing as you progress. The casing, typically made of concrete rings or well tiles, should be lowered into the well and stacked as you continue to dig. This casing not only supports the well walls but also prevents surface contaminants from entering the water supply. Ensure that each section of casing is level and securely placed before proceeding.
4	**Continue Digging** Continue digging until you reach the water table. The depth at which you hit water can vary greatly depending on your location and the time of year. You'll know you've reached groundwater when the bottom of the well begins to fill with water. At this stage, the work becomes more challenging as you'll need to remove water while continuing to dig. A simple hand pump or bucket can be used to bail out water as you deepen the well into the aquifer.
5	**Finish and Secure** Once you've dug at least 10-15 feet into the water table, the well is considered complete. This depth ensures that the well has a sufficient reservoir of water that can recharge even during dry periods. Smooth the bottom of the well to create a level surface where sediment can settle without disturbing the water quality. Finally, secure the top of the well with a well cover or cap to prevent debris, animals, or contaminants from entering the well. If desired, you can also install a hand pump or electric pump to make drawing water easier.

Safety Tips

Digging a well is not without risks. The deeper you dig, the greater the potential hazards, including cave-ins, suffocation from poor air circulation, and the physical demands of the work itself. Here are some crucial safety tips to keep in mind:

- **Shoring and Support:** always ensure the sides of the well are supported by casing as you dig deeper to prevent cave-ins. If you encounter particularly loose or unstable soil, consider reinforcing the well with additional shoring or bracing.
- **Avoid Digging Alone:** never dig a well alone. Always have someone nearby who can assist in case of an emergency. The risk of collapse or other accidents increases significantly with depth, and having a partner can make the work safer and more efficient.

- **Air Quality:** as you dig deeper, the air quality in the well can deteriorate, especially if there is poor ventilation. Consider using a fan or blower to circulate fresh air into the well, and take regular breaks to avoid exhaustion and dizziness.
- **Water Testing:** once the well is complete, have the water tested for contaminants, including bacteria, heavy metals, and chemicals. periodic testing is necessary to guarantee that the water is safe for drinking as well as other uses. If contaminants are found, you may need to install additional filtration or purification systems.
- **Use Proper Lifting Techniques:** when lifting buckets of soil or water, use proper lifting techniques to avoid strain or injury. A pulley system can help reduce the physical demands and prevent accidents.
- **Secure the Well Site:** after the well is completed, secure the area around the well to prevent accidents. Install a fence or barrier if necessary, especially if children or livestock are present on the property.

Alternative Well-Drilling Methods

While hand-dug wells are a viable option for many off-grid homesteaders, there are alternative methods to consider if the conditions are right:

- **Driven Wells:** driven wells involve driving a pipe with a pointed end into the ground until it reaches the water table. This method is suitable for shallow water tables in areas with loose, sandy soils. It's less labor-intensive than digging but is limited by depth and soil type.
- **Borehole Drilling:** borehole drilling uses a mechanical drill to reach deeper water sources. While this method requires specialized equipment and expertise, it's ideal for accessing water at greater depths and in rocky or hard soils. Boreholes can be drilled using hand-powered augers for shallower depths or motorized rigs for deeper wells.
- **Jetting:** it involves using a high-pressure stream of water to cut through soil and sediment, allowing a well pipe to be lowered into place. This method is effective in sandy or loose soils and can be quicker than traditional digging.

Case Study: Wells in Remote Villages

In remote villages in Africa and Asia, hand-dug wells remain a vital water source, especially in areas where modern drilling equipment is unavailable or too expensive. Community-led projects often spearhead the construction of these wells, with local knowledge and collective effort driving the success of the project. These wells, sometimes dug by entire communities over weeks or months, become the center of village life, providing water for drinking, cooking, and irrigation. The skills passed down through generations ensure that even in the absence of advanced technology, people can continue to access clean, reliable water.

Securing Your Water Independence with a Well

Building a well is one of the most fundamental steps in achieving true water independence on your off-grid homestead. Whether you choose to hand-dig a well or explore alternative drilling methods, the process requires careful planning, physical effort, and a commitment to safety. By understanding the principles of groundwater and taking the necessary precautions, you can create a reliable water source that will sustain your homestead for generations.

In embracing this age-old practice, you're not just digging a well; you're tapping into a tradition that has sustained human societies for millennia. The water you draw from your well is more than just a resource—it's a symbol of your self-reliance, your connection to the land, and your dedication to living sustainably and independently.

Greywater Recycling: Sustainable Water Management

Water conservation is a fundamental principle of sustainable living, especially in off-grid scenarios where every drop counts. Greywater recycling is an effective strategy to reuse water from sinks, showers, and laundry (excluding toilet waste) for purposes such as irrigation, flushing toilets, or even recharging groundwater. By recycling greywater, you can significantly reduce your overall water consumption, making your homestead more efficient and environmentally friendly. This section delves into the intricacies of greywater recycling, offering a comprehensive guide to setting up and maintaining your system.

The Importance of Greywater Recycling

In an off-grid environment, water scarcity can be a significant challenge. Greywater recycling offers a sustainable solution by maximizing the utility of water before it is released back into the environment. This practice not only conserves water but also reduces the strain on natural water sources, which is particularly crucial in arid regions or during droughts. Moreover, greywater recycling is beneficial to your plants, as it often contains nutrients that can enhance soil fertility, promoting healthier plant growth.

Historically, water reuse has been a cornerstone of water management in civilizations around the world. For instance, the ancient Romans, known for their advanced engineering, were masters of water management and practiced water recycling in their aqueducts and urban water systems. Used water from public baths, fountains, and public buildings was often redirected to flush public latrines or irrigate gardens. This efficient use of water allowed Roman cities to support large populations and maintain green spaces even in relatively dry climates. The principles behind this ancient water recycling are still relevant today, particularly in the context of sustainable off-grid living.

Understanding Greywater Systems

Greywater systems can range from simple, low-cost setups to more complex and automated systems depending on your needs, budget, and the scale of your homestead. Here's a closer look at the different types of greywater systems you can implement:

1. **Direct Use Systems:**
   - **Overview:** In direct use systems, greywater is immediately routed from sinks, showers, or washing machines to the garden or another use area without treatment. These systems are the simplest to install and can be highly effective if managed correctly.
   - **Advantages:** Simple installation and low cost. These systems work well in climates where over-saturation of soil is not a concern and where greywater is used regularly.
   - **Challenges:** Requires careful management to avoid overloading the soil with water, which can lead to waterlogging, root rot, or nutrient leaching.
2. **Treatment Systems:**
   - **Overview:** Treatment systems involve filtering and sometimes disinfecting greywater before it is reused. These systems are more complex and are often used when greywater will be applied to edible plants or stored for later use.
   - **Advantages:** Provides cleaner greywater, reducing the risk of contamination when used for irrigation of food crops. It also allows for more flexible use of greywater, including storage and later application.
   - **Challenges:** Higher initial cost and more maintenance required to keep the system functioning properly.

DIY Project 9: Building a Greywater Recycling System

Creating a greywater recycling system on your homestead can be a straightforward process if you follow a clear plan. Below is a detailed guide to help you build a basic greywater system suitable for irrigation, with options to expand or modify the system for other uses.

Cost	$$	Difficulty	★★★

Materials:

- Piping: To route greywater from your home to the garden. PVC or polyethylene pipes are commonly used due to their durability and ease of installation.
- Valves: To control the flow of greywater and direct it either to the garden or to the septic system if necessary.
- Filtration Materials: Gravel, sand, and activated carbon can be used for basic filtration to remove larger particles and reduce organic load.
- Distribution System: Drip irrigation lines or perforated hoses can be used to distribute the greywater evenly across your garden.

Tools:

- **Wrench:** For assembling and securing the pipes.
- **Saw:** To cut pipes to the correct length.
- **Drill:** For creating holes in the pipes or containers.

1	**Identify Greywater Sources**

	Begin by determining which greywater sources in your home you want to recycle. The most common sources include the bathroom sink, shower, and washing machine. Make sure that the greywater has no trace of dangerous chemicals or impurities that may harm plants or soil. If necessary, switch to biodegradable, non-toxic soaps and detergents to protect your greywater system and garden.
2	**Install Diverters** Diverters are essential for directing greywater either to the greywater system or to the septic system/sewer, depending on your needs. Install diverters on the drainpipes of your greywater sources. This setup allows you to control when and where the greywater is used, giving you the flexibility to manage water distribution more effectively.
3	**Route the Water** Use piping to route the greywater from the diverters to the garden or your chosen greywater storage. Ensure that the pipes are securely connected and sloped appropriately to allow gravity to move the water efficiently. If your system includes a treatment phase, route the greywater through the filtration unit before it reaches the garden.
4	**Filter the Greywater** If you're concerned about particles or contaminants in the greywater, set up a simple filtration system. This could involve a container filled with layers of gravel, sand, and activated carbon. The gravel and sand filter out larger particles, while the activated carbon helps to reduce organic compounds and odors. Filtered greywater is safer for use in irrigation, particularly for food crops
5	**Distribute the Water** In the garden, use drip lines or a perforated hose to distribute the greywater evenly. This helps prevent over-saturation of the soil and ensures that all plants receive adequate moisture. Drip irrigation is particularly effective because it delivers water directly to the root zone, minimizing evaporation and maximizing water efficiency.

Considerations and Tips:

- **Avoid Toxic Soaps:** only use biodegradable, non-toxic soaps and cleaners in sinks or showers that feed into your greywater system. Traditional soaps and detergents can contain chemicals that harm plants or accumulate in the soil, potentially leading to long-term contamination or reduced soil fertility.

- **Regular Maintenance:** greywater systems require regular maintenance to prevent clogs, leaks, or signs of contamination. Check filters and pipes regularly and clean or replace them as needed to ensure the system runs smoothly. Over time, organic matter can build up in the pipes and filters, reducing efficiency, so periodic cleaning is essential.

- **Legal Considerations:** before installing a greywater system, check local regulations. Some areas have specific rules governing the use of greywater, particularly when it comes to using greywater for food crops. You may need to obtain permits or adhere to certain guidelines to ensure your system is legal and safe.
- **Managing Salinity:** greywater can sometimes contain higher levels of salts, particularly if using water from laundry. High salinity can damage soil structure and harm plants. If salinity is a concern, consider mixing greywater with fresh water or using plants that are more tolerant to salty conditions, such as certain types of grasses or shrubs.
- **Seasonal Adjustments:** in regions with distinct wet and dry seasons, you may need to adjust your greywater usage accordingly. During the rainy season, you might reduce the use of greywater in the garden to prevent waterlogging. In the dry season, however, greywater can be an invaluable resource to keep your garden thriving.
- **Design for Flexibility:** consider designing your greywater system with flexibility in mind. For example, you might include a manual override or bypass option that allows you to divert greywater to different parts of your garden or switch to fresh water if needed. This flexibility can help you manage water use more effectively throughout the year.

Advanced Greywater Systems: Taking It Further

For those who want to maximize the utility of their greywater system, there are more advanced options that can further enhance water conservation and sustainability:

Constructed Wetlands: a constructed wetland is a natural filtration system that uses plants, soil, and microorganisms to treat greywater. Greywater is routed into a shallow bed planted with reeds, cattails, or other water-loving plants. As the water flows through the bed, the plants and microorganisms break down contaminants and absorb nutrients, effectively cleaning the water. The treated water can then be used for irrigation or released into the environment. Constructed wetlands are particularly useful for large-scale greywater systems and can double as an attractive landscape feature.

Biological Filters: biological filters use a combination of gravel, sand, and biofilms (layers of microorganisms) to treat greywater. As the greywater passes through the filter, the biofilms break down organic matter and reduce pathogens, resulting in cleaner water. These systems can be integrated into existing greywater setups, providing an additional layer of purification before the water is reused.

Greywater Heat Recovery: greywater heat recovery systems capture the heat from used water (like from showers or laundry) and use it to preheat incoming cold water. This process reduces the energy needed to heat water, saving both energy and money. While this system doesn't treat greywater for reuse, it adds another dimension to water conservation by making better use of the energy embedded in your water.

Automated Systems: for those who prefer a more hands-off approach, automated greywater systems can be set up with sensors and controls that monitor water quality and manage the flow of greywater based on preset criteria. These systems can adjust irrigation schedules, switch between greywater and fresh water sources, and alert you to maintenance needs, ensuring your greywater system operates efficiently without constant oversight.

The Future of Sustainable Water Use

Greywater recycling is a powerful tool in the arsenal of sustainable living. By implementing a greywater system, you not only reduce your reliance on fresh water but also contribute to the overall health and resilience of your homestead. Whether you opt for a simple direct use system or invest in more advanced greywater treatment, the key is to understand your water needs, monitor your system regularly, and adapt it to your specific environment and lifestyle.

Incorporating greywater recycling into your off-grid living plan is more than just a practical step—it's a commitment to a sustainable future where resources are used wisely and responsibly. With careful planning and attention to detail, your greywater system can provide you with years of reliable, efficient, and environmentally friendly water use, making your homestead a model of self-sufficiency and sustainability.

Securing Your Water Independence

Water is the foundation of life, and securing a reliable, clean water supply is one of the most critical aspects of off-grid living. By mastering these techniques—filtration, well-building, and greywater recycling—you can ensure that your homestead remains self-sufficient, resilient, and sustainable. Each project requires careful planning, dedication, and a willingness to learn, but the rewards are immense: peace of mind, independence from external water supplies, and a secure, sustainable lifestyle.

As you implement these systems, remember that you're not just providing for your current needs; you're also building a legacy of self-reliance and environmental stewardship that can sustain future generations.

Chapter 4 - Off-Grid Food Production, Preservation, Cooking and Consumption

One of the most empowering aspects of off-grid living is the ability to produce your own food. Imagine walking outside your door to a garden full of fresh vegetables or collecting eggs from your chickens each morning. Not only does this provide you with the freshest, most nutritious food possible, but it also ensures that you're not dependent on external systems that can fail or become disrupted. In this chapter, we'll delve into the essentials of growing your own food, raising livestock, and preserving your harvest to ensure you have a reliable food supply all year round. By the end, you'll be well on your way to achieving true food self-sufficiency.

Growing Your Own Food

Why should you grow your own food? The answer is simple: control, security, and sustainability. When you grow your own food, you control what goes into it—no harmful pesticides, no GMOs, and no reliance on long-distance transportation that contributes to environmental degradation. It's also about security. In uncertain times, food supply chains can be disrupted, prices can skyrocket, and access to fresh produce can become limited. Remember the empty grocery store shelves during the COVID-19 pandemic? Those who had their own gardens were less affected by these shortages.

Growing your own food is not just a practical choice; it's a sustainable one. By cultivating a garden, you're reducing your carbon footprint, preserving natural habitats by reducing the demand for mass-produced crops, and contributing to biodiversity. And let's not forget the satisfaction that comes from eating a meal you've grown yourself—it's a connection to the land that few modern conveniences can match.

For example, in Detroit, Michigan, where urban decay has left many vacant lots, residents have turned these spaces into thriving urban gardens. Raised beds are commonly used due to the poor soil quality and the need to avoid contaminants in the ground. These gardens not only provide fresh produce to communities but also serve as a beacon of hope and renewal in areas that have faced economic hardship.

Planning Your Garden: What to Grow and Where

So, where do you start? The first step is planning your garden. The success of your garden hinges on thoughtful planning—choosing the right crops for your climate, understanding your soil, and deciding on the layout of your garden.

Questions to Consider:

1. **What's Your Climate?** Your local climate will heavily influence what you can grow. For example, if you live in a region with hot, dry summers, you might focus on drought-tolerant crops like tomatoes, peppers, and beans. In cooler climates, root vegetables like carrots, potatoes, and beets might thrive.
2. **What Do You Like to Eat?** It might seem obvious but grow what you love to eat. Make a list of your favorite fruits and vegetables and prioritize them in your garden.
3. **How Much Space Do You Have?** Whether you have a large backyard or a simply a small balcony there's a gardening solution for you. If you have limited space, consider vertical or container gardening. For larger spaces, you might want to consider a traditional row garden or raised beds.
4. **What's the Condition of Your Soil?** Soil quality is crucial for a healthy garden. Do you have clay, loamy or sandy soil? Each variety has unique drainage and nutrient-holding characteristics. Conduct a soil test to determine its pH and nutrient levels, which will guide you in amending your soil for the best growing conditions.

Easy-to-Grow Vegetables and Fruits

Choosing the right plants for your garden can make the difference between a bountiful harvest and a disappointing season. Here are some of the most resilient and easy-to-grow vegetables and fruits, particularly suited for those new to gardening or living in challenging climates.

Vegetables:

1. **Tomatoes:**
   - **Growing Conditions:** Tomatoes thrive in warm weather and require full sun. Once established, they are relatively drought-tolerant. However, they require constant watering.
   - **Why They're Easy:** Tomatoes are highly adaptable and can be grown in the ground, in containers, or even in hanging baskets. They also have a relatively short growing season, making them ideal for many climates.
2. **Zucchini:**
   - **Growing Conditions:** Zucchini prefers warm weather and full sun. It needs well-drained soil and regular watering.
   - **Why They're Easy:** Zucchini is known for its prolific production. One or two plants can produce more than enough for a small family, and they require minimal care once established.
3. **Carrots:**
   - **Growing Conditions:** Carrots do well in cooler climates and prefer loose, sandy soil. They require continuous moisture but are generally low maintenance.
   - **Why They're Easy:** Carrots are relatively pest-resistant and can be left in the ground until you're ready to harvest, making them a flexible crop for busy gardeners.
4. **Kale:**
   - **Growing Conditions:** Kale thrives in cool weather and can tolerate light frosts, which actually improve its flavor. It prefers well-drained, fertile soil.

50

- o **Why They're Easy:** Kale is a hardy vegetable that can be grown almost year-round in many climates. It's also a cut-and-come-again crop, meaning you can harvest leaves as needed and the plant will continue to produce.

5. **Beans:**
   - o **Growing Conditions:** Beans prefer warm weather and full sun. They are relatively drought-tolerant and do well in average soil.
   - o **Why They're Easy:** Beans are one of the easiest vegetables to grow. They don't require much fertilizer, and once established, they need minimal care. Plus, they fix nitrogen in the soil, improving fertility for future crops.

Fruits:

1. **Strawberries:**
   - o **Growing Conditions:** Strawberries need full sun and well-drained soil and they can be grown in the ground, in raised beds or in containers.
   - o **Why They're Easy:** Strawberries are perennials, meaning they come back year after year, and they can produce fruit quickly and require low maintenance.
2. **Raspberries:**
   - o **Growing Conditions:** Raspberries prefer cool climates and well-drained, slightly acidic soil. They require a sunny location and constant watering.
   - o **Why They're Easy:** Raspberries are perennial and can produce fruit for many years. They are relatively hardy and can thrive with minimal intervention once established.
3. **Blueberries:**
   - o **Growing Conditions:** Blueberries require acidic soil and full sun. They need consistent moisture and well-drained soil.
   - o **Why They're Easy:** Blueberries are another perennial that, with the right soil conditions, can produce fruit for decades. They are also relatively pest-resistant.
4. **Apple Trees:**
   - o **Growing Conditions:** Apple trees thrive in temperate climates with well-drained soil. They need full sun and regular watering, especially when young.
   - o **Why They're Easy:** While apple trees take a few years to start producing fruit, they require relatively low maintenance once established. They are long-lived and can provide a consistent harvest for many years.
5. **Fig Trees:**
   - o **Growing Conditions:** Figs prefer warm, dry climates and well-drained soil. They need full sun and minimal watering once established.
   - o **Why They're Easy:** Fig trees are incredibly resilient, drought-tolerant, and can produce abundant fruit with minimal care. They are also suitable for growing in containers.

Let me conclude this Section with an historical anecdote: during World War II, the U.S. government encouraged citizens to grow "Victory Gardens" to supplement their rations and reduce pressure on the public food supply. These gardens produced nearly 40% of the fresh vegetables consumed in the

U.S. by 1944. The Victory Garden movement is a powerful example of how individuals can collectively contribute to food security in times of crisis. Imagine how self-sufficient you could be by cultivating a modern-day victory garden, filled with these resilient, easy-to-grow crops.

DIY Vegetable Garden

Good soil is the foundation of any successful garden. But what if your soil isn't perfect? That's where soil preparation and composting come in. Composting is one of the best ways to improve your soil, adding nutrients and improving its structure. Plus, it's an excellent way to recycle your kitchen scraps and yard waste.

How to Start Composting:

1. **Choose a Location:** Find a spot in your yard that's easily accessible but not too close to your living space (to avoid any unpleasant smells). It should be in a location that gets some shade to prevent the compost from drying out too quickly.
2. **Build or Buy a Compost Bin:** You can make a simple compost bin from wood pallets or buy a ready-made bin. The key is to have a structure that allows for good airflow and can retain heat to speed up the composting process.
3. **Start Layering:** Begin by adding a layer of coarse material, like twigs or straw, to help with aeration. Then, alternate between green materials (like fruit and vegetable scraps, coffee grounds and grass clippings) and brown materials (like leaves, straw and paper). Aim for a 50:50 mix of green to brown materials.
4. **Maintain the Pile:** Turn the compost on a frequent basis to help it aerate and decompose faster and keep the pile moist but not saturated. After a few months, you'll have rich, dark compost to mix into your plant beds.

DIY Project 10: Raised Bed Garden Construction

Raised beds are a fantastic option for gardening, especially if your soil is poor or you want to reduce the strain on your back. They allow for better control over soil quality, drainage, and can extend your growing season by warming up faster in the spring.

Cost	$$	Difficulty	★★
Materials:			

- **Wood Planks:** Cedar or redwood are good choices as they resist rot.
- **Soil:** A mix of compost, topsoil, and organic matter.
- **Compost:** Your own homemade compost or store-bought.
- **Mulch:** To retain moisture and suppress weeds.

Tools:

- **Saw:** To cut the wood planks to size.
- **Hammer and Nails:** Or screws and a drill if you prefer.
- **Level:** To ensure your beds are even.
- **Measuring Tape:** For accurate cutting and spacing.

1	**Planning the Size and Location**	Choose a sunny spot in your garden, as most vegetables need at least 6-8 hours of sunlight a day. A standard raised bed is 4 feet wide (so you can reach the center from either side) and 8 feet long, but you can adjust the size based on your space
2	**Cutting the Wood**	Cut your wood planks to the desired lengths. Consider that a 4x8 bed requires two 8-foot planks and two 4-foot planks. If you want the bed to be deeper, you can stack multiple layers of planks.
3	**Assembling the Bed**	Assemble the wood planks into a rectangle using nails or screws. Ensure the corners are square and the bed is level. If stacking, secure each layer of planks to the one below.
4	**Preparing the Ground**	Clear the ground where the bed will be placed. If you have issues with weeds, consider laying down a weed barrier fabric before placing the bed
5	**Filling the Bed**	Fill the bed with a mix of topsoil, compost, and organic matter. Opt for a soil depth of at least 12-13 inches to allow for the development of roots. Rake the surface smooth and water thoroughly before planting.

Sustainable Livestock

Raising livestock is an excellent way to increase your food self-sufficiency and diversify your off-grid homestead. Animals such as chickens, goats, and rabbits are particularly well-suited for small-scale, off-grid living because they don't require large amounts of space and provide a steady source of protein, milk, and other resources. However, there are other animals you can consider raising, each with its own set of benefits and challenges. In this section, we'll explore the basics of raising these animals, the potential issues you might face, and how to overcome them.

Please note that while raising livestock can be incredibly rewarding, it's important to recognize that it's not a task for the faint of heart or the inexperienced. The average person may find the learning curve steep, as it requires a deep commitment to animal care, a solid understanding of their needs, and the ability to respond to challenges that arise—often without immediate outside help. Starting small and gradually building your experience is key to ensuring both your success and the welfare of your animals.

Historical Anecdote: Thomas Jefferson's Monticello Farm

Thomas Jefferson, one of America's Founding Fathers, was also a passionate farmer and livestock keeper. At Monticello, his Virginia estate, Jefferson raised a variety of animals, including sheep, pigs, and poultry, to provide for his household and support his experimental agriculture practices. Jefferson's approach to farming was innovative for his time, focusing on sustainability and self-sufficiency. His dedication to livestock keeping at Monticello is a reminder that even in times of great political and social responsibility, sustainable food production remains a cornerstone of independence.

Chickens: The Gateway to Livestock Keeping

Did you know that during World War II, First Lady Eleanor Roosevelt kept a flock of chickens on the White House lawn? It was part of the Victory Garden effort, and the eggs produced by those chickens helped to supplement the White House kitchen during times of rationing. This anecdote highlights how even small-scale livestock keeping can make a big difference in food self-sufficiency.

Benefits:

- **Eggs and Meat:** Chickens are arguably the most popular choice for backyard livestock due to their ability to provide both eggs and meat. A small flock can keep your family supplied with fresh eggs daily, and extra roosters or older hens can be processed for meat.
- **Insect Control:** Chickens are natural foragers and can help control pests in your garden by eating insects, grubs, and even weeds.
- **Easy to Manage:** Chickens are relatively low maintenance. Once their coop is set up, they need daily feeding, occasional cleaning, and monitoring for health issues.

Challenges:

- **Predators:** Foxes, raccoons hawks, and even neighborhood dogs are among the predators that might harm chickens. Ensuring your coop is predator-proof is crucial.
- **Space Needs:** While chickens don't need much space, overcrowding can lead to stress, disease, and aggressive behavior. Plan for at least 2-3 square feet per chicken inside the coop and 8-10 square feet per chicken in the run.
- **Health Issues:** Chickens can suffer from various health problems, such as mites, lice, and respiratory diseases. For this reason, regular health checks and keeping a clean-living environment are crucial.

DIY Project 11: Build a Chicken Coop

Building a chicken coop is an essential step if you plan to keep chickens. The coop provides shelter from the elements, a safe place to lay eggs, and protection from predators.

Cost	$$	Difficulty	★★★

Materials:

- **Plywood:** For the walls and roof.
- **Chicken Wire:** To create a secure run and ventilation.
- **Nails and Screws:** To assemble the structure.
- **Hinges and Latches:** For doors and windows.
- **Roofing Material:** Such as shingles or metal sheets

Tools:

- **Hammer and Nails:** Or a drill and screws.
- **Saw:** To cut the plywood to size.
- **Measuring Tape:** For accurate cutting.
- **Level:** To ensure the coop is stable.
- **Wire Cutters:** For cutting chicken wire.

1	**Planning the Coop Size** Determine the size of the coop based on the number of chickens you plan to keep. A good rule of thumb is 2-3 square feet per chicken inside the coop and 8-10 square feet per chicken in the run.
2	**Building the Frame** Build the frame of the coop using 2x4s. Start with the floor, then add the walls and roof. Make sure the frame is level and secure
3	**Adding the Walls and Roof** Attach plywood sheets to the frame to create the walls. Cut out openings for windows and doors. Attach the roofing material, ensuring it's weatherproof.
4	**Installing Chicken Wire** Surround the run area with chicken wire, burying the bottom several inches into the ground to prevent predators from digging under. Install the wire over windows for ventilation while keeping the chickens safe
5	**Finishing Touches** Install doors and windows using hinges and latches. Incorporate nesting boxes within the coop and install perches to provide the chickens with a comfortable

	place to roost during the night. Additionally, cover the floor with straw or wood shavings to create suitable bedding

Goats: Versatile and Hardy Livestock

Benefits:

- **Milk and Meat:** Goats are incredibly versatile. They can provide milk, which can be consumed fresh, made into cheese, or used in cooking. Certain breeds are also raised for meat, which is lean and nutritious.
- **Weed Control:** Goats are excellent for clearing overgrown areas. They're natural browsers, preferring shrubs and weeds over grass, which makes them useful for managing vegetation.
- **Hardiness:** Goats are typically resilient creatures capable of flourishing in a wide range of environmental conditions and climates. They're particularly well-suited to dry, arid environments where other livestock might struggle.

Challenges:

- **Fencing:** Goats are notorious escape artists. They're curious, intelligent, and can jump or climb over standard fencing. A strong, high fence with no gaps is necessary to keep them contained.
- **Feeding Needs:** While goats can eat a variety of plants, they need a balanced diet that includes hay, grains, and minerals to stay healthy. They can also be prone to overgrazing, so rotational grazing or providing supplemental feed may be necessary.
- **Health Issues:** Goats can be prone to parasites, particularly if they're kept in damp or muddy conditions. Consistent deworming and vigilant observation for indications of illness are essential.

Tips:

- **Build a Secure Enclosure:** Use tall, sturdy fencing—at least 4 to 5 feet high. Electric fencing can be a good deterrent for escape attempts.
- **Feed and Water Management:** Ensure goats have access to clean water at all times. Invest in high-quality hay and consider a mineral block specifically designed for goats to ensure they get the necessary nutrients.

Rabbits: Quiet and Efficient Protein Source

Benefits:

- **Meat Production:** Rabbits are one of the most efficient animals for meat production. They reproduce quickly, and their meat is lean and high in protein. A small rabbitry can provide a significant amount of meat in a short period.
- **Manure:** Rabbit manure is one of the best fertilizers for your garden. It's rich in nitrogen and can be applied directly to plants without composting, unlike chicken manure, which is too "hot" and needs to break down first.
- **Space-Efficient:** Rabbits require very little space, making them ideal for small homesteads or urban settings. They can be raised in hutches or colonies, depending on your preference and available space.

Challenges:

- **Heat Sensitivity:** Rabbits are sensitive to heat and can suffer from heatstroke in hot climates. Proper ventilation and shade are critical, especially during summer.
- **Predators:** Like chickens, rabbits are vulnerable to predators. Their housing needs to be secure from animals like dogs, foxes, and raccoons.
- **Breeding Management:** While rabbits breed easily, managing their reproduction to prevent overpopulation can be challenging. It's important to have a plan for either processing or selling the offspring.

Tips:

- **Build a Shaded Hutch:** Ensure that your rabbit hutch is well-ventilated and placed in a shaded area. Provide frozen water bottles during hot days to help keep the rabbits cool.
- **Use Wire Floors:** In hutches, wire floors can help keep the living area clean by allowing droppings to fall through. However, provide solid resting areas to prevent sores on their feet.

Ducks: An Alternative to Chickens

Benefits:

- **Egg Production:** Ducks lay large, nutritious eggs that are prized for baking. Unlike chickens, ducks often continue laying through the winter with minimal lighting.
- **Pest Control:** Ducks are excellent foragers and can help control pests like slugs, snails, and insects in your garden.
- **Water Efficiency:** Ducks are less likely than chickens to scratch up your garden, making them a better choice for areas where you want to preserve plant roots.

Challenges:

- **Water Needs:** Ducks need access to water to stay healthy, which can be challenging in dry climates. A small pond or kiddie pool can suffice, but it will need regular cleaning.

- **Messiness:** Ducks are messier than chickens. They enjoy splashing in water, which can turn their living area into a muddy mess if not managed properly.

Tips:

- **Provide Fresh Water:** Ducks need clean water to drink and bathe in. Use shallow tubs or kiddie pools that can be easily emptied and refilled.
- **Build a Secure Duck House:** Ducks need shelter from predators at night. A well-ventilated duck house with a secure door will keep them safe.

Bees: Pollinators and Honey Producers

Benefits:

- **Honey Production:** Bees produce honey, which can be used for personal consumption or sold for profit. Honey is a natural sweetener with a long shelf life.
- **Pollination:** Bees play a crucial role as pollinators for a wide variety of fruits, vegetables and flowering plants. Keeping bees can improve the yield of your garden or orchard.
- **Low Maintenance:** Once established, beehives require relatively low maintenance compared to other livestock.

Challenges:

- **Stings:** Working with bees comes with the risk of being stung, which can be dangerous if you or someone in your household is allergic.
- **Seasonal Management:** Beekeeping is seasonal, with most of the work concentrated in spring and summer. Bees need to be prepared for winter, which involves ensuring they have enough food stored in the hive.
- **Environmental Sensitivity:** Bees are sensitive to pesticides and can be affected by diseases and parasites like Varroa mites. Maintaining a healthy hive requires monitoring and sometimes intervention.

Tips:

- **Start Small:** Begin with one or two hives to learn the basics of beekeeping. Over time, you can expand your apiary.
- **Use Natural Pest Control:** Avoid using chemical pesticides in your garden to protect your bees. Instead, focus on organic and natural pest control methods.

Pigs: A Source of Meat and Composting Helpers

Benefits:

- **Meat Production:** Pigs are an excellent source of meat, and they can be raised on a variety of feeds, including kitchen scraps and garden waste.
- **Land Clearing:** Pigs are natural rototillers. They will dig up roots and turn over soil as they forage, which can help prepare land for planting.
- **Composting:** Pigs are effective at breaking down organic material, which can be composted and used in the garden.

Challenges:

- **Space and Fencing:** Pigs require strong fencing as they are powerful animals that can root under or push through weak barriers. They also need enough space to forage and express natural behaviors.
- **Feeding Needs:** Pigs have high energy and protein needs, requiring a balanced diet. If you're relying on foraging or scraps, you'll need to supplement with grains or commercial pig feed.
- **Odor:** Pigs can be smelly, particularly if their pen isn't managed well. Regular cleaning and composting of waste can mitigate odors.

Tips:

- **Invest in Strong Fencing:** Use electric fencing or hog panels to keep pigs contained. Regularly check for signs of digging or wear.
- **Rotate Pastures:** If possible, rotate pigs between different areas to prevent overgrazing and to manage waste effectively.

Other Livestock Considerations

While these animals provide a solid foundation for a sustainable off-grid homestead, it's essential to consider a few more factors before deciding which animals to raise:

- **Climate:** Some animals are better suited to specific climates. For example, goats and sheep do well in dry, arid environments, while ducks and pigs thrive in wetter conditions.
- **Space:** The amount of space you have will determine how many animals you can comfortably and humanely raise. The phenomenon of overcrowding may result in heightened stress levels, the spread of illness, and diminished productivity.
- **Time and Effort:** Raising livestock requires daily care. Ensure you have the time and resources to commit to feeding, cleaning, and monitoring the health of your animals.
- **Legal Considerations:** It is essential to review the local zoning laws and regulations that pertain to the keeping of livestock. Some areas may have restrictions on the number or type of animals you can keep.

In conclusion, by diversifying the livestock you raise, you can ensure a steady supply of food and other resources while contributing to the overall sustainability of your homestead. Each animal brings unique benefits and challenges, but with careful planning and commitment, they can all play a vital role in your journey toward self-sufficiency. Please always keep in mind that sustainable livestock management is about more than just the animals—it's about creating a balanced system that works in harmony with your land, your resources, and your lifestyle.

Food Preservation Techniques

Growing and raising your own food is only part of the equation—you also need to know how to preserve your harvest to ensure a steady food supply year-round. Proper food preservation techniques are crucial for reducing waste and ensuring that you have access to nutritious food even when fresh produce is out of season. This section will explore some of the most effective and time-tested methods of food preservation: canning, drying, and fermenting. Each method has its unique benefits, challenges, and historical significance.

Canning: Capturing the Harvest in a Jar

Canning was invented by French confectioner Nicolas Appert in the early 19th century. He developed the process in response to a challenge from Napoleon Bonaparte, who needed a way to safely preserve food for his troops. Appert's technique consisted of enclosing food within glass containers and subjecting them to heat in boiling water, a process that established the groundwork for contemporary canning practices. Interestingly, the process was developed before scientists understood the role of bacteria in food spoilage — Appert's method worked, but the reason why wasn't fully understood until later.

Canning is one of the oldest and most reliable methods of food preservation. By sealing food in jars and heating them to a temperature that destroys harmful bacteria, you can store fruits, vegetables, and even meats for years. Canning allows you to enjoy the taste of summer produce in the depths of winter, ensuring your hard work in the garden doesn't go to waste.

Types of Canning:

1. **Water Bath Canning:**
   o **Best For:** High-acid foods such as fruits, pickles, and jams.
   o **Method:** Food is packed into jars, and the jars are submerged in boiling water for a specific amount of time. The heat kills bacteria, yeast, and molds, and creates a vacuum seal as the jars cool.
   o **Pros:** Simple and cost-effective. Requires minimal equipment—a large pot with a lid and a rack to keep the jars off the bottom.
   o **Cons:** Not suitable for low-acid foods due to the risk of botulism, a potentially deadly foodborne illness.
2. **Pressure Canning:**
   o **Best For:** Foods that are low in acidity include items such as vegetables, meats and various types of soups.

- o **Method:** Food is packed into jars and placed in a pressure canner, where it is heated to temperatures above boiling (240°F/116°C). This higher temperature is necessary to safely preserve low-acid foods.
- o **Pros:** Safe for preserving a wide variety of foods, including those that cannot be safely canned using the water bath method.
- o **Cons:** Requires more specialized equipment (a pressure canner), which is an investment. The process is also more complex and time-consuming.

Practical Tips:

- **Sterilization is Key:** Always sterilize your jars and lids before canning to prevent contamination.
- **Follow Recipes Exactly:** Canning recipes are scientifically tested to ensure safety. Altering ingredients, especially the acid levels, can lead to dangerous results.
- **Label Your Jars:** Labeling each jar with the date and contents is critical for successful inventory management and ensuring that older preserves are used before newer ones.

Drying: Nature's Simple Preservation

The process of drying eliminates moisture from food, thereby preventing the proliferation of bacteria, yeasts and molds. This method has been used for thousands of years and is one of the simplest ways to preserve food. Dried foods are lightweight, space-saving, and retain much of their nutritional value. It is possible to dehydrate a variety of items, including fruits, vegetables, herbs, and meats.

Native Americans were experts in drying food to ensure a stable food supply through harsh winters. They created pemmican, a concentrated mixture of dried meat, fat, and sometimes berries. Pemmican was highly nutritious, portable, and could last for years without spoiling. This technique was essential for survival in environments where fresh food was scarce for months at a time and is a testament to the effectiveness of drying as a preservation method.

Solar drying has been used for centuries in other cultures. In Mediterranean regions, figs, grapes (for raisins), and tomatoes have been sun-dried for generations. This simple method preserved these fruits for year-round use and is still in practice today. In fact, many of the dried fruits and vegetables we find in stores are produced using modern versions of these ancient solar drying techniques.

Methods of Drying:

1. **Sun Drying:**
   - o **Best For:** Fruits like grapes (for raisins), apricots, and tomatoes, as well as herbs.
   - o **Method:** Food is arranged in a single layer on trays and allowed to dry under the sun. This technique is most effective in warm, dry areas.
   - o **Pros:** No equipment needed; relies solely on natural sunlight and airflow.

- **Cons:** Dependent on weather; can take several days and is vulnerable to pests and contamination.
2. **Dehydrator Drying:**
   - **Best For:** A wide range of foods, including fruits, vegetables, meats (for jerky), and herbs.
   - **Method:** Food is placed in a dehydrator, a device that circulates warm air at a controlled temperature, speeding up the drying process.
   - **Pros:** Consistent and efficient; can dry food quickly regardless of weather.
   - **Cons:** Requires an initial investment in a dehydrator. Uses electricity, which may be a consideration for off-grid living unless you have a reliable renewable energy source.

Practical Tips:

- **Cut Uniformly:** Ensure that pieces are cut to a consistent size to dry evenly.
- **Pre-Treatment:** Some fruits benefit from pre-treatments like blanching or dipping in lemon juice to preserve color and nutrients.
- **Storage:** Store dried foods in airtight containers in a cool, dark place to maintain their quality.

DIY Project 12: Solar Dehydrator

A solar dehydrator serves as an excellent method for drying fruits, vegetables, and herbs while eliminating the need for electrical power. It harnesses the power of the sun, making it a perfect addition to your off-grid homestead. Building your solar dehydrator can be a rewarding project that reduces your reliance on modern appliances while ensuring you can preserve food sustainably.

Cost	$$	Difficulty	★★
Materials:			
<ul><li>**Glass Panels:** For the top of the dehydrator to let in sunlight.</li><li>**Wood:** For the frame and drying trays.</li><li>**Mesh Trays:** To hold the food while allowing air circulation.</li><li>**Nails and Screws:** To assemble the structure</li></ul>			
Tools:			
<ul><li>**Saw:** To cut the wood to size.</li><li>**Hammer and Nails:** Or screws and a drill.</li><li>**Screwdriver:** To assemble the trays.</li><li>**Measuring Tape:** For accurate cutting.</li></ul>			
1	**Building the Frame**		

	Build a rectangular frame using wood planks. The size depends on how much food you plan to dry at once, but a good starting point is a 2x3 foot frame.
2	**Installing the Glass Top** Attach glass panels to the top of the frame. These panels will trap heat inside the dehydrator, speeding up the drying process. Ensure there's enough ventilation to allow moisture to escape.
3	**Creating the Trays** Build drying trays using wood for the frame and mesh for the bottom. The mesh allows air to circulate around the food, ensuring even drying. Stack the trays inside the frame.
4	**Positioning the Dehydrator** Place the dehydrator in a sunny location, tilted at an angle to maximize sun exposure. The exact angle depends on your latitude—roughly equivalent to your location's latitude for optimal sun exposure.
5	**Drying Your Food** Slice fruits and vegetables into thin, even pieces and place them on the trays. Drying times will vary depending on the food and weather conditions, but expect it to take several hours to a couple of days

Fermenting: Harnessing Nature's Power

Fermentation is a natural preservation method that not only preserves food but also enhances its nutritional value and flavor. By encouraging the growth of beneficial bacteria, fermenting transforms ordinary vegetables into probiotic-rich superfoods like sauerkraut, kimchi, and yogurt.

This method is one of the oldest forms of food preservation, with roots in many ancient cultures. Indeed fermentation has been used for thousands of years across various cultures. In Korea, kimchi — fermented vegetables with spices — has been a staple for over 2,000 years. In ancient Egypt, bread and beer were daily essentials, both products of fermentation. These foods not only provided nutrition but also preserved ingredients that would otherwise spoil in the hot climate. Today, many of these traditional fermented foods are celebrated for their health benefits and remain central to diets worldwide.

Benefits of Fermenting:

- **Improved Digestion:** Fermented foods are rich in probiotics, which support gut health and aid in digestion.

- **Enhanced Nutrition:** this process enhances the bioavailability of nutrients, facilitating the absorption of vitamins and minerals by the body.
- **Extended Shelf Life:** Fermentation preserves food for months, sometimes years, without the need for refrigeration.

Methods of Fermenting:

1. **Lacto-Fermentation:**
   - **Best For:** Vegetables (e.g., sauerkraut, pickles), dairy (e.g., yogurt), and grains.
   - **Method:** Food is submerged in a brine (saltwater solution) and left at room temperature for several days to weeks. The salt inhibits harmful bacteria while allowing beneficial lactic acid bacteria to flourish.
   - **Pros:** Simple to do at home with minimal equipment. The process enhances flavors and adds a tangy taste.
   - **Cons:** Requires careful monitoring of temperature and salt concentration to ensure safety.
2. **Alcohol Fermentation:**
   - **Best For:** Fruits (e.g., wine, cider) and grains (e.g., beer).
   - **Method:** Yeast converts the sugars in food into alcohol and carbon dioxide. This method is used to make alcoholic beverages and certain types of bread (e.g., sourdough).
   - **Pros:** Produces alcoholic beverages that can be stored for long periods. Also used in baking to produce bread with a unique flavor and texture.
   - **Cons:** More complex than lacto-fermentation and requires precise control of conditions to prevent spoilage.

Practical Tips:

- **Use Clean Equipment:** Always use clean jars and utensils to prevent contamination.
- **Monitor Fermentation:** Taste your ferment periodically to check its progress. The flavor will develop over time, and you can stop the process when it reaches your preferred level of tanginess.
- **Store Properly:** Once fermented, store your foods in a cool, dark place or refrigerate them to slow down the fermentation process and maintain quality.

Preserving Food Through Smoking and Curing

When living off-grid, preserving food is not just a convenience—it's a necessity. Smoking and curing are ancient techniques that have been used for centuries to preserve meat, fish, and even some vegetables. These methods not only extend the shelf life of food but also enhance its flavor, making them indispensable skills for anyone seeking a self-sufficient lifestyle. This subsection delves deeper into the art and science of smoking and curing, offering detailed guidance on how to effectively use these techniques in an off-grid environment.

The Science Behind Smoking and Curing

Smoking and curing are both methods of food preservation that rely on reducing moisture and introducing antimicrobial agents to inhibit the growth of bacteria, mold, and yeast. These processes work by altering the environment in which bacteria would typically thrive, making it less hospitable for spoilage organisms.

- **Smoking:** This process involves exposing food to smoke from burning wood, which imparts flavor while drying the surface of the food. The smoke also contains compounds like formaldehyde and phenols that have antimicrobial properties, helping to preserve the food by slowing down the growth of bacteria and mold. There are two primary types of smoking: hot smoking and cold smoking.
- **Curing:** Curing is a process that entails the use of salt, sugar, nitrates or a mixture of these substances to preserve food. Salt is the most critical element in curing because it draws moisture out of the food through osmosis, creating an environment where bacteria cannot survive. Sugar, when used, helps balance the flavor and can aid in the fermentation process, which also acts as a preservative. Nitrates and nitrites, often used in curing meats like bacon and ham, add an extra layer of protection against certain bacteria, such as Clostridium botulinum, which causes botulism.

Why It Matters Off-Grid: In an off-grid situation, where refrigeration might be unreliable or unavailable, smoking and curing become essential for ensuring that your food supplies last. These methods allow you to store large quantities of food without the need for electricity, making them ideal for preserving hunted game or bulk purchases of meat and fish.

The Smoking Process: Hot vs. Cold Smoking

Hot smoking is a process that cooks and preserves food at the same time. The food is exposed to smoke at temperatures ranging from 160°F to 225°F (71°C to 107°C). This method not only infuses the food with a smoky flavor but also cooks it, making it ready to eat immediately after smoking.

- **Best Foods for Hot Smoking:** Meat (like pork, beef, and poultry), fish (especially oily fish like salmon and mackerel), and sausages.
- **The Process:**
    1. **Preparation:** Season the meat or fish with a dry rub or marinade. Let it rest for a few hours or overnight to fully take in the flavors.
    2. **Smoking:** Set up your smoker or make-shift smokehouse. Maintain a temperature between 160°F and 225°F. Place the food on racks or hang it inside the smoker, ensuring it's not touching other pieces to allow even smoke penetration.
    3. **Monitoring:** Smoke the food for several hours, depending on the thickness and type of food. Use a meat thermometer to make sure that the internal temperature reaches at least 160°F for meat and 145°F for fish to ensure safety.

4. **Cooling and Storage:** Once smoked, allow the food to cool before storing it in an airtight container. Hot-smoked food can be eaten immediately or stored for several weeks in a cool, dry place.

Cold Smoking is a longer process that preserves food without cooking it. The food is exposed to smoke at lower temperatures, typically between 68°F and 86°F (20°C to 30°C). Because cold smoking does not cook the food, it must be cured before smoking to prevent bacterial growth.

- **Best Foods for Cold Smoking:** Cured meats (like ham, bacon, and salami), cheese, and fish (especially salmon).
- **The Process:**
    1. **Curing:** Before cold smoking, the food must be cured with salt or a salt-based curing mix to draw out moisture and inhibit bacterial growth. Curing times can vary but typically last several days to weeks, depending on the thickness and type of food.
    2. **Drying:** After curing, rinse the food to remove excess salt and dry it thoroughly. This stage is essential, as any lingering moisture can result in spoilage when cold smoking.
    3. **Smoking:** Set up your cold smoker, ensuring that the smoke is kept at a temperature below 86°F. Hang or place the food in the smoker, and allow it to absorb the smoke for several hours to several days, depending on the desired flavor intensity.
    4. **Aging:** Some cold-smoked foods, like salami or ham, are aged in a cool, dry environment for several weeks or months after smoking to develop their flavor fully.

The Curing Process: Dry Curing vs. Wet Curing

Dry Curing is the process of rubbing food with a mixture of salt, sugar, and sometimes nitrates. The food is then left to cure in a cool, dry place, allowing the salt to draw out moisture and create an inhospitable environment for bacteria.

- **Best Foods for Dry Curing:** Hams, bacon, pancetta, and some fish like salmon.
- **The Process:**
    1. **Preparation:** Mix salt with sugar and any other desired spices (such as pepper, garlic, or juniper berries). Rub the mixture thoroughly onto the surface of the meat or fish, ensuring that every part is covered.
    2. **Curing:** Place the coated food in a non-reactive container (like glass or plastic) and store it in a cool, dry place. The curing time can range from a few days to several weeks, depending on the thickness and type of food.
    3. **Rinsing and Drying:** After curing, rinse the food to remove excess salt, then dry it thoroughly. At this point, the food can be smoked, aged, or cooked as desired.

Wet Curing, or (Brining), entails immersing food in a mixture composed of water, salt, sugar, and occasionally includes spices or nitrates. This method is often used for larger cuts of meat or poultry.

- **Best Foods for Wet Curing:** Poultry, large hams, corned beef, and pastrami.

- **The Process:**
    1. **Preparation:** Dissolve salt and sugar in water to create a brine. The concentration of salt can vary depending on the recipe, but a common ratio is 1 cup of salt to 1 gallon of water. Add spices or other flavorings if desired.
    2. **Curing:** Submerge the food completely in the brine. Use a weight to keep it fully submerged if necessary. Store the container in a cool, dark place, such as a root cellar, for the curing period, which can last from a few days to a few weeks.
    3. **Rinsing and Drying:** After the curing period, rinse the food to remove excess brine, and allow it to dry. Wet-cured foods can be cooked immediately, smoked, or aged further.

Practical Considerations for Off-Grid Smoking and Curing

Setting Up an Off-Grid Smoking Station:

- **Simple Smokers:** Off-grid smokers can be as simple as a pit dug in the ground, covered with a tarp to trap the smoke, or a more elaborate smokehouse built from locally sourced materials. A metal drum smoker is another accessible DIY option that works well in off-grid environments.
- **Choosing Wood for Smoking:** The choice of wood utilized in the smoking process will have a considerable impact on the taste of the food being smoked. Hardwoods like hickory, oak, apple, and cherry are excellent choices. Avoid softwoods like pine or cedar, as they contain resins that can impart a bitter taste and may be harmful when burned.

Curing in Off-Grid Conditions:

- **Cool, Dry Environment:** Whether you're dry curing or wet curing, maintaining a consistent, cool temperature is crucial. If you lack a refrigerator or controlled environment, consider using a root cellar, a shaded outdoor area, or even digging a pit in the ground where temperatures are more stable.
- **Storage:** Once cured and/or smoked, store your food in a cool, dry place. Properly cured and smoked meats can last for months, making them an essential part of your off-grid food storage plan.

Safety Tips:

- **Avoid Over-Smoking:** While it might be tempting to smoke food for extended periods, be mindful of over-smoking, which can lead to a bitter taste. Balance is key to achieving the best flavor and preservation.
- **Check for Mold:** Regularly inspect cured and smoked foods for signs of mold, particularly if stored for long periods. While some surface mold can be scraped off, extensive mold growth is a sign of spoilage.

Smoking and curing are invaluable techniques for anyone living off the grid. These methods not only allow you to preserve food without refrigeration but also enhance its flavor, making your hard-earned provisions even more enjoyable. With practice, you can master these ancient arts and ensure a steady supply of preserved meats and fish to sustain you through any season.

Freezing and Cooling as Off-Grid Food Preservation Techniques

When it comes to preserving food off the grid, many people immediately think of methods like drying, fermenting, or canning. However, freezing and cooling can also be valid and effective alternatives, even in an off-grid setting.

One of the biggest challenges of off-grid living is preserving food without the convenience of a refrigerator. If you've ever wondered how people kept their food fresh before the advent of electricity, you're not alone. The good news is that there are several tried-and-true methods for keeping food cool without relying on power from the grid. These methods are not only energy-efficient but also surprisingly effective, even in hot climates.

For instance, the Zeer Pot is an example of ancient wisdom that has stood the test of time. Similar cooling techniques were used by the Egyptians, who stored food and water in porous clay jars that were kept cool through evaporation. In rural parts of Nigeria, the Zeer pot has been reintroduced in recent decades as a low-cost solution to food spoilage in areas without access to electricity. This simple technology has made a significant impact, allowing farmers to store produce for longer periods, reducing waste, and increasing food security.

But why is off-grid refrigeration so important? In a self-sufficient lifestyle, wasting food is not an option. Whether you're storing the bounty from your garden or preserving meat from a recent hunt, keeping your food fresh is essential to minimizing waste and ensuring that you have enough to eat throughout the year. Without refrigeration, food spoilage can quickly become a major issue, leading to both wasted resources and lost time. Preserving food effectively is a cornerstone of off-grid living, and mastering these techniques is key to maintaining a steady supply of nutritious meals.

DIY Project 13: Zeer Pot Refrigerator

The Zeer pot, also known as a pot-in-pot refrigerator, is an ingenious device that uses the principles of evaporative cooling to keep food cool in hot climates. This ancient technology, which dates back to early civilizations in the Middle East and Africa, requires no electricity and is easy to build with basic materials.

Why choose a Zeer pot? The Zeer pot is an excellent example of how ancient wisdom can meet modern needs. In a world where we often rely on high-tech solutions, it's refreshing to find a method that works just as well with nothing more than natural materials and a bit of water. It's particularly useful in arid regions where other cooling methods may not be practical.

Cost	$	Difficulty	★

Materials:

- **Clay Pots:** Two unglazed clay pots, one smaller than the other.
- **Sand:** Fine, clean sand to fill the space between the pots.
- **Water:** For wetting the sand and creating the evaporative cooling effect.
- **Cloth or Towel:** To cover the pots and retain moisture.

Tools: none

1	**Choosing the Pots** Select two unglazed clay pots, one that fits inside the other with a few inches of space between them. The outer pot should be large enough to hold a substantial amount of sand, while the inner pot should be spacious enough to store your food items.
2	**Preparing the Pots** Soak both pots in water for several hours before assembly. This will saturate the clay, which is essential for the evaporative cooling process. After soaking, place the smaller pot inside the larger one, ensuring it is centered.
3	**Adding the Sand** Fill the space between the two pots with fine, clean sand. Pack the sand tightly and evenly, leaving no gaps. Once the sand is in place, pour water over it until it is fully saturated. The water will slowly evaporate through the porous clay, drawing heat away from the inner pot and cooling the contents inside.
4	**Covering and Using the Zeer Pot** Cover the top of the pots with a damp cloth or towel. This helps to retain moisture and enhance the cooling effect. Place the Zeer pot in a well-ventilated, shaded area where it can receive a breeze. The cooling effect works best in dry, hot climates, where the evaporation rate is higher. Store fruits, vegetables, and other perishables in the inner pot, and check the sand daily to ensure it remains moist.

Additional Tips:

- **Maximize Ventilation:** Place the Zeer pot in an area with good airflow to enhance the evaporative cooling effect. A constant breeze will help keep the inner pot cooler.
- **Use in Conjunction with Other Methods:** The Zeer pot is great for fruits and vegetables, but for meat and dairy, you may need to combine it with other preservation methods like salting, drying, or smoking.
- **Monitor Moisture Levels:** Check the sand regularly to ensure it stays moist. The cooling effect diminishes as the sand dries out, so keep a supply of water nearby for regular top-ups.

Other Off-Grid Refrigeration Methods

If the Zeer pot doesn't meet all your cooling needs, there are several other off-grid refrigeration methods that can be equally effective, depending on your environment and resources.

Root Cellars

Root cellars are a time-honored method of keeping food cool. These underground storage spaces take advantage of the earth's natural insulating properties to maintain a stable, cool temperature year-round. Root cellars are ideal for storing root vegetables, canned goods, and other perishables. They can be as simple as a dug-out pit or as complex as a fully constructed underground room with ventilation and shelving.

Why a root cellar? Imagine having a naturally cool space that doesn't rely on electricity and can store large quantities of food for months. A root cellar is more than just a storage space—it's an insurance policy against food spoilage. In a well-constructed root cellar, your harvest will stay fresh long after the growing season has ended, providing you with a steady food supply throughout the winter.

DIY Tip: If you're building a root cellar, consider digging into a north-facing slope, where the earth's temperature remains more consistent and cooler. Ensure good ventilation to prevent moisture buildup, which can lead to rot and spoilage.

Spring Houses

A spring house is a small structure built over a natural spring or stream, where the cool water helps to keep food fresh. These were commonly used before refrigeration became widespread and can still be effective in areas with accessible fresh water. The constant flow of water around stored food keeps the temperature low, ideal for dairy products, meat, and vegetables.

Why use a spring house? If you have access to a reliable spring or stream, a spring house can be an incredibly effective and sustainable way to keep food cool. The naturally cold water does the hard work for you, maintaining a low temperature that's ideal for preserving perishable items. It's a method that has been used for centuries and is still relevant today.

DIY Tip: When building a spring house, make sure it is well-shaded and that the water flow is consistent. The structure should also be well-ventilated to prevent mold and mildew.

Solar-Powered Refrigerators

For those who can afford a more modern solution, solar-powered refrigerators offer the convenience of electric refrigeration without the grid. These units are powered by solar panels and can be highly efficient, especially in sunny climates. They are particularly useful for storing food that requires lower temperatures, such as dairy and meat.

Why go solar? If you're living off-grid in an area with abundant sunshine, a solar-powered refrigerator might be your best option. It provides all the benefits of a conventional refrigerator while staying true to your off-grid principles. Solar refrigeration is particularly useful for preserving meat, dairy, and other perishables that require more precise temperature control.

DIY Tip: When setting up a solar-powered refrigerator, consider the placement of your solar panels to maximize sunlight exposure. Ensure that the refrigerator is properly insulated to reduce energy consumption and make the most of your solar power.

The Salt and Ice Refrigeration Method

Did you know that you can refrigerate water—and keep food cool—using salt? This method isn't about creating drinkable water, but rather about leveraging the properties of salt to lower the temperature of ice, thereby creating a simple, off-grid refrigeration method.

How does it work? When salt is added to ice, it lowers the melting point of the ice, causing it to melt faster while absorbing heat from its surroundings. This process results in a mixture of ice and water that is colder than ice alone, which can be used to keep food cool for extended periods.

Cost	$	Difficulty	★
Materials:			

  - **Ice:** Enough to fill a container or bucket.
  - **Salt:** Coarse salt works best, but any salt will do.
  - **Container:** A bucket or cooler to hold the ice and salt mixture.
  - **Water (optional):** For faster cooling.

Proportions: for every 5 pounds of ice, use approximately 1 pound of salt. This ratio provides an effective balance for lowering the temperature of the ice-water mixture.

1	**Prepare the Ice and Salt Mixture** Fill your container with ice, leaving some space at the top. Sprinkle the salt evenly over the ice, ensuring that it's well distributed. The salt will begin to lower the temperature of the ice, creating a super-cold brine solution.

2	**Use the Ice and Salt Mixture** Place the food or items you want to keep cool into a separate container or bag, then submerge it in the ice and salt mixture. Alternatively, you can place the food in a cooler and surround it with the ice-salt mixture. This method is particularly useful for keeping dairy products, meat, or beverages cold for extended periods.
3	**Monitor the Temperature** Check the temperature periodically. The ice and salt mixture should keep the contents cool for several hours, depending on the ambient temperature and the amount of ice used

Additional Tips:

- **Use Large Blocks of Ice:** Large blocks of ice melt more slowly than smaller pieces, providing longer-lasting cooling. If possible, freeze water in large containers in advance to create bigger ice blocks.
- **Keep It Insulated:** To maximize the effectiveness of this method, keep your ice-salt mixture in an insulated container, such as a cooler. This will slow down the melting process and maintain a lower temperature for a longer period.
- **Safety Note:** Remember that this method is for cooling purposes only; the water in the ice-salt mixture is not drinkable due to its high salt content.

Historical Anecdote: Salt Preservation Techniques

The use of salt to preserve and refrigerate food isn't new. Before the advent of modern refrigeration, people commonly used salt to preserve meats and fish, especially during long sea voyages where fresh supplies were scarce. The same principles apply today in off-grid living. By lowering the temperature of ice with salt, you can create a makeshift refrigerator that's surprisingly effective in keeping food fresh.

Combining Methods for Maximum Efficiency

One of the keys to successful off-grid living is the ability to combine different techniques to meet your needs. When it comes to refrigeration, you can use multiple methods to create a system that's tailored to your environment and lifestyle.

For example:

- **Start with the Zeer Pot:** Use it for everyday fruits and vegetables, taking advantage of its low-tech, reliable cooling power.

- **Supplement with a Root Cellar:** Store larger quantities of food, especially those that need long-term storage, like potatoes, carrots, and canned goods.
- **Add a Spring House:** If you have access to a spring or stream, use it to keep milk, cheese, and other dairy products fresh.
- **Use Solar-Powered Refrigeration:** For items that need precise temperature control, such as meat, eggs, and dairy, especially during the hot summer months.
- **Utilize Salt and Ice:** For temporary cooling, like keeping beverages cold during a hot day or maintaining a low temperature during power outages if you're using a hybrid off-grid system.

By strategically combining these methods, you can create a comprehensive off-grid refrigeration system that ensures your food stays fresh, your drinks stay cool, and your lifestyle remains sustainable.

Mastering Off-Grid Refrigeration

Off-grid refrigeration is about more than just keeping your food cold; it's about creating a resilient, adaptable system that meets your needs without relying on modern conveniences. Whether you're using ancient techniques like the Zeer pot, leveraging the natural coolness of the earth with a root cellar, or combining ice and salt for an effective DIY refrigerator, you're tapping into time-tested methods that have sustained people for centuries.

Living off the grid doesn't mean sacrificing comfort or convenience—it means finding smart, sustainable ways to achieve the same results. By mastering these off-grid refrigeration techniques, you're not just preserving your food; you're preserving your independence, your connection to the land, and your ability to thrive in any environment.

Off-Grid Cooking: Essential Techniques and Safety Considerations

Cooking in an off-grid environment requires a combination of ingenuity, resourcefulness, and a keen awareness of safety. Without the conveniences of modern kitchen appliances, you'll need to rely on tried-and-true methods that have sustained people for centuries. This chapter will guide you through essential off-grid cooking techniques, from igniting a fire and making homemade charcoal to constructing and using a variety of DIY cooking devices like solar ovens, tin can stoves, and gallon drum smokers.

Whether you're preparing a meal after a successful hunt, preserving food for the winter, or simply enjoying the simplicity of cooking in nature, understanding how to safely manage heat and fire is crucial. We'll cover the basics of fire safety, explore the art of building efficient cooking tools, and delve into practical tips for creating delicious meals without the need for electricity. By mastering these skills, you'll be better equipped to cook nourishing, flavorful food in any off-grid situation, ensuring both your safety and self-sufficiency.

Guide: Igniting Fire Through Friction

Fire has been an essential survival tool for humanity since ancient times, providing warmth, light, and the ability to cook food. One of the most primal methods of creating fire is through friction, a technique that requires skill, patience, and the right materials. While it may seem challenging, learning how to ignite a fire using friction is a valuable skill for off-grid living, camping, or survival situations. This guide will walk you through the steps to create fire using the bow drill method, one of the most reliable friction-based techniques.

Materials:

- **Bow:** A sturdy, curved piece of wood (approximately the length of your arm) with a strong cord or string attached.
- **Drill (Spindle):** A straight, firm and dry wood piece that measures aboute one inch in diameter and twelve inches in length.
- **Fireboard (Hearth):** A flat, softwood board with a carved notch and a small depression where the drill will spin.
- **Socket (Handhold):** A small, hard and smooth stone or wood piece having a dip to accommodate the spindle's top.
- **Tinder Bundle:** Dry, fine material like grass, bark, or leaves to catch the ember and start the flame.

Tools:

- **Knife:** For carving the fireboard, spindle, and socket.

	• **(Optional) Gloves** to protect your hands while using the bow drill
1	**Prepare the Materials** • Select dry, seasoned wood for the fireboard and spindle. Softwoods like cedar, cottonwood, or willow are excellent for the fireboard, and for the spindle hardwoods like hickory or oak are recommended. • Carve the spindle so it has a rounded point at both ends, reducing friction at the socket and increasing friction at the fireboard. • Carve a small depression near the edge of the fireboard and cut a notch leading from the edge to the center of the depression. This notch will collect the hot dust that forms as you drill.
2	**Assemble the Bow Drill** • String the bow with a strong, non-elastic cord. Tie the cord tightly but leave enough slack to loop it around the spindle. • Place the spindle into the bowstring, looping the string around the spindle once. • Position the spindle's bottom point into the fireboard's depression and hold the top with the socket
3	**Create Friction** • Kneel with one foot on the fireboard to keep it steady. • Hold the socket with one hand, applying downward pressure on the spindle, and grip the bow with the other hand. • Begin to move the bow back and forth in a sawing motion, spinning the spindle rapidly in the fireboard's notch. Maintain consistent pressure and speed.
4	**Form an Ember** • Continue the back-and-forth motion until you see smoke and a small pile of dark, hot dust forming at the notch. This dust will eventually begin to glow, indicating that an ember has formed. • Carefully remove the spindle while keeping the fireboard steady.
5	**Transfer the Ember** • Gently tap the fireboard to drop the ember into your prepared tinder bundle.

	• Blow softly on the ember as you fold the tinder around it, gradually increasing the intensity of your breaths until the tinder ignites into a flame.
6	**Build the Fire** Once you have a flame, carefully place it under your kindling (small sticks or dry wood) and gradually add larger pieces of wood to build your fire.

Additional Tips:

- **Wood Selection:** The choice of wood is crucial. Ensure both the fireboard and spindle are dry, as moisture will make it much harder to create an ember.
- **Tinder Bundle:** You want your tinder bundle to be as fine and dry as possible. Fluffy, fibrous materials like dry grass, bark shavings, or cotton work best.
- **Practice:** Making fire through friction requires practice. Don't be discouraged if you don't succeed on the first try—keep refining your technique.

Learning to ignite fire through friction is an essential and rewarding survival skill. While it may be challenging, mastering this technique gives you a reliable method of starting a fire in any situation, using only natural materials.

Guide: Creating Homemade Charcoal

Charcoal is a valuable resource for cooking, heating, and even as a filtration medium. Unlike regular wood, charcoal burns hotter and cleaner, making it an excellent fuel for various off-grid applications. While you can purchase charcoal, making it yourself from natural materials is a sustainable and cost-effective option. This guide will walk you through the steps to create your own charcoal using a simple method known as the "earth mound" or "pit" method, which has been used for centuries.

Materials:
<ul><li>**Hardwood Logs or Branches:** Choose dense, dry hardwoods like oak, hickory, or maple, which produce the best quality charcoal.</li><li>**Shovel:** For digging the pit or mound.</li><li>**Metal Drum (Optional):** To create a more controlled environment for charcoal production.</li><li>**Greenery or Grass:** To cover the pit or drum, controlling the airflow.</li><li>**Matches or Lighter:** To ignite the wood.</li></ul>
Tools:
<ul><li>**Axe or Saw:** to cut the wood into small enough pieces.</li></ul>

• **Rake:** For spreading dirt or managing the fire.	
1	**Prepare the Wood:** Cut your hardwood logs or branches into pieces that are roughly 12-18 inches long. The wood should be dry, as wet or green wood will not convert to charcoal effectively. If using a metal drum, ensure it has ventilation holes at the bottom and a removable lid.
2	**Choose the Method:** • **Pit Method:** Dig a shallow pit in the ground, about few feet deep (2 or 3) and wide enough for holding your wood. This method allows you to cover the wood with soil to control the burn. • **Mound Method:** Alternatively, you can stack the wood on the ground and cover it with soil or green material, creating a mound. This method is ideal if you don't want to dig a pit.
3	**Stack the Wood:** Arrange the wood tightly in the pit or drum. The tighter the wood is packed, the better the resulting charcoal will be. If using a metal drum, fill it with the wood and place the lid loosely on top.
4	**Ignite the Wood:** Light a small fire at the bottom of the pit or drum using kindling and small pieces of wood. Allow the fire to spread slowly through the stacked wood. Once the fire is established, cover the pit or drum with soil, leaving small gaps for airflow. This reduces the oxygen supply, causing the wood to smolder rather than burn completely.
5	**Control the Burn:** Monitor the burn closely. You want the wood to smolder and slowly convert to charcoal over several hours. If flames begin to escape from the gaps, reduce the airflow by covering the gaps with more soil or green material. The smoldering process can take anywhere from 6 to 24 hours, depending on the size of the pit and the density of the wood.
6	**Harvest the Charcoal:**

	• Once the wood has fully converted to charcoal, carefully uncover the pit or drum. Be cautious of any remaining hot spots. • Allow the charcoal to cool completely before handling because charcoal that is still warm can reignite when exposed to air.
7	**Store the Charcoal:** Store the cooled charcoal in a dry, airtight container to keep it from absorbing moisture. Properly stored, homemade charcoal can last indefinitely and is ready to use for cooking, heating, or other purposes.

Additional Tips:

- **Wood Selection:** The quality of the charcoal depends heavily on the type of wood used. Hardwoods like oak, hickory, and maple produce dense, high-quality charcoal, while softwoods like pine may result in lighter, less effective charcoal.
- **Safety:** When working with fire, always keep a water source and a fire extinguisher handy. Ensure that the area is clear of flammable materials, and never leave the smoldering wood unattended.
- **Uses for Charcoal:** Besides cooking and heating, charcoal can be used as a soil amendment, in water filtration, and even as a drawing medium for art projects.

Creating your own charcoal is a practical and rewarding skill that enhances your self-reliance. With a bit of time and effort, you can produce high-quality charcoal right at home, ready for use in a variety of off-grid applications.

DIY Project 14: Solar Oven Construction

Harnessing the power of the sun to cook food is not only eco-friendly but also incredibly practical, especially for off-grid living. A solar oven is a simple device that uses sunlight as its energy source, allowing you to cook meals without the need for electricity, gas, or firewood. This project involves creating a basic solar oven using accessible materials, making it an excellent addition to your sustainable living toolkit.

Cost	$	Difficulty	★★
Materials:			

- **Cardboard Boxes** (2): One larger and one smaller, with the smaller box able to fit inside the larger box with some space around it.
- **Aluminum Foil:** To line the interior of the boxes and reflect sunlight.
- **Black Construction Paper:** To line the bottom of the inner box and absorb heat.
- **Glass or Plastic Sheet:** To cover the top of the oven, trapping heat inside.

- **Insulating Material**: Such as crumpled newspaper, cotton batting, or straw, to fill the space between the two boxes.
- **Clear Plastic Wrap**: As an alternative or additional cover to trap heat.
- **Tape or Glue**: To secure the materials in place.

Tools:

- **Box Cutter or Utility Knife**: For cutting the cardboard.
- **Ruler**: To measure and ensure straight cuts.
- **Scissors**: For cutting aluminum foil and construction paper.
- **Marker or Pen**: For marking measurements on the cardboard.

1	**Prepare the Boxes:** - Begin by selecting two cardboard boxes: one larger and one smaller. The smaller box should fit comfortably inside the larger box, leaving a gap of about 2-3 inches on all sides. - Use a box cutter or utility knife to carefully cut the top flaps off both boxes.
2	**Line the Inner Box:** - Line the inside of the smaller box with aluminum foil, using tape or glue to secure it. The foil will reflect sunlight and concentrate heat inside the oven. - Use black construction paper to line the bottom of the inside box. Black absorbs more heat, helping to increase the oven's temperature.
3	**Insulate the Oven:** Place the smaller box inside the larger box. Fill the space between the two boxes with insulating material such as crumpled newspaper, cotton batting, or straw. This insulation helps to retain heat within the inner box. Make sure the insulating material is packed tightly and evenly around the sides and bottom of the inner box.
4	**Create the Oven Lid:** Measure and cut a piece of glass or clear plastic to fit over the top of the inner box. This will act as the oven door, allowing sunlight in while trapping heat inside.

	If you don't have access to glass or plastic, you can use clear plastic wrap stretched tightly over the top of the inner box as a makeshift lid. Secure it with tape around the edges.
5	**Construct a Reflector:** • Cut a flap in the lid of the larger box, leaving one side attached so that it can be propped up to reflect sunlight into the oven. Line the inside of this flap with aluminum foil to maximize reflection. • Position the flap to angle sunlight directly into the oven, helping to increase its efficiency.
6	**Test and Use the Solar Oven:** • Place the solar oven outside in direct sunlight, ideally during the peak sun hours of the day. • Adjust the reflector flap to direct the maximum amount of sunlight into the oven. The internal temperature should rise as sunlight is concentrated inside. • Use a thermometer to monitor the temperature inside the oven. Depending on the weather and sunlight intensity, the oven can reach temperatures of 200°F (93°C) or higher—sufficient for slow-cooking meals, baking, or heating water. • Place your food inside the oven on a heat-resistant tray or dish and cover it with the glass or plastic lid. Monitor the cooking process and adjust the reflector as needed.

Additional Tips:

- **Cooking Times:** Solar ovens cook more slowly than conventional ovens. Plan for longer cooking times, especially for baking or roasting.
- **Safety:** Always handle the oven carefully, especially when removing the lid, as it can get quite hot.
- **Weather Considerations:** Solar ovens work best in direct sunlight. On cloudy days or in the late afternoon, the oven's efficiency may decrease.
- **Portability:** This solar oven is lightweight and portable, making it easy to move around to capture the best sunlight throughout the day.

How to Use a Solar Oven

Using a solar oven is a straightforward process, but it requires an understanding of how to harness and utilize solar energy effectively. Here's a detailed guide on how to get the most out of your DIY solar oven, from setup to cooking techniques.

1. Positioning the Solar Oven

- **Choose the Right Location:** Place your solar oven in a spot that receives direct sunlight for several hours a day. The best times for solar cooking are between 10 a.m. and 3 p.m., when the sun is at its highest and most intense.
- **Adjust the Reflector:** The reflector flap should be angled to capture as much sunlight as possible and direct it into the oven. As the sun moves across the sky, you may need to adjust the flap periodically to maintain maximum efficiency.
- **Level the Oven:** Ensure the solar oven is placed on a stable, level surface. This will prevent any spills and ensure that the food inside cooks evenly.

2. Preheating the Oven

- **Preheat for Best Results:** Just like a conventional oven, a solar oven benefits from preheating. Allow the oven to sit in direct sunlight for about 20-30 minutes before placing your food inside. This ensures that the oven reaches its optimal cooking temperature, typically between 200°F to 250°F (93°C to 121°C).
- **Use a Thermometer:** If possible, place an oven thermometer inside the solar oven to monitor the temperature. This will give you a better idea of when the oven is ready for cooking.

3. Cooking with a Solar Oven

- **Cooking Techniques:** Solar ovens are excellent for slow cooking, baking, and heating food. They can be used to prepare a wide variety of dishes, including stews, casseroles, bread, and even desserts like cookies or fruit crisps.
  - **Slow Cooking:** For dishes like stews and casseroles, solar ovens provide an ideal low and slow cooking environment. The gradual increase in temperature helps to tenderize meats and blend flavors.
  - **Baking:** Solar ovens can bake bread, cakes, and other baked goods, though they may require longer cooking times than conventional ovens. Be patient and monitor your baked goods closely to avoid overcooking.
  - **Reheating:** Leftovers and pre-cooked foods can be easily reheated in a solar oven. This is particularly useful for off-grid living, where traditional heating methods might not be available.
- **Use Dark, Thin Pans:** Dark, thin pans absorb heat more efficiently, helping your food cook faster. Avoid using shiny or reflective cookware, as it can reflect the sunlight away from the food.
- **Check and Stir:** Every 30 minutes or so, check on your food and stir if necessary. This helps to ensure even cooking and prevents any hot spots from forming.

- **Cooking Time:** Solar cooking takes longer than conventional cooking. Plan for extended cooking times—typically 1.5 to 2 times longer than in a regular oven. However, the slow and steady heat often results in more flavorful and tender dishes.

4. Maintaining the Solar Oven's Efficiency

- **Rotate the Oven:** To capture the most sunlight, rotate the solar oven periodically throughout the day. This is especially important if you're cooking something that requires a longer time, as it ensures the oven maintains a consistent temperature.
- **Keep the Lid Clear:** Ensure that the glass or plastic lid stays clean and free from condensation or debris. A clear lid allows maximum sunlight to enter the oven, improving its efficiency.
- **Monitor Water Content:** For dishes that require moisture, such as stews or casseroles, keep an eye on the water level. Solar ovens lose less moisture than conventional ovens, so you may need to adjust liquid amounts to prevent dishes from becoming too watery.

5. Safety Considerations

- **Handle with Care:** Even though the temperatures in a solar oven are lower than in conventional ovens, the surfaces inside can still become very hot. Use oven mitts or gloves when handling food or adjusting the reflector.
- **Ventilation:** If you're cooking for an extended period, occasionally lift the lid to release steam and prevent too much pressure from building up inside the oven.
- **Cooking During Cloudy Weather:** Solar ovens work best in clear, sunny conditions. On cloudy days, the oven may not reach high enough temperatures to cook food safely. Plan your solar cooking on days with strong, consistent sunlight, and have an alternative cooking method ready for cloudy days.

6. Cleanup and Maintenance

- **Easy Cleanup:** The slow, steady cooking in a solar oven usually results in less splatter and mess. Clean the inside of the oven with a damp cloth after each use to keep it in good condition.
- **Store Properly:** When not in use, store your solar oven in a dry place to protect it from the elements. This prolongs its lifespan and ensures it's ready to use whenever you need it.
- **Check Insulation:** Periodically inspect the insulation materials to ensure they haven't shifted or degraded. Proper insulation is key to maintaining the oven's efficiency.

A solar oven is a versatile and sustainable cooking tool that can easily become a favorite in your off-grid living setup. With a bit of practice and the right conditions, you can enjoy a wide variety of dishes cooked using nothing but the power of the sun.

DIY Project 15: Tin Can Rocket Stove

The Tin Can Rocket Stove, often referred to as a Hobo Rocket Stove, is an efficient and portable cooking device that can be made from a few simple materials. It's an ideal solution for off-grid living, camping, or emergency situations where traditional cooking methods might not be available. This stove uses small amounts of fuel, like twigs or small branches, to create a high-temperature, smokeless fire. The design maximizes airflow, allowing the fire to burn hot and efficiently, making it perfect for boiling water or cooking meals with minimal resources.

Cost	$	Difficulty	★★

Materials:

- **Large Tin Can:** This will be the main body of the stove. A large coffee can or a similar-sized can works well.
- **Smaller Tin Can:** This will serve as the fuel intake and air passage. A soup can or vegetable can is ideal.
- **Metal Pipe or Duct (Optional):** Can be used to create a more durable fuel intake, but a smaller tin can will suffice.
- **Insulation Material:** This could be perlite, sand, or even small pebbles to fill the space around the internal pipe or can.
- **Metal Grate:** A small metal grill or mesh to place on top of the stove for cooking.
- **Metal Shears or Tin Snips:** For cutting the cans.
- **Gloves:** To protect your hands while working with sharp metal edges.
- **Marker:** For marking cutting lines on the cans.

Tools:

- **Metal Shears or Tin Snips:** For cutting the tin cans to create openings for the fuel intake and airflow.
- **Gloves:** To protect your hands from sharp edges while cutting and assembling the tin cans.
- **Marker:** For marking cutting lines on the cans to ensure accurate cuts.
- **Drill (Optional):** If you decide to add ventilation holes or secure the parts with screws.
- **File or Sandpaper (Optional):** For smoothing any rough edges after cutting the metal cans.

1	Prepare the Large Tin Can: Start by thoroughly cleaning out the large tin can. Remove any labels and wash the inside to remove any remaining food or residue. Use a marker to outline a square near the bottom of the large tin can. This square

	should be slightly smaller than the diameter of the smaller tin can, as it will serve as the opening where the smaller can or metal pipe will be inserted.
2	**Cut the Opening for the Fuel Intake:** Using metal shears or tin snips, carefully cut out the square marked on the large tin can. This opening will allow you to insert the smaller tin can or metal pipe into the large can. Be cautious of sharp edges, and wear gloves to protect your hands.
3	**Prepare the Smaller Tin Can:** Clean the smaller tin can and remove any labels. Cut off one end of the can entirely, leaving the other end intact. This will allow you to insert it into the larger can, creating a passage for fuel and air. If using a metal pipe instead of a smaller can, cut the pipe to fit the size of the opening in the large can.
4	**Assemble the Rocket Stove:** Insert the smaller tin can or metal pipe into the opening you cut in the large can. The open end should extend slightly into the center of the large can, while the intact end remains outside, allowing you to feed fuel into the stove. Once the intake pipe or can is securely in place, fill the space around it inside the large can with insulation material (perlite, sand, or small pebbles). This insulation helps to retain heat and directs airflow, making the stove more efficient.
5	**Create the Cooking Surface:** Place a small metal grate or mesh on top of the large tin can. This will serve as the cooking surface where you can place pots or pans. Ensure the grate is stable and covers the entire opening to prevent pots from tipping over.
6	**Test the Stove:** Before using the stove for cooking, test it by lighting a small fire. Place some kindling or small twigs into the fuel intake (the smaller tin can or pipe) and light them. The design should allow air to flow through the intake, feeding the fire and creating a strong upward draft. Once the fire is burning steadily, you can add larger sticks or small branches to the fuel intake. The insulated design of the stove should concentrate the heat and produce a hot, efficient fire with minimal smoke.
7	**Cooking with the Rocket Stove:**

| | • Place your pot or pan on the metal grate and begin cooking. The concentrated heat from the rocket stove should bring water to a boil quickly or cook food efficiently. |
| | • Monitor the fire and add fuel as needed. The design of the stove allows it to burn small amounts of fuel for an extended period, making it an excellent option for off-grid cooking. |

Additional Tips:

- **Fuel Choice:** Dry, small-diameter sticks and twigs work best in a tin can rocket stove. Avoid using wet or green wood, as it will produce more smoke and burn less efficiently.
- **Portability:** The tin can rocket stove is light and simple to travel, making it ideal for camping or emergency use. Consider making a carrying handle or packing it with your off-grid survival gear.
- **Maintenance:** After each use, clean out any ash or debris from the stove to ensure it continues to function efficiently.

Building a Tin Can Rocket Stove is a practical and straightforward project that provides a reliable cooking method using minimal resources. Whether you're living off the grid, camping, or preparing for emergencies, this stove offers an efficient and eco-friendly way to cook food and boil water.

DIY Project 16: Gallon Drum Smoker Construction

Smoking meat and other foods is a time-honored tradition that adds incredible flavor and preserves food for longer periods. Building a smoker from a gallon drum is an excellent DIY project for those who enjoy the art of smoking and want to add a practical and rustic piece of equipment to their off-grid homestead. This project involves converting a metal drum into a functional smoker that can be used to smoke meats, fish, and even vegetables.

Cost	$	Difficulty	★★★
Materials:			

- **55-Gallon Metal Drum**: This will serve as the main body of the smoker. Ensure it is clean and free from any hazardous materials.
- **Grill Grates**: Metal grates that fit inside the drum to hold the food.
- **High-Temperature Paint**: To prevent the drum from rusting and wearing.
- **Chimney Pipe**: For venting smoke.
- **Temperature Gauge**: To monitor the internal temperature.
- **Metal Hinges and Latch**: For the door.
- **Metal Legs or Bricks**: To elevate the drum off the ground.

- **Firebox**: Optional, for creating indirect heat (can be an additional small metal box or barrel).
- **Handle**: For the door.
- **Smoker Chips or Wood Chunks**: For flavoring the smoke.

Tools:

- **Drill with Metal Bits**: For making holes for the chimney, hinges, and temperature gauge.
- **Angle Grinder or Metal Saw**: To cut the drum and make openings.
- **Metal File**: For smoothing rough edges.
- **Wrench**: For securing bolts and attachments.
- **Wire Brush**: To clean the drum

1	**Prepare the Drum:** • Start by thoroughly cleaning the 55-gallon metal drum. If it has been used previously, make sure it is free of any chemicals or residues. Use a wire brush to remove rust or paint from the surface. • Rinse and let the drum dry completely.
2	**Cut the Door:** • Using an angle grinder or metal saw, cut out a rectangular door from the side of the drum. This door should be large enough to allow easy access to the grill grates and food inside the smoker. • Smooth the edges of the cut with a metal file to prevent injury. • Attach metal hinges to one side of the door and a latch to the other side. Add a handle to the door for easy opening and closing.
3	**Install the Grill Grates:** • Inside the drum, measure and mark where you want the grill grates to be placed. Typically, you'll want two levels: one higher up for food and one lower for the charcoal or wood. • Drill holes along the inside of the drum to hold metal brackets or bolts that will support the grill grates. Ensure the grates are level and secure.
4	**Add the Chimney:** • Cut a hole at the top of the drum for the chimney pipe. The chimney allows smoke to escape and controls airflow inside the smoker.

	• Attach the chimney pipe securely to the hole. Ensure it fits snugly to prevent smoke from escaping around the edges. • Optional: Install a damper in the chimney pipe to regulate the amount of smoke and heat inside the smoker.
5	**Install the Temperature Gauge:** • Drill a hole on the front of the drum near the top, just above where the food will be placed. • Place the temperature gauge in the hole and secure it tightly. This gauge will allow you to monitor the internal temperature and make adjustments as needed.
6	**Paint the Drum:** • Apply a coat of high-temperature paint to the exterior of the drum to protect it from rust and wear. Ensure that the paint is appropriate for metal surfaces and intense heat. • Allow the paint to dry completely before proceeding.
7	**Elevate the Smoker:** Elevate the drum off the ground using metal legs or place it on a set of bricks. This ensures proper airflow and makes it easier to manage the fire and food.
8	**Create the Firebox (Optional):** • For indirect heat smoking, you can create a separate firebox attached to the side of the drum. This can be done using a smaller metal box or barrel. • Cut a hole in the side of the drum and attach the firebox using metal brackets or welding. This allows smoke and heat to enter the drum without direct contact with the food.
9	**Season the Smoker:** It's important to season the smoker before using it for meals. This involves coating the interior with a thin layer of cooking oil and running a hot fire in the smoker for several hours. This process helps to seal the metal and burn off any remaining residues
10	**Start Smoking:**

	<ul><li>Once the smoker is seasoned, it's ready to use. Place charcoal or wood chips in the lower grate, light the fire, and wait until the temperature stabilizes.</li><li>Place your food on the upper grate, close the door, and monitor the temperature using the gauge. Adjust the vents and chimney as needed to control the smoke and heat.</li></ul>

Additional Tips:

- **Wood Selection:** Different types of wood chips provide different flavors to the food. Experiment with apple, hickory, mesquite or cherry wood to find your preferred flavor profile.
- **Temperature Control:** Maintaining a consistent temperature is key to successful smoking. Use the chimney and any additional vents to regulate airflow and temperature.
- **Cleaning:** After each use, clean the grates and remove ashes to keep the smoker in good working condition. Regular maintenance will prolong the life of your smoker.
- **Safety:** Always use heat-resistant gloves when handling the smoker and place it in a well-ventilated area away from flammable materials.

Cooking Safety in Off-Grid Living: Understanding Temperatures, Bacteria, and Viruses

In an off-grid situation, where access to modern conveniences like refrigeration, controlled cooking environments, and processed foods may be limited, the importance of food safety becomes paramount. Whether you're relying on hunted game, foraged plants, or homegrown produce, understanding the risks associated with bacteria, viruses, and parasites in food is crucial to preventing illness. This section will provide detailed guidance on safe cooking temperatures, the risks posed by various pathogens, and the best practices for ensuring that your food is safe to eat.

Risks Associated with Off-Grid Food Sources

Understanding Pathogens: When living off-grid, your food sources might include wild game, fish, foraged plants, and homegrown vegetables. These sources can potentially harbor harmful bacteria, viruses, and parasites, especially if they are not handled or cooked properly. Knowing the risks and how to mitigate them is key to staying healthy.

- **Bacteria:** Common bacteria that can contaminate food include E. coli, Campylobacter, Listeria and Salmonella. These bacteria can cause severe foodborne illnesses, often with symptoms like nausea, vomiting, abdominal cramps and diarrhea.
- **Viruses:** Hepatitis A and Norovirus are viruses that can contaminate food and water. They often cause symptoms like vomiting, diarrhea, and jaundice and can be particularly severe in off-grid situations where medical care might be less accessible.

- **Parasites:** Parasites like Trichinella (found in undercooked wild game), Giardia (in contaminated water), and Toxoplasma (from raw or undercooked meat) can lead to serious health issues, including digestive problems, muscle pain, and even neurological effects.

Hunted Game and Foraged Foods:

- **Wild Game:** Animals like deer, elk, rabbit, and wild birds can carry bacteria and parasites not commonly found in domesticated animals. Trichinella, for example, is a parasitic worm found in the muscle of wild animals, particularly in bear, boar, and some birds. Consuming undercooked meat from these animals can lead to trichinosis, a potentially serious disease.
- **Foraged Plants:** While plants themselves are less likely to carry harmful pathogens, they can be contaminated by animals, insects, or waterborne pathogens. It's essential to wash and cook foraged plants thoroughly to minimize risks.

Safe Cooking Temperatures and Pathogen Elimination

Cooking to Kill Bacteria and Viruses: Cooking food to the correct temperature is the most reliable way to kill harmful bacteria, viruses, and parasites. Below are the recommended internal temperatures for different types of food, specifically tailored to an off-grid lifestyle where food sources might be more varied.

- **Poultry (Chicken, Turkey, Game Birds):**
  - *Safe Temperature:* At least 165°F (74°C).
  - *Why It's Important:* This temperature kills Salmonella, Campylobacter, and the Avian Influenza virus, which can be present in both domesticated and wild birds.
- **Ground Meat (Beef, Pork, Wild Game):**
  - *Safe Temperature:* At least 160°F (71°C).
  - *Why It's Important:* Ground meat is more susceptible to bacterial contamination because bacteria can be mixed throughout the meat. Cooking to 160°F effectively kills E. coli, Salmonella, and other bacteria.
- **Whole Cuts of Meat (Beef, Pork, Lamb, Wild Game):**
  - *Safe Temperature:* At least 145°F (63°C) with a rest time of 3 minutes.
  - *Why It's Important:* Cooking to this temperature kills surface bacteria like E. coli and Salmonella. The rest period allows the heat to penetrate deeper into the meat, further reducing the risk of bacterial contamination.
- **Wild Game (Bear, Boar, Venison):**
  - *Safe Temperature:* At least 160°F (71°C).
  - *Why It's Important:* Wild game can carry Trichinella parasites, which cause trichinosis. Cooking to 160°F is crucial to killing these parasites.
- **Fish:**
  - *Safe Temperature:* At least 145°F (63°C).
  - *Why It's Important:* This temperature ensures that harmful parasites and bacteria present in wild-caught fish are eliminated. Fish should be opaque and flake easily with a fork.

- **Eggs:**
  - *Safe Temperature:* At least 160°F (71°C).
  - *Why It's Important:* Cooking eggs until both the yolk and white are firm helps to prevent Salmonella infection, which can be present on the shell or inside the egg.
- **Foraged Plants and Wild Edibles:**
  - *Safe Practice:* Boil or cook thoroughly.
  - *Why It's Important:* Boiling kills most waterborne pathogens like Giardia and Cryptosporidium, which can contaminate foraged plants, particularly those found near water sources.

Cooking Methods in Off-Grid Situations

Open Fire Cooking: Cooking over an open fire is a common method in off-grid living, but it requires careful attention to ensure food reaches safe temperatures.

- **Monitoring Temperature:** Use a meat thermometer to check the internal temperature of your food, especially when cooking thick cuts of meat or whole birds. Ensure the fire is hot enough to cook food evenly.
- **Rotating Food:** When grilling or roasting over an open flame, rotate the food frequently to ensure even cooking. This helps prevent undercooked areas where bacteria and parasites might survive.
- **Cooking in Pots:** When boiling or stewing, ensure the water or broth maintains a rolling boil throughout the cooking process. This is particularly important for wild game or foraged foods that might be contaminated.

Wood Stoves: Wood stoves offer a more controlled environment for cooking but still require monitoring to maintain consistent temperatures.

- **Simmering and Slow Cooking:** Use the wood stove for simmering soups, stews, and slow-cooked dishes. These methods allow heat to penetrate deeply into the food, ensuring bacteria and parasites are killed.
- **Baking and Roasting:** When baking or roasting, preheat the stove to the desired temperature, and use a thermometer to verify that the food has reached safe cooking temperatures.

Solar Ovens: Solar ovens are effective for cooking food without fuel, but they rely on consistent sunlight and take longer to cook food.

- **Extended Cooking Times:** Solar ovens may take longer to reach safe cooking temperatures, so plan for extended cooking times, especially for meats and poultry.
- **Use a Thermometer:** Always use a thermometer to check that food has reached the recommended internal temperature. Solar ovens can vary in effectiveness depending on the weather.

Symptoms of Foodborne Illness: Foodborne illnesses can manifest with symptoms like nausea, vomiting, diarrhea, abdominal cramps, and fever. In severe cases, especially when caused by pathogens like E. coli, Salmonella, or Trichinella, foodborne illnesses can lead to long-term health complications or even be life-threatening.

Emergency Measures:

- **Hydration:** If you or someone in your group shows signs of foodborne illness, ensure they stay hydrated. Diarrhea and vomiting can quickly lead to dehydration, which is especially dangerous in off-grid situations.
- **Seek Medical Attention:** In severe cases, such as prolonged vomiting, high fever, or signs of dehydration, seek medical attention immediately. If you're in a remote area, have a plan for emergency transport to the nearest healthcare facility.

Proactive Measures:

- **Regularly Inspect and Rotate Stored Food:** Periodically check stored food supplies for signs of spoilage, mold, or pests. Rotate your stock to ensure you use older items first.
- **Boil Water:** Always boil water before drinking or cooking if you're unsure of its purity, especially when collecting water from natural sources.
- **Avoid Raw or Undercooked Foods:** Given the higher risk of contamination in off-grid settings, it's safer to avoid consuming raw or undercooked meats, fish, and eggs.

In an off-grid living situation, ensuring food safety is critical to maintaining your health and well-being. By understanding the risks associated with various food sources and adhering to safe cooking temperatures, you can significantly reduce the risk of foodborne illnesses. Proper preparation, vigilant monitoring, and the right cooking techniques will help you safely enjoy the fruits of your labor, whether it's from hunting, foraging, or home gardening.

Cultivating Food Self-Sufficiency in Off-Grid Living

The journey toward off-grid living is deeply rooted in the ability to sustain oneself, and food production plays a pivotal role in this journey. Throughout this chapter, we've explored the multifaceted aspects of growing, preserving, and preparing your own food—a crucial step toward true independence. The freedom that comes from harvesting your own fruits and vegetables, collecting eggs from your chickens, or preserving the bounty of your garden ensures that you remain resilient and self-sufficient in any situation.

By cultivating your own food, you take control of what you eat, reducing your reliance on external systems that are often vulnerable to disruption. The COVID-19 pandemic, with its empty grocery store shelves and soaring prices, served as a stark reminder of the importance of self-sufficiency. When you grow your own food, not only are you providing the freshest, most nutritious produce for your family, but you are also ensuring a stable food supply even in uncertain times.

Moreover, the techniques covered in this chapter—from planning your garden and raising livestock to preserving your harvest through canning, drying, and fermenting—are all about sustainability. These practices reduce your carbon footprint, minimize waste, and help you create a thriving, self-sustaining homestead that can weather the ups and downs of modern life.

The DIY projects detailed in this chapter, such as building a raised bed garden, constructing a chicken coop, or making a solar dehydrator, are designed to empower you with the skills and knowledge needed to succeed in off-grid living. They offer practical, hands-on solutions that are both cost-effective and environmentally friendly, helping you to create a sustainable lifestyle that aligns with your values of self-reliance and ecological stewardship.

Raising livestock, another key component of off-grid food production, not only diversifies your food sources but also adds a layer of security and independence. Whether you're keeping chickens for eggs and meat, raising goats for milk, or tending to bees for honey, each animal contributes to the sustainability of your homestead. However, as with any aspect of off-grid living, it's essential to approach livestock management with care, ensuring that you have the time, resources, and knowledge to provide for the well-being of your animals.

Food preservation techniques such as canning, drying, and fermenting are not just about keeping food from spoiling; they are about maintaining a year-round supply of healthy, homegrown food. These methods have been practiced for generations, allowing people to survive and thrive in environments where fresh food was not always available. By mastering these techniques, you ensure that your efforts in the garden or with your livestock do not go to waste, and you build a pantry that can sustain you through any season.

In conclusion, the ability to produce, preserve, and prepare your own food is at the heart of off-grid living. It is a journey that connects you to the land, fosters resilience, and ensures that you and your family can thrive independently. As you continue to explore the world of off-grid living, remember that each step you take toward food self-sufficiency brings you closer to a life of true freedom and sustainability.

Chapter 5 - Off-Grid Waste Management

Living off-grid isn't just about generating your own power or growing your own food—it's about managing all aspects of your life independently, and that includes waste. When you're living closer to nature, your impact on the environment becomes much more apparent. Suddenly, what you throw away and how you dispose of it takes on a new level of importance. Have you ever wondered what happens to your waste when you're off the grid? Unlike city living, where waste simply disappears into a system you don't have to think about, off-grid living requires you to deal with waste directly. This chapter is dedicated to exploring efficient, sustainable, and eco-friendly ways to manage waste when you're living off-grid.

Composting Toilets: Turning Waste into Resource

Let's start with one of the most basic yet essential aspects of waste management—dealing with human waste. When you're off the grid, conventional flush toilets connected to a sewage system are often not an option. Even if they were, the amount of water they waste would be impractical for a self-sufficient lifestyle. So, what's the solution? Enter the composting toilet—a hygienic, eco-friendly alternative that turns what we typically think of as waste into a valuable resource.

But why should you consider a composting toilet? Imagine being able to produce rich, fertile compost from your toilet waste, all while conserving water and reducing your environmental footprint. Composting toilets don't just solve a problem; they transform it into an opportunity to enhance your off-grid life.

A Historical Perspective: The Humanure Movement

The concept of exploiting human waste as a resource is not new. Indeed, it has been done in various ways for ages. The term "humanure" was popularized by Joseph Jenkins in his 1994 book, *The Humanure Handbook*, which advocates for the safe composting of human waste to create rich soil for growing food. This practice, though still unconventional in many places, offers a sustainable solution to waste management that is particularly suited to off-grid living.

How Does a Composting Toilet Work?

A composting toilet works by creating the right conditions for the natural decomposition of human waste into compost. This process is facilitated by the presence of oxygen, moisture, and carbon-rich materials like sawdust or leaves. Over time, the waste breaks down into a nutrient-rich substance that can be used to fertilize gardens and landscapes.

But how exactly does this process work? Picture a traditional compost pile, where kitchen scraps, yard waste, and other organic materials break down into rich, dark compost. The same principles apply to human waste—when managed correctly, it can decompose safely and naturally, turning what is often considered a liability into an asset.

Historical Anecdote: The Outhouse

Before the invention of modern plumbing, outhouses were the standard method of waste disposal in rural America and many other parts of the world. These simple, unventilated structures often produced unpleasant odors and attracted flies. However, by applying the principles of composting—such as regularly covering waste with dirt or ash—these issues can be mitigated. The composting toilet is essentially a modern, more refined version of the outhouse, designed with both hygiene and sustainability in mind.

Think back to the 19th century: Imagine a time when the average person's waste disposal solution was a simple wooden shack in the backyard. These outhouses were not particularly hygienic by today's standards, but they got the job done. Now, imagine taking that basic concept and refining it with modern knowledge and materials to create a system that not only manages waste but also recycles it into something beneficial for your garden. That's the power of the composting toilet.

DIY Project 17: Build a Composting Toilet

Building your own composting toilet is a manageable project that doesn't require advanced carpentry skills, just a basic understanding of the principles involved and some simple tools.

Cost	$$	Difficulty	★★
Materials:			

- **Wood:** To build the frame and structure of the toilet.
- **Sawdust or other carbon-rich material:** Essential for covering waste after each use.
- **Toilet Seat:** For comfort and functionality.
- **Bucket:** To collect waste, ideally a 5-gallon bucket.
- **Vent Pipe:** To allow gases to escape and prevent odors.

Tools:

- **Saw:** For cutting the wood to size.
- **Drill:** To assemble the structure.
- **Screwdriver:** For securing the seat and other components.

1	**Building the Frame** Start by constructing a sturdy frame for your toilet. Use durable wood that can withstand moisture and frequent use. The frame should be large enough to house a 5-gallon bucket beneath the toilet seat. The height and dimensions will depend	

on your comfort and space, but a typical height is around 18 inches, similar to a standard toilet.

Why use wood? Wood is not only a renewable resource but also easy to work with and customize. It's strong, insulating, and when treated or painted, it can last for years in a composting toilet setup. Consider this: in the early days of rural America, pioneers often built their entire homes from the timber they cut themselves. Wood has always been a reliable material for those who value self-sufficiency.

2	**Installing the Seat** Once the frame is built, install the toilet seat on top. Ensure that it's securely fastened and comfortable to use. The seat should align with the opening that leads directly into the bucket below.
3	**Preparing the Bucket** Place the bucket inside the frame, directly under the toilet seat. After each use, you'll cover the waste with a layer of sawdust, leaves, or other carbon-rich material. This helps to reduce odors, balance the carbon-nitrogen ratio and speed up the composting process. **Why sawdust?** Sawdust is a natural byproduct of woodworking and is readily available in many rural areas. It's also highly absorbent, which helps to manage moisture and control odors in the composting process. In the early days of sawmills, sawdust was often discarded as waste—until people realized its value in gardening and composting.
4	**Adding a Vent Pipe** To minimize odors, install a vent pipe that extends from the back of the toilet structure and runs outside. This pipe allows gases to escape, which keeps the air inside your shelter fresh and prevents the buildup of potentially harmful gases.
5	**Maintenance and Usage** Using a composting toilet is simple. After each use, cover the waste with sawdust or leaves. When the bucket is full, it can be removed and added to your compost pile, where it will break down further into safe, usable compost. Regularly clean the toilet and ensure the vent pipe remains unobstructed

Additional Tips:

- **Use Biodegradable Toilet Paper:** If possible, use biodegradable toilet paper to ensure everything breaks down smoothly in the composting process.
- **Compost Regularly:** Make sure you have a designated composting area where the waste can continue to decompose. This process can take several months, but the result is nutrient-rich compost that can be used to enrich soil.
- **Monitor Moisture Levels:** The compost pile should be moist but not wet. Excess moisture can slow down the composting process and produce smells.

Why is moisture control so important? Moisture is a critical factor in composting. Excessive water can produce an anaerobic environment, leading to slow decomposition and unpleasant odors. On the other hand, too little moisture can cause the composting process to stall. By maintaining the right balance, you ensure that your composting toilet remains efficient and odor-free.

Managing Household Waste: Reduce, Reuse, Recycle

When you're living off-grid, you're directly responsible for all the waste your household generates. Unlike urban living, where waste is whisked away weekly by garbage trucks, off-grid living forces you to confront the reality of your consumption. Have you ever considered how much garbage you generate in a day, week or year? The good news is that with a bit of planning and creativity, you can significantly reduce the amount of waste you generate—and even find ways to reuse or recycle much of it.

Why is managing household waste so crucial off-grid? Waste isn't just an inconvenience; it's a potential hazard. Accumulated trash can attract pests, produce unpleasant odors, and even contaminate your living space if not properly managed. Moreover, a high volume of waste often reflects inefficiencies in your lifestyle—whether it's from overconsumption, poor planning, or not making full use of available resources.

A Tale of Two Campsites: Lessons in Waste Management
Consider this: Two groups of people go camping in the wilderness. One group leaves behind a trail of trash—cans, plastic wrappers, and food waste scattered everywhere. The other group leaves no trace, carefully packing out everything they brought in. Which group would you rather emulate in your off-grid life? The latter group not only respects their environment but also ensures that it remains clean and safe for themselves and others. The same principles apply to off-grid living: effective waste management isn't just about cleanliness — it's about respect for your surroundings and a commitment to sustainability.

Reducing Waste: The First Step

The most efficient strategy to manage trash is to avoid creating it in the first place. In fact, the first step toward trash reduction is conscientious consumption. When you're living off-grid, every item you bring into your home should have a purpose. If it doesn't, it's just taking up space and will eventually become waste.

Ask yourself:

- **Do I really need this?** Before purchasing anything, consider whether it's necessary. Can you make do with something you already have?
- **Can this item be reused or repurposed?** Items that can be used multiple times or for multiple purposes are always preferable to single-use products.

Reusing and Repurposing: Give New Life to Old Items

Before you throw something away, consider whether it can be reused or repurposed. Many items that would otherwise end up in the trash can be given a second life with a bit of creativity.

Common Items to Repurpose:

- **Glass Jars:** Perfect for storing dried goods, homemade jams, or even as drinking glasses.
- **Old Clothing:** Torn or worn-out clothing can be cut up and used as cleaning rags, or repurposed into quilts or other crafts.
- **Wooden Pallets:** These can be turned into furniture, compost bins, or garden planters.

DIY Project 18: Build a DIY Compost Bin

During World War II, "Victory Gardens" became a popular way for citizens to contribute to the war effort by growing their own food. Alongside these gardens, composting became a common practice to recycle organic waste and enrich the soil. The government even distributed pamphlets on how to compost effectively. Today, the same principles apply to off-grid living — composting not only reduces waste but also enhances your ability to grow your own food.

Composting is a powerful way to repurpose organic waste. By turning kitchen scraps, garden clippings, and other biodegradable materials into compost, you create a nutrient-rich soil amendment that can be used to enhance your garden. Building your own compost bin is a simple project that can be completed in a day.

Cost	$	Difficulty	★
Materials:			

- **Wooden Pallets:** Typically free or inexpensive and easy to find.

- **Chicken Wire:** To line the inside and keep the compost contained.
- **Hinges:** For a simple lid to keep pests out.
- **Nails and Screws:** To assemble the structure.

Tools:

- **Hammer:** For driving nails.
- **Drill:** For screws and attaching the lid.
- **Saw:** For cutting the pallets if necessary.

1	**Construct the Frame** Arrange the wooden pallets to form a three-sided structure, with an open front for easy access. Secure the pallets together with nails or screws. If you want to add a bit of durability, you can use a few extra pieces of wood to reinforce the corners. **Why use pallets?** Wooden pallets are often discarded after use, making them an ideal material for upcycling. They're sturdy, easy to work with, and provide plenty of airflow to help your compost decompose efficiently.
2	**Line with Chicken Wire** Cover the inside of the compost container with chicken wire. This keeps the compost contained and allows for proper airflow, which is essential for the composting process.
3	**Add a Lid** If you're concerned about animals getting into your compost, add a simple hinged lid using a piece of wood and some hinges. This will keep pests out while still allowing you to easily add new material and turn the compost.
4	**Start Composting** Begin adding organic material to your compost bin. This includes fruit and vegetable scraps, eggshells, coffee grounds, leaves, grass clippings and more. Avoid adding meat, dairy or oily foods, as these can attract pests and take longer to decompose.

Additional Tips:

- **Turn the Compost Regularly:** Turning your compost periodically helps aerate it and speed up the decomposition process.
- **Balance Your Compost:** For the best compost, aim for a balance of "greens" (nitrogen-rich materials like vegetable scraps) and "browns" (carbon-rich materials like leaves and straw).
- **Monitor Moisture Levels:** Compost should contain roughly the same moisture content as a wrung-out sponge. Too much water can make the compost anaerobic and stinky, while too little may slow down decomposition.

Recycling: Closing the Loop

Recycling is the final piece of the waste management puzzle. While reducing and reusing are preferable, recycling ensures that the materials you do use don't go to waste. In an off-grid setting, recycling might look a little different from what you're used to. Instead of relying on curbside pickup, you may need to find creative ways to recycle materials yourself or take them to local recycling centers.

Ask yourself:

- **What can I recycle on-site?** Glass bottles can be crushed and used as a filler in construction projects. Aluminum cans can be melted down and then repurposed. Even plastic can be turned into durable, reusable items with the right tools.
- **What needs to be taken to a recycling center?** Items like certain plastics, metals, and batteries may need to be taken to a local recycling facility. Plan your trips carefully to minimize fuel use and make the most of each visit.

For instance, metal cans can be recycled not only to reduce waste but also to transform a common household item into something valuable and practical. Recycling metal cans can be more than just a fun craft project; it can also be a practical way to create useful items for your off-grid lifestyle. In the next pages you will discover how to turn metal cans into practical tools and items that can help you manage waste and make the most of available resources.

DIY Project 19: Turn Metal Cans into a Herb Planter

Growing herbs in recycled metal cans is an easy way to start a small, sustainable garden even if you have limited space. Herbs like basil, parsley and mint are perfect for small planters and can provide fresh flavors for your off-grid meals.

Cost	$	Difficulty	★
Materials:			

- **Metal cans** (various sizes)
- **Potting soil**
- **Herb seeds or seedlings**
- **Paint or markers** (optional for decoration)

	• **Small rocks or pebbles** (for drainage)	

Tools:

- Hammer and nail
- Can opener (if needed)
- Paintbrushes (if decorating)

1	**Prepare the Cans:** Clean the cans thoroughly and remove any sharp edges using the can opener if necessary. Use a hammer and nail to punch a few drainage holes in the bottom of each can.
2	**Decorate the Cans (Optional):** Use paint or markers to decorate the outside of the cans. This step is optional but adds a personal touch to your planters.
3	**Plant Your Herbs:** • Place a layer of small rocks or pebbles at the bottom of each can to aid in drainage. • Fill the cans with potting soil, leaving about an inch of space at the top. • Plant your herb seeds or seedlings in the soil and water lightly.
4	**Maintain Your Planters:** Put the planters in a sunny area and water them regularly. Rotate the cans occasionally to ensure even sunlight exposure.

DIY Project 20: Make a Mini Tool Organizer

A mini tool organizer made from recycled cans helps keep your workspace tidy and ensures that your tools are always within reach. It's a simple, cost-effective way to manage your supplies in an off-grid setting.

Cost	$	Difficulty	★
Materials:			

	• **Metal cans** (various sizes) • **Strong adhesive or screws** • **Wood plank or sturdy base**

Tools:

• **Drill** (if using screws)
• **Hammer and nails** (for additional support)

1	**Prepare the Cans:** Clean the cans and remove any sharp edges. Optionally, paint or label the cans to indicate what tools will go inside.
2	**Attach the Cans to a Base:** • Arrange the cans on a wood plank or other sturdy base in a way that makes sense for the tools you plan to store. • Secure the cans to the base using strong adhesive or screws. If using screws, drill a small hole in the can and screw it into the base.
3	**Organize Your Tools:** Once the adhesive or screws are set, use the cans to store small tools like screwdrivers, pliers, and nails. The cans can be arranged by tool type or size.
4	**Mount the Organizer (Optional):** If you want to save space, mount the entire organizer on a wall in your workshop or storage area.

Waste Management as a Pillar of Off-Grid Living

Waste management is a fundamental aspect of off-grid living that goes beyond mere cleanliness—it's about sustainability, resourcefulness, and self-reliance. In this chapter, we've explored how to transform waste into valuable resources, reduce consumption, and creatively reuse materials, all of which are vital to minimizing your environmental impact and enhancing your independence.

Composting toilets, for example, turn human waste into rich compost, conserving water and reducing your ecological footprint. Managing household waste by reducing, reusing, and recycling ensures that every item serves a purpose, minimizing the waste you generate. The DIY projects presented, such as building compost bins and repurposing materials, offer practical ways to integrate these principles into your daily life.

Ultimately, waste management in off-grid living is about creating a sustainable system that aligns with your values. By effectively managing your waste, you contribute to a healthier environment and a more self-sufficient lifestyle, paving the way for a sustainable future.

Chapter 6 - Maintaining Hygiene in Off-Grid Living

Living off-grid offers freedom, self-sufficiency, and a closer connection to nature, but it also presents unique challenges—one of the most important being the maintenance of personal and household hygiene. Without access to modern conveniences like running water, sewage systems, or store-bought cleaning products, how do you ensure that you and your living space remain clean, healthy, and comfortable? In this chapter, we'll explore the essential aspects of maintaining hygiene in an off-grid environment, from personal cleanliness to sanitation, and from DIY cleaning solutions to sustainable waste management.

Maintaining proper hygiene isn't just about comfort — it's a critical component of your health and well-being. In an off-grid setting, where access to medical care might be limited, preventing illness and infection becomes even more important. How can you effectively clean and sanitize when you don't have access to store-bought products or municipal water systems? What strategies can you use to manage waste and maintain a clean-living environment? These are the questions we'll answer, offering practical solutions and DIY projects that ensure you stay healthy and clean, even when living off the grid.

Personal Hygiene in Off-Grid Living

When you're living off the grid, maintaining personal hygiene is not just about looking good—it's about staying healthy. Without easy access to showers, hot water, and soap, how do you prevent the buildup of dirt, sweat, and bacteria that can lead to skin infections, rashes, or worse? In this section, we'll discuss the critical role personal hygiene plays in your overall health, and why it should never be overlooked, even in the most rugged environments.

DIY Project 21: Making Homemade Soap

Making your own soap at home is a fulfilling and creative process that allows you to control the ingredients and tailor the product to your skin's needs. Whether you're looking to avoid harsh chemicals or simply want to enjoy the benefits of natural ingredients, homemade soap offers a more personal and sustainable alternative to store-bought options. This guide will walk you through the basics of making cold-process soap, a traditional method that produces high-quality bars.

Cost	$	Difficulty	★
Materials:			

- **Lye (Sodium Hydroxide):** Essential for the saponification process that turns oils into soap. Handle with care, as it is a caustic substance.
- **Distilled Water:** To dissolve the lye. Always use distilled water to ensure purity.

- **Oils (Olive Oil, Coconut Oil, and Palm Oil):** These are the base oils for the soap, each contributing different properties such as moisturizing, lathering, and hardness.
- **Essential Oils (Optional):** For fragrance, use natural essential oils like lavender, eucalyptus, or peppermint.
- **Additives (Optional):** Herbs, oatmeal, or clays can be added for texture and additional skin benefits.

Tools:

- **Digital Scale:** To measure ingredients accurately.
- **Heat-Resistant Glass or Plastic Bowls:** For mixing the lye solution and oils.
- **Stainless Steel Pot:** For melting oils.
- **Stick Blender:** To blend the soap mixture to trace.
- **Soap Mold:** Silicone molds or a wooden box lined with parchment paper.
- **Rubber Gloves & Safety Goggles:** For protection when handling lye.
- **Thermometer:** To monitor the temperature of the lye and oils.
- **Spatula:** For stirring and scraping the mixture.

1	**Prepare Your Work Area:** Ensure you are working in a well-ventilated area and to prevent spillage cover your workplace with newspaper or a plastic Lye sheet. Wear rubber gloves and safety goggles to protect your skin and eyes from lye.
2	**Measure and Mix the Solution:** • Using a digital scale, measure the appropriate amount of lye (Sodium Hydroxide) based on your recipe (e.g., 4.5 oz of lye for a basic batch). • Slowly add the lye to a heat-resistant bowl containing the measured amount of distilled water (e.g., 10 oz of water). Never add water to lye since this may result in a dangerous reaction. Stir gently until the lye is completely dissolved. The solution will heat up quickly and release fumes, so keep your face away from the bowl.
3	**Melt the Oils:** In a stainless-steel pot, measure and melt your oils over low heat. A typical recipe might include 16 oz of olive oil, 10 oz of coconut oil, and 6 oz of palm oil. Stir the oils together until they are fully melted and combined. Remove from heat.
4	**Combine Lye and Oils:** • Allow the lye solution and the melted oils to cool to about 100-110°F. Use a thermometer to check the temperatures.

	• Slowly pour the lye solution into the oils. Use a stick blender to mix the ingredients. Blend in short bursts to avoid splashing, stirring between bursts until the mixture reaches "trace", that is the point at which the mixture thickens and leaves a trail on the surface when dripped from the blender.
5	**Add Fragrance and Additives (Optional):** If desired, add essential oils for fragrance (e.g., 1 oz of lavender essential oil) and any additives like oatmeal, dried herbs, or clay. Stir these in thoroughly but quickly, as the soap will begin to set.
6	**Pour into Molds:** Pour the soap mixture into your prepared molds, using a spatula to scrape all the mixture from the pot. To eliminate air bubbles, gently tap the molds on the counter.
7	**Cure the Soap:** • Cover the molds with a towel or lid and let them sit undisturbed in a warm area for 24-48 hours. Once the soap has hardened, remove it from the molds and cut it into bars if necessary. • Place the bars on a drying surface or in a well-ventilated space to cure for 4-6 weeks. This curing procedure hardens the soap and entirely saponifies the lye, resulting in mild, long-lasting bars.
8	**Store and Use:** Once cured, store your soap in a cool, dry place. Homemade soap bars can last several months when stored properly. Enjoy your handmade soap, knowing it's free from synthetic additives and tailored to your preferences

Additional Tips:

- **Soap Calculator:** Use an online soap calculator to adjust the lye and water amounts based on the specific oils you choose.
- **Safety First:** <u>Lye is a caustic substance</u> that can cause burns or injury if mishandled, so <u>always handle it with caution</u>. Wear safety clothing, operate in a well-ventilated environment, and keep vinegar available to neutralize any lye leaks.
- **Customization:** Experiment with different oils, scents and ingredients to create a make that is completely yours. In addition, almond oil, cocoa and shea are great options for added moisture.

Where to Retrieve Lye (Sodium Hydroxide)

1. **Hardware Stores:** Lye is commonly found in hardware stores, especially in the plumbing section. It's often sold as a drain cleaner, but you need to ensure it's 100% sodium hydroxide without any additives.
2. **Online Retailers:** Lye can be purchased from various online retailers, and specialty soap-making supply websites. When buying online, always check that it's food-grade or at least pure sodium hydroxide.
3. **Soap-Making Supply Stores:** Specialty stores that cater to soap makers often carry lye. These stores may be physical locations or online, and they provide lye specifically intended for soap-making.
4. **Chemical Supply Stores:** Chemical supply stores or scientific suppliers might also carry lye, but it may be sold in larger quantities. Make sure it's pure sodium hydroxide and not mixed with other chemicals.
5. **Local Farmers' Markets or Artisanal Shops:** Some artisanal soap makers sell soap-making kits that include small quantities of lye. These kits can be a good option if you're looking to make a limited batch of soap.

Alternatives to Lye for Soap Making

While traditional cold process soap requires lye, there are alternatives if you want to avoid handling sodium hydroxide directly:

1. **Melt and Pour Soap Bases:**
   o Melt and pour soap bases are pre-made soaps that have already gone through saponification. You can melt the base, add your own scents, colors, and additives, and then pour it into molds. This method is ideal for beginners or those who want to avoid handling lye.
   o These bases are readily available at craft stores, online retailers, and soap-making supply shops.
2. **Castile Soap:**
   o Instead of making your soap from scratch, you can use pure Castile soap (made from olive oil) as a base. Melt the Castile soap and add additional oils, fragrances, and other ingredients to customize it.
   o Castile soap can be found in health food stores, some supermarkets, and online.
3. **Soap Rebatching:**
   o Rebatching involves grating an existing bar of soap, melting it down, and adding new ingredients like essential oils or herbs. This method allows you to customize soap without directly handling lye.
   o You can use leftover soap scraps or purchase unscented soap bars for rebatching.

While these alternatives provide safer and easier methods of making soap, they do not allow for the same level of customization as starting from scratch with lye. However, they are excellent options for those who want to create handmade soap with less risk and effort.

Making your own soap at home is a rewarding process that allows you to control the ingredients and create a product tailored to your skin's needs. With practice, you can experiment with different recipes, scents, and additives to produce beautiful, natural soap bars that are perfect for personal use or gifting.

DIY Project 22: Making Homemade Toothpaste

Your teeth and gums are just as important as the rest of your body when it comes to hygiene. Without regular brushing, plaque and bacteria can lead to tooth decay, gum disease, and other serious health issues. But in an off-grid situation, you may not have access to commercial toothpaste. Don't worry—this section will teach you how to make your own effective, natural toothpaste using simple ingredients like baking soda, coconut oil, and essential oils. Not only is it easy to make, but it's also free from harmful chemicals and can be tailored to your specific oral health needs.

Cost	$	Difficulty	★
Materials: • **Baking Soda:** A natural abrasive that helps remove plaque and stains. • **Coconut Oil:** Has antibacterial qualities and provides a smooth texture. • **Essential Oil (Peppermint or Spearmint):** Adds flavor and a refreshing scent, while also offering antibacterial benefits. • **Xylitol (Optional):** A natural sweetener that helps to prevent cavities and adds a mild sweetness to the toothpaste. • **Salt (Optional):** Adds additional abrasive qualities and helps to kill bacteria.			
Tools: • **Mixing Bowl:** To combine the ingredients. • **Spoon or Spatula:** For mixing. • **Small Container with Lid:** To store the finished toothpaste.			
1	**Combine the Dry Ingredients:** In a mixing bowl, add 2 tablespoons of baking soda. If you choose to use salt, add about 1/4 teaspoon of fine sea salt. Stir to combine.		
2	**Add the Coconut Oil:** • Add 2 tablespoons of coconut oil to the dry ingredients. Coconut oil is solid at room temperature but melts easily. If your coconut oil is too solid, you can warm it slightly to make it easier to mix.		

	• Use a spoon or spatula to thoroughly mix the baking soda and coconut oil until you achieve a smooth, paste-like consistency.
3	**Add Flavor and Sweetener:** • If using, add 1 teaspoon of xylitol to the mixture. This natural sweetener not only enhances flavor but also promotes dental health by reducing bacteria that cause cavities. • Add 5-10 drops of peppermint or spearmint essential oil for flavor. Adjust the number of drops to your taste preference but be cautious as essential oils are potent.
4	**Mix Thoroughly:** Stir the mixture thoroughly until all ingredients are well combined. The final texture should be a smooth, spreadable paste.
5	**Store the Toothpaste:** Transfer the homemade toothpaste to a small container with a lid. Store it in a cool, dry place. Coconut oil may harden in cooler temperatures, so you might need to warm the container slightly before use.
6	**Use the Toothpaste:** To use, dip a clean toothbrush into the paste or use a small spoon to apply a pea-sized amount to your toothbrush. Brush as usual, and rinse your mouth thoroughly with water

Additional Tips:

- **Customization:** Feel free to experiment with other essential oils like cinnamon, clove, or tea tree oil for additional antibacterial properties and flavor variations.
- **Storage:** Keep the toothpaste in an airtight container to prevent it from drying out. It can last up to a few weeks, depending on storage conditions.
- **Remineralizing Option:** For added benefits, consider adding a small amount of calcium carbonate powder to help remineralize teeth.

This homemade toothpaste is a natural, chemical-free alternative that can help you maintain oral hygiene while aligning with a more sustainable lifestyle. It's simple to make, customizable, and a great addition to your daily routine.

1.4 DIY Project: Building an Outdoor Shower

Staying clean without indoor plumbing can be a challenge, but an outdoor shower offers a practical solution. In this project, we'll show you how to build a simple, yet effective, outdoor shower using basic materials like a gravity-fed water system, a showerhead, and a solar water heater. This shower setup allows you to wash away the dirt and grime after a long day of work, and can be a refreshing addition to your off-grid homestead. We'll also discuss ways to ensure your shower water is reused responsibly, such as diverting it to a greywater system for your garden.

DIY Project 23: Natural Deodorants

Worried about body odor in the absence of modern deodorants? You can create your own natural deodorants using ingredients that are gentle on your skin and the environment. Commercial deodorants often contain chemicals like aluminum and parabens, but natural alternatives offer a safer and more sustainable option.

Cost	$	Difficulty	★

Ingredients:

- 1/4 cup baking soda
- 1/4 cup arrowroot powder or cornstarch
- 4 tablespoons coconut oil (solid)
- 10-15 drops of essential oil (optional, for scent)

Tools:

- **Mixing Bowl:** A small to medium-sized bowl for combining the ingredients.
- **Measuring Cups:** Used to measure out the baking soda, arrowroot powder (or cornstarch), and coconut oil accurately.
- **Spoon or Spatula:** For mixing the ingredients together into a smooth paste.
- **Small Jar or Empty Deodorant Stick Container:** To store the finished deodorant. If using a jar, make sure it has a tight-fitting lid. If using an empty deodorant stick, ensure it's clean and dry.
- **Measuring Spoons:** To measure the essential oils accurately if you choose to add them.
- **Small Spatula or Spoon (Optional):** For applying the deodorant, especially if stored in a jar.

1	**Mix Dry Ingredients:** In a bowl, combine the baking soda and arrowroot powder (or cornstarch).
2	**Add Coconut Oil:**

	Slowly add the coconut oil and mix until the ingredients form a smooth paste. The coconut oil acts as a natural antibacterial agent and moisturizer.
3	**Essential Oils:** For an appealing scent, add a few drops of essential oil. Lavender, tea tree, and peppermint oils are popular choices for their antibacterial properties
4	**Store and Use:** Transfer the mixture to a small jar or an empty deodorant stick. To apply, use your fingers or a small spatula to spread a thin layer under your arms.

Why Use Natural Deodorants?

- **Chemical-Free:** Avoids exposure to potentially harmful chemicals found in commercial products.
- **Eco-Friendly:** Uses biodegradable ingredients that are safe for the environment.
- **Cost-Effective:** Made from affordable, readily available ingredients.

Natural deodorants are not only effective but also align with the principles of sustainable, off-grid living. They help you stay fresh without relying on store-bought products, giving you peace of mind about what you're putting on your skin.

DIY Project 24: Creating Homemade Wet Wipes

Homemade wet wipes are a convenient solution when you need a quick clean-up but didn't have access to soap and water. Whether you're out in the field, on a long hike, or just conserving water, these DIY wipes are perfect for freshening up on the go.

Cost	$	Difficulty	★
Materials:			

- A roll of strong, absorbent paper towels (preferably reusable cloths for an eco-friendly option)
- 2 cups distilled water.
- 2 tablespoons coconut oil or olive oil
- 1 tablespoon Castile soap or a mild liquid soap
- 10-15 drops of essential oil (lavender, tea tree, or lemon for antibacterial properties)
- A container with a tight-sealing lid

Tools:

- **Sharp Knife:** For cutting the roll of paper towels in half, if using paper towels. A serrated knife or bread knife works well for this task.
- **Cutting Board:** To safely cut the paper towel roll on and protect your work surface.
- **Mixing Bowl:** For mixing the distilled water, oil, soap, and essential oils together.
- **Measuring Cups:** To measure the correct amount of distilled water and oil.
- **Measuring Spoons:** For measuring the Castile soap or liquid soap and essential oils.
- **Spoon or Whisk:** For stirring the liquid mixture until well combined.
- **Container with Tight-Sealing Lid:** A container to store the wet wipes, ensuring they stay moist and ready for use. The container should be large enough to hold the half roll of paper towels or reusable cloths.
- **Spoon or Tongs (Optional):** For pressing down the paper towels into the container as they soak up the liquid mixture.

1	**Cut the Paper Towels:** If using paper towels, cut the roll in half with a sharp knife to create two smaller rolls that fit your container.
2	**Mix the Solution:** In a bowl, mix the distilled water, oil, soap, and essential oils. Stir until well combined.
3	**Soak the Towels:** Place the half roll of paper towels (or cloths) in the container and pour the liquid mixture over it. Allow the towels to soak up the solution.
4	**Store and Use:** Seal the container with the lid. When you need a wipe, simply pull one from the center of the roll.

Benefits of Homemade Wet Wipes:

- **Convenience:** Provides an easy way to clean your hands, face, or body without needing a full wash.
- **Customizable:** You may customize the ingredients to your skin type or preferences.
- **Portable:** Ideal for keeping in your bag, car, or backpack when you're on the go.

These homemade wipes are versatile and can be used for a variety of purposes, from personal hygiene to cleaning surfaces. They're especially useful in off-grid situations where water is a precious resource.

DIY Project 25: No-Water Shaving Cream

How do you stay groomed without running water? Shaving is one aspect of personal hygiene that can be challenging off-grid, but with the right approach, it's entirely manageable. Waterless shaving creams or oils allow you to shave comfortably without needing a basin of water.

Cost	$	Difficulty	★

Ingredients:

- 1/4 cup coconut oil
- 1/4 cup shea butter
- 2 tablespoons jojoba oil or olive oil
- 5-10 drops of essential oil (optional for scent

Tools:

- **Small Pot or Saucepan:** For melting the coconut oil and shea butter over low heat.
- **Spoon or Spatula:** To stir the oils and mix in the jojoba oil and essential oils.
- **Hand Mixer or Whisk:** For whipping the mixture into a light, fluffy consistency once it has cooled slightly.
- **Measuring Cups:** To accurately measure the coconut oil, shea butter, and jojoba or olive oil.
- **Measuring Spoons:** For measuring the essential oils, if you choose to add them.
- **Mixing Bowl:** For whipping the cooled mixture into the desired consistency.
- **Jar with Lid:** To store the finished shaving cream. The jar should have a tight-fitting lid to keep the cream fresh and prevent it from drying out.

1	**Melt and Mix:** In a small pot, melt the coconut oil and shea butter over low heat. Once melted, remove from heat and stir in the jojoba oil and essential oils.
2	**Cool and Whip:** Allow the mixture to cool slightly, then whip it with a hand mixer or whisk until it becomes light and fluffy.
3	**Store:** Transfer the whipped shaving cream to a jar with a lid. It will solidify as it cools but will soften when applied to the skin.

Benefits of No-Water Shaving Cream:

- **Moisturizing:** The oils in the cream help to moisturize the skin, reducing irritation and razor burn.
- **Convenient:** Can be used without water, making it perfect for shaving in off-grid conditions or on the move.
- **Eco-Friendly:** Made from natural, biodegradable ingredients.

No-water shaving cream is an excellent addition to your off-grid hygiene toolkit, ensuring you can maintain your grooming routine even when water is scarce.

DIY Project 26: Building a Hand-Powered Washing Machine

A hand-powered washing machine is a simple device that uses manual force to agitate clothes in water, simulating the action of a modern washing machine. It's ideal for off-grid living, requiring no electricity and very little water.

Cost	$	Difficulty	★★

Materials:

- **5-Gallon Bucket with a Lid:** A standard 5-gallon bucket will serve as the washing chamber. The lid should fit tightly to prevent water from splashing out during use.
- **Toilet Plunger or Similar Agitator:** A standard toilet plunger works well as an agitator. You may also use any other type of manual agitator that can create sufficient movement to wash clothes.
- **Drill with Hole Saw Bit:** A drill with a hole saw bit (approximately 1-2 inches in diameter) is needed to create a hole in the bucket lid for the plunger handle.
- **Rubber Grommets (Optional):** Rubber grommets can be used to seal the hole around the plunger handle, preventing leaks. These are optional but recommended for a more secure and leak-proof fit.
- **Detergent:** Any laundry detergent suitable for hand washing can be used. Be sure to use a small amount, as the manual washing process requires less detergent than a traditional machine.
- **Clothesline or Drying Rack:** A place to hang your clothes to dry after washing. A simple clothesline or portable drying rack will suffice.

Tools:

- **Drill:** Needed to create the hole in the bucket lid. A standard electric drill is fine, and if you're off-grid, a hand-crank drill could also work.
- **Hole Saw Bit:** Used with the drill to create a hole in the bucket lid. The size of the bit should match the diameter of the plunger handle.
- **Utility Knife or Scissors:** Useful for making any adjustments or cleaning up the edges of the hole in the lid after drilling.

- **Screwdriver:** Depending on your plunger or other components, a screwdriver might be needed for minor adjustments.
- **Wrench (Optional):** A wrench might be needed if any nuts or bolts are involved in securing the plunger or other components.
- **Marker (Optional):** To mark the center of the bucket lid before drilling.

1	**Preparing the Bucket:** Start by selecting a sturdy 5-gallon bucket with a tight-fitting lid. Drill a hole in the center of the lid that is just large enough for the handle of the plunger to fit through.
2	**Modifying the Plunger:** Take the toilet plunger and use the drill or a utility knife to create several small holes in the rubber plunger head. These holes will allow water and detergent to flow through more easily, improving the washing action
3	**Assembling the Washing Machine:** Place the clothes you want to wash in the bucket, add water, and a small amount of detergent. Insert the plunger through the hole in the lid, ensuring it fits snugly. If necessary, use rubber grommets to seal the hole around the plunger handle.
4	**Washing the Clothes:** Secure the lid on the bucket. Move the plunger up and down vigorously to agitate the clothes inside. The plunger's action simulates the agitation of a washing machine, helping to remove dirt and grime. Continue this action for 5-10 minutes, depending on the level of dirtiness.
5	**Rinsing and Drying:** After washing, remove the clothes and rinse them thoroughly in clean water. Wring out excess water by hand or using a wringer. Finally, hang the clothes on a clothesline or drying rack to air dry.

This hand-powered washing machine is an efficient and eco-friendly way to clean clothes without electricity, making it ideal for off-grid living or emergency situations.

DIY Project 27: Building a DIY Clothes Wringer

A clothes wringer is a simple device that helps remove excess water from clothes after washing, making them easier to dry. This project will guide you through building a hand-cranked wringer using basic materials.

Cost	$$	Difficulty	★★★

Materials:

- **Two Wooden Rolling Pins or Cylindrical Wooden Dowels:** These will serve as the rollers for squeezing out the water from clothes. Rolling pins are ideal because they are already shaped and smooth, but cylindrical wooden dowels can also be used if you prefer to cut and shape them yourself.
- **Metal Brackets and Screws:** Metal brackets will be used to mount the rolling pins to the frame securely. Screws will be needed to attach the brackets to the frame and secure other components.
- **Hand-Crank Handle:** This is essential for manually turning the rolling pins. You can repurpose a handle from an old machine, like an old meat grinder or other hand-cranked devices or purchase a hand-crank mechanism specifically for this purpose.
- **Springs:** Springs are necessary to apply consistent pressure to the rolling pins, ensuring they squeeze out the water effectively. The springs should be strong enough to maintain tension but flexible enough to adjust as needed.
- **Sturdy Frame (Wood or Metal):** The frame holds the entire wringer together. It needs to be strong and stable enough to support the rolling pins and withstand the force applied during operation. Wood is easier to work with, but metal offers more durability.

Tools:

- Two wooden rolling pins (or cylindrical wooden dowels)
- **Saw:** For cutting wood or metal to create the frame and possibly for shaping the rolling pins or dowels.
- **Drill:** For making holes in the frame, brackets, and rolling pins to attach components. A drill is also used to attach the hand-crank and to secure screws.
- **Screwdriver:** For driving screws into the frame and securing the metal brackets, hand-crank handle, and other components.
- **Wrench:** A wrench may be needed to tighten bolts or adjust the hand-crank mechanism.
- **Measuring Tape:** To measure and ensure proper spacing and alignment of the rolling pins within the frame.
- **Clamps (Optional):** Clamps can be helpful for holding components in place while you drill or screw them together.
- **Level:** To ensure the rolling pins are aligned correctly and the frame is stable and even.
- **Pliers (Optional):** For bending or adjusting metal brackets or springs as needed.

1	**Constructing the Frame:**

	Build a sturdy frame to hold the two rolling pins in place. The frame should be tall enough to allow the pins to sit parallel, with enough space between them for clothes to pass through. Use wood or metal for the frame, ensuring it is stable and strong.
2	**Attaching the Rolling Pins:** Mount the rolling pins horizontally on the frame using metal brackets. The pins should be close enough that when clothes are passed between them, they are squeezed tightly. Attach the hand-crank handle to one of the pins, so that when you turn the handle, both pins rotate.
3	**Adding Springs for Pressure:** Install springs on either side of the frame to apply pressure to the rolling pins. This pressure is what forces the water out of the clothes as they pass through the wringer. Adjust the tension on the springs to ensure the wringer works effectively.
4	**Operating the Wringer:** To use the wringer, simply feed wet clothes between the two rolling pins while turning the hand-crank. The pressure from the pins will squeeze out excess water, making the clothes much easier to dry.
5	**Final Adjustments:** Test the wringer with a small load of clothes and make any necessary adjustments to the tension or alignment of the pins. Once the wringer is working smoothly, it can be used regularly as part of your off-grid laundry routine.

DIY Project 28: Outdoor Shower Construction

Incorporating an outdoor shower into your off-grid living setup can be both a practical and refreshing addition. Whether you're rinsing off after a day of working outdoors or simply enjoying the experience of showering under the open sky, an outdoor shower is a simple yet rewarding project. This shower can be constructed with basic materials, and it's a great way to utilize rainwater or a gravity-fed water system. Plus, it provides a sustainable bathing option that's perfect for an off-grid lifestyle.

Cost	$$	Difficulty	★★★
Materials:			

- **Wooden Posts** (4x4): For the frame.
- **PVC Pipe** (1/2 inch): For the plumbing.
- **Showerhead**: A basic model that can be attached to the PVC pipe.
- **Valve or Faucet**: To control water flow.

- **Gravel or Flat Stones**: For the shower floor.
- **Plastic or Metal Barrel**: Optional, for a gravity-fed water source.
- **Screws & Nails**: For assembling the frame.
- **Tarp or Shower Curtain**: For privacy.
- **Concrete Mix**: To secure the posts in the ground.

Tools:

- **Drill**: For creating holes in the posts and securing the showerhead.
- **Saw**: For cutting the wooden posts to size.
- **Level**: To ensure the posts are vertical.
- **Shovel**: For digging holes for the posts.
- **Pipe Cutter**: For cutting the PVC pipe to the correct length.
- **Wrench**: For securing the showerhead and valve.

1	**Choose the Location:** Select a location that offers privacy and adequate drainage. Ideally, the shower should be placed near a water source and in a spot that receives ample sunlight to keep the area warm.
2	**Build the Frame:** - Cut the wooden posts to your desired height for the shower (typically around 7 feet). - Dig four holes at the corners of the intended shower area. Each hole should be about 2 feet deep to secure the posts. - Place the posts into the holes and use a level to ensure they are vertical. Fill the holes with concrete mix to anchor the posts securely. - Allow the concrete to set for 24 hours before proceeding.
3	**Install the Floor:** Lay a bed of gravel or flat stones on the ground inside the frame to create a solid and drainable shower floor. This prevents water from pooling and helps with drainage.
4	**Set Up the Plumbing:** - Measure and cut the PVC pipe to create the plumbing system. - Attach the showerhead to the top of the PVC pipe.

	- If using a gravity-fed system, position the barrel above the shower (such as on a platform) and connect the PVC pipe to it, leading the pipe down to the shower area. - Install a valve or faucet at a convenient height to control the water flow. - Use the wrench to ensure all connections are tight and secure.
5	**Add Privacy Features:** Attach a tarp or shower curtain to the frame using nails or screws, creating a privacy barrier around the shower. You can also use natural materials like bamboo or wooden slats for a more aesthetic touch.
6	**Test the System:** - Once everything is in place, test the water flow by filling the barrel (if using) and turning on the faucet. Check for leaks in the plumbing and ensure that the water drains properly from the shower floor. - Adjust the positioning of the showerhead and valve as needed for comfort.

Additional Tips:

- **Water Source:** If you don't have a gravity-fed system, you can connect the shower to a garden hose or install a simple solar-heated water tank for warm showers.
- **Seasonal Use:** Consider disassembling or winterizing the shower if you live in a region with freezing winters to prevent damage to the pipes and materials.
- **Customization:** Personalize your outdoor shower with hooks for towels, a shelf for soap, or decorative elements like plants or stones.

Alternative Personal Hygiene Method: Dry Brushing - A Waterless Cleaning Solution

When living off-grid, you may find yourself in situations where water is scarce, or you need to freshen up quickly without the luxury of a full shower. Maintaining personal hygiene in such conditions requires creativity and resourcefulness. This section will delve into alternative hygiene methods that are both practical and effective, ensuring you stay clean and healthy even when water is in short supply. These techniques are essential for water conservation and provide valuable options when you're on the move or in a situation where traditional bathing isn't feasible.

Have you ever felt grimy but didn't have enough water to shower? Dry brushing could be the answer. Dry brushing is an ancient technique used to exfoliate the skin, stimulate blood circulation, and promote lymphatic drainage—all without a drop of water. It involves using a natural bristle brush to remove dead skin cells and impurities from the surface of your skin.

How to Dry Brush:

1. **Choose the Right Brush:** Select a brush with natural bristles, which are firm but not too abrasive. Long-handled brushes are ideal for reaching your back and other hard-to-reach areas.
2. **Brush Before Showering:** Dry brushing is particularly effective on dry skin prior to bathing. Begin with your feet and move upwards toward your heart in long, sweeping gestures. This orientation increases circulation and aids in the movement of lymphatic fluid.
3. **Gentle, Consistent Pressure:** Apply gentle pressure, adjusting based on your skin's sensitivity. Avoid brushing areas with cuts, sunburn, or rashes.
4. **Brush Daily:** Incorporate dry brushing into your daily routine. It not only cleanses the skin but also invigorates the body, making it a refreshing start to your day.

Benefits of Dry Brushing:

- **Exfoliation:** Removes dead skin cells, leaving your skin smoother and softer.
- **Circulation:** Enhances blood flow and promotes the elimination of toxins.
- **Energy Boost:** Many people find dry brushing to be invigorating, giving them a natural energy boost.

Dry brushing is an excellent way to maintain hygiene when water is limited. It's quick, effective, and requires no additional resources beyond a simple brush.

Adapt and Thrive with Alternative Hygiene Methods

In an off-grid living situation, maintaining personal hygiene requires adapting to new methods and thinking creatively about how to stay clean and healthy. Whether you're using dry brushing to exfoliate, natural deodorants to stay fresh, or homemade wet wipes for a quick clean-up, these alternative hygiene techniques are essential for thriving in a water-limited environment. By incorporating these practices into your daily routine, you can ensure that you remain comfortable and confident, no matter how far off the grid you go.

Household Hygiene

A clean-living environment is essential for preventing the spread of germs and maintaining a healthy home. But how do you clean effectively without commercial cleaners or endless supplies of water? In this section, we'll discuss the importance of household hygiene in off-grid living and introduce simple, effective methods for keeping your space tidy and sanitized. Whether it's sweeping floors, wiping down surfaces, or managing clutter, these basic practices are key to creating a healthy, comfortable living environment.

DIY Project 29: Make Your Own Natural Cleaning Products

Why rely on store-bought cleaners filled with chemicals when you can make your own natural, eco-friendly cleaning products? In this project, we'll guide you through the process of creating homemade cleaning solutions using common household items like vinegar, baking soda, lemon juice, and essential oils. These cleaners are safe, effective, and versatile—perfect for everything from disinfecting countertops to scrubbing toilets. We'll also provide recipes for specific cleaning tasks, such as a powerful all-purpose cleaner, a gentle surface polish, and a natural disinfectant spray.

Cost	$	Difficulty	★

Materials:

- **White Vinegar:** A natural disinfectant and deodorizer.
- **Baking Soda:** Great for scrubbing and neutralizing odors.
- **Essential Oils:** For aroma and added antimicrobial qualities.
- **Reusable Spray Bottle:** Preferably glass or durable plastic.

Tools:

- **Measuring Cups:** To ensure proper ratios.
- **Mixing Bowl:** For combining ingredients.

1	**Mix Your Ingredients** For a basic all-purpose cleaner, mix equal parts white vinegar and water in a reusable spray bottle. Add a few drops of essential oil for fragrance. For tougher cleaning jobs, like scrubbing sinks or tubs, mix baking soda with a small amount of water to form a paste.
2	**Store and Use** Store your homemade cleaning products in clearly labeled bottles. Use the vinegar mixture for countertops, windows, and general cleaning. The baking soda paste is ideal for scouring surfaces and removing stains. **Why make your own?** Not only does this reduce waste, but it also ensures that no harmful chemicals are entering your off-grid environment. Plus, it's cost-effective—vinegar and baking soda are inexpensive and versatile.

Embracing a Hygienic Off-Grid Lifestyle

Maintaining hygiene in an off-grid environment is not just about staying clean—it's essential for your health, well-being, and overall comfort. By adopting the strategies and DIY projects discussed in this chapter, you can effectively manage personal and household hygiene without relying on modern conveniences.

From creating your own soap and natural cleaning products to building an outdoor shower and understanding alternative hygiene methods, each step you take enhances your self-sufficiency and resilience. Hygiene off the grid requires creativity, resourcefulness, and a proactive approach, but with the right knowledge, you can ensure a clean, healthy, and sustainable living space.

Incorporating these practices into your daily routine not only protects you and your family from illness but also aligns with a lifestyle of independence and respect for your environment. As you continue your off-grid journey, let these hygiene practices be a foundation for a thriving, self-sufficient life.

Chapter 7 - Off-Grid Power Solutions

Power is one of the most crucial aspects of off-grid living. Without a reliable energy source, your off-grid life can quickly become difficult, especially when you're trying to maintain modern comforts like lighting, refrigeration, or even just charging your phone. In this chapter, we'll explore various renewable energy sources that can power your off-grid home, guide you through setting up your own solar power system, and discuss wind energy as a supplementary option. We'll also cover essential backup power solutions to ensure you're never left in the dark. Remember, an off-grid power solution isn't just about convenience—it's a wise investment in your future, safeguarding you against the uncertainties of external power supplies.

Introduction to Renewable Energy

When you decide to live off the grid, one of the first questions you'll face is: "How will I generate electricity"? The answer usually lies in renewable energy sources. Unlike traditional fossil fuels, renewable energy is sustainable, environmentally friendly, and often more cost-effective in the long run. But which renewable energy source is right for you? Let's break down the three main options: solar, wind, and micro-hydro power.

But before we dive into the details, let me ask you this: Do you remember what happened during the 2003 Northeast Blackout? This massive power outage affected over 50 million people across the United States and Canada, plunging entire cities into darkness for days. It was a stark reminder of how vulnerable our modern power grid can be. Now imagine being completely unaffected by such a catastrophe because your home is powered by the sun, the wind, or a flowing stream nearby. That's the real power of going off-grid—freedom from the fragility of external power systems.

Overview of Solar, Wind, and Micro-Hydro Power

Solar Power

Solar power harnesses energy from the sun using photovoltaic (PV) panels. This is the most common choice for off-grid living because it's scalable, reliable, and has become increasingly affordable over the years. Solar panels are versatile; they can be mounted on your roof, placed on the ground, or even integrated into your building materials.

The concept of using the sun for energy isn't new. Did you know that ancient civilizations like the Romans and Greeks designed their buildings to capture the sun's heat during the winter? This early form of passive solar energy was crucial for heating their homes. Fast forward to the 21st century, and we now have the technology to convert sunlight directly into electricity, making solar power one of the most effective and sustainable energy sources for off-grid living.

Pros:

- **Reliability:** Solar power works anywhere the sun shines, making it a viable option in most parts of the world.
- **Low Maintenance:** Once installed, solar panels require very little maintenance.
- **Scalability:** You can start small and expand your system as your energy needs grow.

Cons:

- **Initial Cost:** The upfront cost can be high, though this is mitigated over time through savings on energy bills.
- **Weather Dependency:** Solar power is less effective on cloudy days and not productive at night, necessitating a battery system for energy storage.
- **Space Requirements:** You need adequate space to install enough panels to suit your energy requirements..

Wind Power

Wind power is another viable option, especially if you live in a location with consistent wind speeds. Wind turbines convert kinetic energy from the wind into electricity, which can then be used to power your home or stored in batteries for later use.

Wind energy has been harnessed for centuries. Think about the iconic windmills of the Netherlands, which were used as far back as the 12th century to pump water and grind grain. Today's wind turbines are a far cry from those early machines, but the principle remains the same capturing the power of the wind to do useful work.

Pros:

- **Efficient in Windy Areas:** In locations with high wind speeds, wind turbines can generate a significant amount of electricity.
- **Complementary to Solar:** Wind power may supplement solar energy by supplying power when the sun is not shining.

Cons:

- **Variable Output:** Wind energy production can be inconsistent, depending on the weather.
- **Noise and Aesthetics:** Wind turbines may be noisy and might not be visually appealing.
- **Maintenance:** Wind turbines have moving parts, which means they require more maintenance than solar panels.

Micro-Hydro Power

If you have access to a flowing water source on your property, micro-hydro power might be the best option for you. This system converts the energy of moving water into electricity, providing a consistent power source.

Hydropower is one of the earliest types of energy used by humanity. Water wheels powered mills in ancient Greece and Rome, and later, during the Industrial Revolution, water turbines became a cornerstone of industry. While the technology has evolved, the principle remains the same— harnessing the power of moving water to generate electricity.

Pros:

- **Continuous Power:** Unlike solar and wind, which depend on weather conditions, micro-hydro can provide a constant supply of electricity.
- **High Efficiency:** Micro-hydro systems are very efficient, often producing more power for less cost compared to solar or wind.

Cons:

- **Site-Specific:** You need a suitable water source, which isn't available to everyone.
- **Environmental Impact:** Altering the flow of water can impact local ecosystems.
- **Complex Installation:** Micro-hydro systems can be complex to install and may require permits.

Real Example: The Hytte Solar Community in Norway

The Hytte Solar Community in Norway is a successful example of using solar energy in a challenging environment. Despite long winters with limited sunlight, the community has installed efficient solar systems coupled with large battery banks. They've also incorporated backup generators for periods of extreme weather. This project demonstrates how even in less-than-ideal conditions, renewable energy can be the backbone of off-grid living.

DIY Solar Power System

Now that you have a basic understanding of the different renewable energy sources, let's focus on setting up a solar power system. Solar power is the most accessible and practical solution for many off-grid homes, and with the right knowledge, you can build your own system. Plus, investing in a solar power system isn't just about ensuring your independence; it's also a smart financial decision. Over time, it pays for itself by eliminating your electricity bills and shielding you from rising energy costs.

Basics of Solar Energy: Panels, Batteries, Inverters

Solar Panels

Solar panels, also known as photovoltaic (PV) panels, are the core component of any solar power system. They convert sunlight directly into electricity. When choosing panels, consider the efficiency, durability, and warranty. The most common types are monocrystalline, polycrystalline, and thin-film panels.

- **Monocrystalline Panels:** These are the most efficient and space-efficient, making them ideal if you have limited roof space. They are also more durable and have a longer lifespan, but they are more expensive.
- **Polycrystalline Panels:** These are less efficient but less expensive. They require more room to generate the same quantity of power as monocrystalline panels.
- **Thin-Film Panels:** These are less common for residential use. They are lightweight and flexible but also less efficient and generally require more space.

Batteries

Since solar panels only generate electricity when the sun is shining, you'll need a way to store energy for use at night or on cloudy days. This is where batteries come in. The two main types of batteries used in solar systems are lead-acid and lithium-ion.

- **Lead-Acid Batteries:** These are cheaper and have been used for decades. They come in two types: flooded and sealed. Flooded lead-acid batteries require maintenance (checking and topping off the water levels), while sealed ones are maintenance-free. They have a shorter lifetime and lower depth of discharge (DoD) than lithium-ion batteries.
- **Lithium-Ion Batteries:** These are more expensive initially but have a longer lifespan, better efficiency, and require minimal maintenance. They may also be discharged at a higher depth of discharge (DoD) without causing battery damage.

Inverters

Most home appliances run on alternating current (AC), but solar panels generate direct current (DC) electricity. The inverter is the component that converts the DC electricity generated by solar panels or batteries into AC electricity that your home can use.

- **Pure Sine Wave Inverters:** These produce a smooth and consistent wave of AC power, which is ideal for sensitive electronics like computers and TVs.
- **Modified Sine Wave Inverters:** These are less expensive but they emit a harsher wave that might interfere with some appliances and devices.

DIY Project 30: Build Your Own Solar Power Generator

Let's get practical. Here's how you can build your own solar power generator to provide electricity for your off-grid home. This project is a great way to dip your toes into solar power and can be expanded as your needs grow.

Cost	$$$$	Difficulty	★★★★

Materials:

- **Solar Panels:** Determine how many panels you need based on your energy consumption (more on that below). A good starting point for a small off-grid system might be three 300W panels.
- **Deep-Cycle Batteries:** Start with two to four batteries, depending on your budget and energy storage needs.
- **Inverter:** A 3000W pure sine wave inverter is a good choice for most small to medium off-grid systems.
- **Charge Controller:** This device adjusts the voltage that flows from the solar panels to the batteries to prevent overcharging
- **Wiring and Connectors:** Proper gauge wiring is critical. Thicker wires are required for higher current. You'll also need connectors and fuses for safety.

Tools:

- **Wire Cutters/Strippers:** Essential for preparing the cables.
- **Soldering Iron:** To secure the connections, ensuring low resistance and longevity.
- **Multimeter:** For testing the voltage and current at different points in your system.
- **Drill:** For mounting components.
- **Screwdrivers and Wrenches:** To assemble and secure your system.

1	**Estimate Your Power Consumption** Before you start building, you need to know how much power you'll need. Grab a notepad or a spreadsheet and list all the electrical devices you plan to use, along with their wattage and estimated hours of use per day. For instance: - **LED Light Bulb (10W):** 5 bulbs x 4 hours/day = 200 Wh/day - **Refrigerator (150W):** 24 hours/day = 3600 Wh/day - **Laptop (60W):** 5 hours/day = 300 Wh/day Add up the total watt-hours (Wh) per day to determine your daily energy consumption. This number will guide you in selecting the size of your solar system. **Electrician's Tip:** Always overestimate your energy needs by 20-30% to account for inefficiencies and unforeseen increases in consumption. If your daily usage is 4000 Wh, consider designing your system for 5000 Wh to 6000 Wh.
2	**Sizing Your Solar Panels** To calculate the number of panels you need, divide your daily energy consumption by the average sunlight hours in your area and then by the wattage of the panels.

	Example: If you need 5000 Wh/day and you get 5 hours of peak sunlight, you need at least 1000 watts of solar panels (5000 Wh / 5 hours = 1000W). If each panel is 300W, you'll need about 3 to 4 panels.
3	**Installing the Panels** Choose a location with maximum sunlight exposure, ideally facing south if you're in the Northern Hemisphere. Mount the panels on your roof or on a ground-based rack. Ensure they are tilted at the right angle based on your latitude to maximize solar gain.
4	**Wiring the System** Connect the panels in series or parallel, depending on the voltage and current requirements of your system. Parallel connections increase current while series connections increase voltage. Use proper gauge wires to handle the current safely. **Electrician's Tip:** Use a multimeter to check the voltage and current after connecting the panels but before connecting them to the charge controller. This ensures there are no faults in the wiring.
5	**Connecting the Charge Controller** The charge controller goes between your solar panels and your batteries. It regulates the voltage from the panels to prevent overcharging the batteries. Connect the panels to the input terminals and the batteries to the output terminals.
6	**Setting Up the Batteries** Place your batteries in a ventilated area to prevent the build-up of gases. Connect the batteries in series to increase the voltage, or in parallel to increase the capacity, depending on your system design.
7	**Installing the Inverter** Connect the inverter to the battery bank. This inverter will convert the DC stored in the batteries into AC, which powers your home appliances. Make sure the inverter's output matches your home's electrical system (usually 120V in the US).
8	**Testing and Troubleshooting** Once everything is connected, test your system. Use a multimeter to check the voltage at different points. Ensure that the inverter is producing the correct AC voltage and that all connections are secure.

Wind Power for Beginners

If you live in an area with consistent winds, wind power can be an excellent complement to your solar system. Wind turbines can generate power during the night or on cloudy days, helping to balance your energy production.

Before investing in a wind turbine, it's crucial to evaluate your location's wind potential. Ideally, you should have average wind speeds of at least 10-12 mph (16-19 kph) to make a wind turbine viable.

- **Site Assessment:** Use an anemometer to measure wind speeds at different times of the day and year. Data from local weather stations can also provide insight into the wind potential.
- **Height Matters:** Wind speeds increase with height. Placing your turbine on a tall tower (30-50 feet above nearby obstructions) can significantly improve performance.

For instance, in Texas with average wind speeds of 15 mph, a turbine can generate enough electricity to power a home during windy days, significantly reducing the reliance on an additional solar system. This hybrid approach can allow a family to enjoy a stable power supply year-round.

DIY Project 31: DIY Wind Turbine

Building your own wind turbine can be a rewarding project that contributes significantly to your off-grid power supply.

Cost	$$$	Difficulty	★★★

Materials:

- **PVC Pipes:** For making the blades.
- **DC Motor or Generator:** To convert the rotational energy into electricity.
- **Tower or Mast:** A sturdy pole to mount the turbine.
- **Charge Controller:** To regulate the voltage from the turbine.
- **Batteries:** To store the generated power.
- **Inverter:** To convert the DC electricity to AC.

Tools:

- **Drill:** For assembling the turbine.
- **Saw:** For cutting the PVC pipes.
- **Wrench:** To secure the turbine to the mast.
- **Multimeter:** For testing electrical connections

1	**Building the Blades** Cut the PVC pipes into three or four equal-length pieces, shaping them into blades. The blades should be tapered to capture the wind effectively. Sand the edges smooth to reduce drag.	
2	**Attaching the Blades to the Hub**	

	Mount the blades onto a hub that is attached to the DC motor or generator. The hub should be balanced to avoid wobbling when the turbine spins.
3	**Constructing the Tower** Install a sturdy tower to mount your wind turbine. Use a guyed mast for stability, especially in high-wind areas. The higher the tower, the better the turbine will perform.
4	**Wiring the System** Connect the wires from the generator to the charge controller, which regulates the voltage going into the batteries. Use heavy-duty wiring to handle the current and include a fuse for safety. **Electrician's Tip:** When wiring, make sure to use weatherproof connectors and enclosures to protect the system from the elements.
5	**Installing the Batteries and Inverter** Connect the charge controller to your battery bank. The batteries store the electricity generated by the wind turbine. From the batteries, connect an inverter to convert the stored DC power into AC for household use
6	**Testing and Adjustments** After setting up the turbine, monitor its performance. Use a multimeter to measure the output and adjust the blade angle if necessary to maximize efficiency

Backup Power Options

Even with a well-designed solar or wind system, there may be times when you need additional power. A backup power system ensures you're never left without electricity, especially during periods of low solar or wind activity.

Remember what happened in Texas during the winter storm of 2021? The power grid failed under the stress of unprecedented cold, leaving millions without electricity, heat, or water. An off-grid power solution with a reliable backup system could have been a lifeline in such a situation.

I report the example of a homeowner in Northern Arizona, who installed a comprehensive off-grid power system, including a solar array, wind turbine, and a large battery bank. By carefully monitoring and maintaining their batteries, they've achieved a reliable power supply that allows them to live comfortably without connection to the grid. Their backup system, including a propane generator, provides peace of mind during extended cloudy periods or windless days.

Batteries are the heart of any off-grid power system, storing energy for use when your renewable sources aren't generating electricity. Proper maintenance is crucial for ensuring their longevity and reliability.

- **Battery Types:** As discussed earlier, lead-acid and lithium-ion are the most common types. Each has its own maintenance requirements.
- **Maintenance Tips:** Check the water levels in lead-acid batteries on a regular basis and top up with distilled water. Keep the connections clean and keep the batteries somewhere cold and dry. Lithium-ion batteries require less care, although they should be checked for charge and temperature.

DIY Project 32: Battery Bank Setup

Setting up a battery bank allows you to store excess energy generated by your solar or wind system.

Cost	$$$	Difficulty	★★★

Materials:

- **Batteries:** Choose based on your energy needs and budget.
- **Connectors:** Heavy-duty cables to connect the batteries.
- **Fuse Box:** For safety and circuit protection.
- **Battery Monitor:** To track the state of charge and health of your battery bank.

Tools:

- **Wrench:** For tightening connections.
- **Multimeter:** To check voltages and ensure proper wiring.
- **Screwdrivers:** For assembling the fuse box and battery monitor.

1	**Designing Your Battery Bank** Determine the total storage capacity you need based on your daily energy consumption and desired autonomy (days you can go without recharging). For example, if you use 5000 Wh/day and want 3 days of autonomy, you need 15,000 Wh of storage
2	**Connecting the Batteries** Connect the batteries in series to increase voltage or in parallel to increase capacity, depending on your system's design. Use proper connectors and ensure all connections are tight.
3	**Installing the Fuse Box**

	A fuse box protects your system from overloads and short circuits. Install it between the battery bank and the inverter. Use fuses rated for the current your system will handle.
4	**Adding a Battery Monitor** A battery monitor helps you keep track of the state of charge, voltage, and overall health of your battery bank. Install it in a visible location for easy monitoring.
5	**Testing the System** After everything is connected, test the system by charging the batteries and then using them to power your home. Monitor the battery levels and ensure the fuse box and connections are functioning correctly.

Powering Your Off-Grid Life with Confidence

Off-grid power solutions are the backbone of a self-sufficient lifestyle. By embracing renewable energy sources like solar, wind, and micro-hydro, you not only gain independence from the grid but also protect yourself from the unpredictability of external power supplies. This chapter has equipped you with the knowledge and practical steps to design, build, and maintain your own off-grid power system, ensuring that you can enjoy modern comforts no matter how far off the beaten path you choose to live.

Whether you're harnessing the sun's rays with a DIY solar setup, supplementing your energy needs with wind power, or ensuring reliable backup power with a well-maintained battery bank, these solutions provide the stability and resilience essential for off-grid living. The projects and strategies discussed are more than just technical guides—they are investments in your security, sustainability, and freedom.

As you move forward, remember that a successful off-grid power system is built on careful planning, smart choices, and ongoing maintenance. By taking these steps, you're not just keeping the lights on— you're securing a future of independence and peace of mind in your off-grid home.

Chapter 8 - Off-Grid Security

When you think about living off the grid, your mind might naturally gravitate towards the freedom and self-sufficiency it brings. The idea of being independent, relying on your own resources, and living closer to nature is incredibly appealing. But with that independence comes the responsibility of ensuring your safety and security. Have you ever considered what it would mean to be truly self-reliant in terms of protecting yourself and your property? In remote areas, far from the immediate help of law enforcement or neighbors, security becomes an essential aspect of your off-grid life.

However, the need for security isn't just a concern for those intentionally living off-grid. There are situations where people are forced into an "off-grid" state due to emergencies or disasters. In such scenarios, when public security forces are stretched thin and focused on managing the crisis, criminals may exploit the situation. This has happened in the past during natural disasters or large-scale power outages, where looting and home invasions have increased due to the absence of law enforcement. Therefore, having a solid security plan is crucial, whether you've chosen an off-grid lifestyle or are temporarily thrust into one.

Securing Your Off-Grid Home

Living in a remote area comes with a unique set of security challenges. Unlike urban environments where there's almost always someone nearby, off-grid living often means isolation. This isolation can be both a blessing and a curse. On one hand, it offers peace, privacy, and a connection to nature. On the other hand, it can make you more vulnerable to intruders, whether they're curious wildlife, potential thieves, or even just lost hikers.

But what about when you're forced off-grid by a situation beyond your control? During times of crisis, when law enforcement is overburdened or unable to respond, how would you protect your home and family from those who might take advantage of the situation? History has shown that during major emergencies, such as hurricanes, floods, or widespread power outages, there can be a spike in criminal activity. For instance, during Hurricane Katrina, numerous reports of looting and home invasions were documented as police were overwhelmed by the scale of the disaster. Being prepared for such scenarios is essential.

A Real-Life Example: The Importance of Preparedness

Consider the story of a couple who decided to live off-grid in the remote mountains of Colorado. They built a beautiful, self-sustained cabin surrounded by forests, miles from the nearest town. One night, they heard noises outside — rustling in the bushes, strange sounds that weren't part of the usual night-time wildlife chorus. With no neighbors for miles and limited cell service, they realized they were completely unprepared for a security breach. Fortunately, the noise turned out to be nothing more than a deer wandering too close for comfort, but it served as a wake-up call. They quickly implemented a comprehensive security plan, including motion sensors, floodlights, and a sturdy perimeter fence.

This story highlights a crucial point: while off-grid living offers many benefits, it's essential to be prepared for the unexpected. Security isn't just about keeping others out; it's about creating peace of mind and ensuring that your sanctuary remains just that—a safe, secure place for you and your loved ones.

The concept of security systems has evolved significantly over time, yet the underlying principles have remained remarkably consistent. In ancient civilizations, perimeter defenses such as walls and fences, like the Great Wall of China or medieval city walls, were vital for protecting settlements. These barriers not only served to keep invaders out but also acted as the first line of defense, providing early warnings of approaching threats. Similarly, early detection mechanisms were employed within these fortifications—trip wires and alarm bells, for instance, were used in historical fortresses to alert inhabitants to potential dangers. Today's motion sensors are the modern equivalents of these early warning systems, continuing the age-old practice of safeguarding one's territory through prompt detection and response. While the technology has advanced, from physical barriers to sophisticated electronic systems, the fundamental goal remains the same: preventing security breaches before they escalate into serious threats.

DIY Project 33: Perimeter Security System

One of the first steps in securing your off-grid home is to establish a strong perimeter. This not only serves as a deterrent to potential intruders but also gives you early warning if someone—or something—approaches your property.

Cost	$$$	Difficulty	★★★
Materials:			

- **Motion Sensors:** These are the eyes of your security system, detecting movement around your property. These sensors can be found at most hardware stores, online retailers, or specialty security shops. They range from basic, low-cost models to more sophisticated ones that can be integrated into a larger security system.
- **Alarm System:** A basic alarm that can alert you to any disturbances. Many pre-configured, low-cost house alarm systems are available that don't require advanced skills to install. These systems often come with a simple setup guide and can be purchased from electronics stores or online.
- **Floodlights:** Motion-activated lights that illuminate your property when triggered. Floodlights can be found at most home improvement stores and are a key part of your perimeter defense.

- **Fencing Materials:** For creating a physical barrier around your home. Depending on your needs and budget, you can use anything from barbed wire to wooden posts.
- **Wiring and Connectors:** To set up and connect your sensors and alarms.

Tools:

- **Drill:** For installing sensors and lights.
- **Screwdrivers:** For securing devices and connecting wires.
- **Wire Cutters:** Essential for sizing and connecting wires.
- **Shovel:** If you're installing a physical fence.

1	**Assess Your Property** Begin by walking the perimeter of your property. Identify potential entry points where an intruder might approach—these could be natural paths, driveways, or any clearings that lead towards your home. Consider the visibility and how easy it would be for someone to approach unnoticed. **Why is this important?** Knowing your property's vulnerabilities is the first step in securing it. Just like a medieval castle, your home's defense begins at its outermost boundaries.
2	**Install Motion Sensors** Position motion sensors around the perimeter of your property, focusing on those key entry points you identified. These sensors should be set at a height that detects human-sized intruders but avoids small animals like rabbits or squirrels to reduce false alarms.
3	**Set Up Floodlights** Pair your motion sensors with floodlights. When the sensors detect movement, the floodlights should automatically illuminate the area. This sudden burst of light can startle intruders and alert you to their presence.
4	**Install the Alarm System** Connect your motion sensors to a central alarm system. This could be as simple as a loud siren or as complex as a system that sends notifications to your smartphone. Many of these systems are available in pre-configured kits that don't require any advanced technical skills to set up. They can be purchased from online

	retailers or electronics stores. **Why an alarm?** In a remote location, the sound of an alarm can be a powerful deterrent. It not only scares off intruders but also gives you crucial time to react.
5	**Build a Fence** If your budget and property layout allow, consider installing a sturdy fence around your property. While it won't stop a determined intruder, it serves as a physical barrier that can slow down their progress and force them to reveal their presence.
6	**Use Refurbished Smartphones for Surveillance** Did you know that an old smartphone can be turned into a security camera? With the help of surveillance apps available for download, you can repurpose a refurbished smartphone to monitor your property. These apps typically allow you to set up the phone to detect motion and even send alerts or live feeds directly to another device. This is an economical solution that utilizes technology you might already have on hand.

Additional Tips:

- **Use Reflective Tape:** Placing reflective tape on your fence or around your property can make it more visible at night, especially when illuminated by your floodlights.
- **Secure Entry Points:** Gates, doors, and windows should be reinforced and locked at all times. Consider using heavy-duty locks or even installing secondary barriers like bars or shutters.
- **Regular Maintenance:** Check your sensors, lights, and alarms regularly to ensure they're functioning properly. Replace batteries and repair any damage immediately.

Rudimentary Security Systems

While technology offers numerous advantages in securing your property, sometimes simpler, low-tech solutions can be just as effective. If you're on a tight budget or prefer not to rely on electronics, consider these rudimentary security methods:

- **Noise-Making Barriers:** A simple, yet effective deterrent can be created using tin cans, metal chains, or even gravel. Hanging tin cans on string along a perimeter fence or placing gravel around windows and doors can create noise if someone tries to sneak onto your property. The sound can alert you to their presence before they even get close.
- **Barbed Wire and Thorny Bushes:** Historically, barbed wire has been used as a simple but

effective barrier to deter intruders. Planting thorny bushes around your home's perimeter also adds a natural layer of security, making it more difficult for intruders to approach without getting scratched or tangled.

- **Traps and Warning Devices:** While less common today, some people still use rudimentary traps or warning devices. For example, tripwires attached to noise-making devices, such as bells or cans, can serve as early warning systems. However, be cautious with this approach to ensure safety and legality.

Firearms and Self-Defense

Living off-grid often means being far from help, so self-defense is a critical consideration. Whether it's protecting yourself from wildlife or deterring potential human intruders, being prepared is essential. But before you start stocking up on weapons, it's important to understand that self-defense isn't just about having a firearm—it's about being aware of your surroundings, knowing how to use any tools you choose to carry, and understanding the legal implications of using force.

Ask yourself: Are you truly prepared to defend yourself and your property? Have you thought about what you would do in a worst-case scenario? These aren't pleasant questions, but they're necessary ones.

Consider the case of a homesteader in Alaska, who lived miles from the nearest town. One evening, he noticed movement outside his cabin. A large bear was prowling around, clearly interested in the scent of food. With no time to wait for help, he had to rely on his training and the firearms he kept on hand. By remaining calm and following the safety protocols he'd practiced, he was able to scare the bear off without injury to himself or the animal. This incident illustrates the importance of being prepared—not just with weapons, but with the knowledge and composure to use them effectively.

Legal Considerations and Safety Tips

Before deciding to keep firearms or other weapons on your off-grid property, <u>you need to be aware of the laws in your area</u>. Firearms laws vary widely depending on your location, and it's crucial to know what's legal, what's required for safe storage, and under what circumstances you're permitted to use force.

Ask yourself:

- **What are the local laws regarding firearm ownership and use?**
- **Do I have the proper training to handle firearms safely?**
- **How will I securely store firearms to prevent accidents?**

DIY Project 34: Safe Gun Storage

In the days of the Wild West, guns were a common part of everyday life. However, responsible gun owners understood the importance of safe storage. Many homes had a designated area, often reinforced and secure, where firearms were kept when not in use. This practice not only prevented accidents but also protected valuable firearms from theft.

If you choose to keep firearms on your property, proper storage is essential. <u>A gun safe or lockbox is a must, especially if you have children or other people living with you.</u> Building a simple, secure storage space can be done with basic materials and tools.

Cost	$$$	Difficulty	★★★

Materials:

- **Heavy-Duty Metal or Wood:** For the structure of the safe.
- **Padlock or Electronic Lock:** For secure access.
- **Foam Padding:** To protect firearms from scratches and damage.

Tools:

- **Drill:** For assembling the structure.
- **Screwdriver:** For attaching the lock and securing the safe.
- **Saw:** If you're cutting wood or metal to size.

1	**Build the Structure** Construct a secure box or cabinet using heavy-duty materials like thick wood or metal. Ensure the structure is robust enough to resist break-ins. If you're using wood, consider reinforcing it with metal sheets for added security.
2	**Install the Lock** Attach a reliable locking mechanism. A combination lock or electronic keypad offers more security than a simple padlock. Ensure the lock is installed securely and functions properly.
3	**Add Padding** Line the interior of the safe with foam padding to prevent your firearms from being scratched or damaged. This also helps to absorb any impact if the safe is jostled.
4	**Secure the Safe** Position the safe in a discreet location that is not easily visible or accessible. Bolt

	it to the floor or wall to prevent it from being moved or stolen.

<u>Safety First</u>:

- **Never point a firearm at anything you don't intend to shoot.**
- **Keep your finger off the trigger until you're ready to fire.**
- **Always treat every firearm as if it's loaded.**
- **Store firearms unloaded, with ammunition stored separately.**

Building a Safe Room

In some situations, the best defense is a strong offense—in other cases, it's the ability to retreat to a safe location until the danger has passed. This is where a safe room, or panic room, comes into play. A safe room is a fortified area within your home designed to protect you and your family from threats such as intruders, natural disasters, or even chemical attacks.

But have you considered what you would do in an emergency situation? Where would you go if an intruder breached your home or if a severe storm made it unsafe to remain in the main living area? A safe room provides a secure place to shelter until help arrives or the threat subsides.

Historical Example: The Siege of Masada

In the first century, Jewish rebels took refuge in the fortress of Masada to protect themselves from the Roman army. The fortress, located on a plateau, was virtually impregnable and allowed the rebels to hold out for years. While a safe room isn't meant to withstand a years-long siege, the principle is the same: having a strong, defensible position can give you the time and security you need in a crisis.

A Real-Life Example: The Importance of a Safe Room

During the 2011 Joplin tornado in Missouri, one family survived the devastating storm by taking refuge in their safe room—a reinforced concrete structure within their home. While the rest of their house was destroyed, the safe room withstood the tornado's powerful winds, saving their lives. This example underscores the value of having a dedicated space where you can ride out emergencies, whether they're natural disasters or human-made threats.

DIY Project 35: Panic Room Construction

Building a panic room requires careful planning and sturdy materials. This isn't just a small project; it's an investment in your safety and peace of mind.

Cost	$$$$$	Difficulty	★★★★★

Materials:

- **Reinforced Steel Door:** A must for securing the entrance to your safe room.
- **Concrete or Cinder Blocks:** For constructing the walls.
- **Steel Reinforcements:** To strengthen the walls and door frame.
- **Locks and Bolts:** High-quality locks and bolts for securing the door.
- **Ventilation System:** To ensure fresh air supply in case you're in the room for an extended period.

Tools:

- **Drill:** For installing locks and bolting the door.
- **Saw:** For cutting any additional materials.
- **Welding Machine:** If you're incorporating steel reinforcements.
- **Trowel:** For laying concrete or mortar.

1	**Choose the Location** The ideal location for a safe room is in the interior of your home, away from exterior walls and windows. A basement or a central room on the lowest level of the house is often the best choice. The location should also be easily accessible from the main living areas, so you can reach it quickly in an emergency. **Why this location?** In emergencies, every second counts. Placing your safe room in a central, easily accessible location ensures you can reach safety as quickly as possible. Historically, fortresses were built with strongholds or keeps at their centers—areas that were the last line of defense if outer walls were breached. Your safe room serves a similar purpose.
2	**Build the Walls** Construct the walls of your safe room using concrete or cinder blocks, reinforced with steel bars. These materials are strong enough to withstand significant force, whether from intruders or natural disasters. Ensure that the walls are at least 6 inches thick and reinforced with steel for maximum protection.
3	**Install the Door** The door is the most critical part of your safe room. Install a heavy-duty, reinforced steel door with high-security locks. The door frame should also be reinforced with steel to prevent it from being breached. The door should open

	inward, preventing it from being blocked by debris outside.
4	**Add Ventilation** A good safe room should be airtight enough to protect against chemical threats but still provide sufficient ventilation to keep the air fresh. Install a ventilation system that includes a hand-crank or battery-operated fan to ensure you have a continuous supply of air. Some systems also include air filtration units to protect against airborne toxins.
5	**Equip Your Safe Room** Outfit your safe room with the essentials you would need to survive for at least 24-72 hours. This includes water, non-perishable food, first-aid supplies, a battery-operated radio, flashlights, extra batteries, and a means of communication, like a cell phone or two-way radio.

Additional Tips:

- **Test Your Safe Room:** Once the room is complete, run a drill with your family to ensure everyone knows how to reach the safe room quickly and lock it securely.
- **Consider Communication:** Keep a backup means of communication, such as a satellite phone, inside the safe room in case local networks go down.
- **Maintain Supplies:** Regularly check the supplies in your safe room, replacing food, water, and batteries as needed to ensure they're always ready in an emergency.

Fortifying Your Off-Grid Sanctuary

Security is a fundamental aspect of off-grid living, ensuring that the freedom and self-sufficiency you cherish are protected from unforeseen threats. Whether you're living in a remote area by choice or thrust into an off-grid situation due to emergencies, the responsibility of safeguarding your home and loved ones rests squarely on your shoulders. This chapter has provided you with the tools and knowledge to build a robust security plan tailored to the unique challenges of off-grid life.

By establishing a secure perimeter, utilizing both modern technology and simple, effective methods, and preparing for self-defense, you're not just protecting your property—you're creating a haven where you can thrive independently. The projects and strategies outlined here, from building a safe room to implementing DIY security systems, are designed to give you peace of mind and the confidence to face any situation head-on.

Living off-grid is about embracing freedom and independence, but it's also about being prepared for the unexpected. By taking proactive steps to secure your home, you ensure that your off-grid lifestyle remains a source of peace and fulfillment, allowing you to fully enjoy the serenity and connection to nature that drew you to this path in the first place. With a well-thought-out security plan, you can confidently navigate the challenges of off-grid living, knowing that your sanctuary is protected.

Chapter 9 - Communication and Networking

When you think of living off-grid, you might envision a lifestyle free from the constant buzz of emails, social media, and the endless distractions of modern communication. However, staying connected is still crucial, whether it's for safety, maintaining relationships, or keeping up with the world beyond your homestead. Have you ever considered how you would communicate in an off-grid situation, especially if an emergency strikes or if you need to coordinate with others nearby? In this chapter, we'll explore various ways to establish reliable communication networks, from simple radio setups to more sophisticated local networks, ensuring that you're never truly isolated, even when living off the grid.

Staying Connected Off-Grid

Living off-grid often means being far from the conveniences of urban life, including reliable communication networks. But even in the most remote locations, staying connected can be vital. Whether it's reaching out for help during an emergency, coordinating with neighbors, or simply staying in touch with family and friends, having a reliable communication system is essential.

But what if the power grid goes down, and cell towers are out of service? This scenario isn't far-fetched—natural disasters, severe weather, or even technical failures can disrupt traditional communication networks, leaving you cut off from the outside world. This is where off-grid communication tools become invaluable. From radios to satellite communication, there are several ways to ensure you're never truly alone, even when the world around you goes silent.

A Real-Life Example: The Role of Communication During Disasters

Consider the 2017 hurricane season, which included devastating storms like Hurricane Maria. In Puerto Rico, the hurricane knocked out the entire island's power grid, leaving millions without electricity or communication. For weeks, people struggled to reach loved ones, and emergency responders faced immense challenges coordinating relief efforts. In many cases, those who had alternative communication methods, such as satellite phones or ham radios, were able to maintain contact and provide crucial information to rescue teams.

This example highlights the importance of having reliable communication tools, especially in situations where traditional networks fail. Whether you're living off-grid by choice or necessity, being prepared with the right communication equipment can make all the difference.

Options for Off-Grid Communication

There are several options for maintaining communication when living off-grid, each with its own advantages and limitations. Let's explore some of the most common methods:

- **CB Radios: Citizens Band (CB) radios** are a popular choice for off-grid communication. They're relatively inexpensive, easy to use, and don't require a license in most countries. CB radios operate on shortwave frequencies, typically in the 27 MHz band, making them suitable for local communication over a few miles. This is particularly useful for communicating with neighbors or coordinating activities within a community.
    - o **Pros:** No license required, easy to use, affordable.
    - o **Cons:** Limited range, prone to interference.

- **Ham Radios, or amateur radios,** offer more power and range than CB radios, making them ideal for long-distance communication. However, operating a ham radio typically requires a license, which involves passing an exam. With the right setup, ham radios can communicate across continents, making them a powerful tool for staying connected, even in remote locations.
    - o **Pros:** Long-range communication, access to multiple frequencies, strong community support.
    - o **Cons:** Requires a license, more complex setup.

- **Satellite Phones** are an excellent choice for those who need reliable communication, regardless of their location. In contrast to cell phones that depend on ground-based towers for connectivity, satellite phones establish a direct link with satellites positioned in Earth's orbit, thereby offering coverage in nearly all locations. They're particularly useful in areas without cell service or in disaster situations where the cell network is down.
    - o **Pros:** Global coverage, independent of local infrastructure.
    - o **Cons:** Expensive, requires a clear view of the sky.

- **Two-Way Radios, also known as walkie-talkies,** are another practical option for short-range communication. These devices are ideal for coordinating activities within a homestead or communicating with nearby neighbors. They are user-friendly and do not necessitate extensive technical expertise.
    - o **Pros:** Simple operation, no license needed for some models, portable.
    - o **Cons:** Limited range, subject to interference.

- **Internet-Based Communication, for those who still want to stay connected to the internet,** options like satellite internet or long-range Wi-Fi can provide access in remote areas. These services are generally more expensive and slower than traditional broadband, but they allow you to stay online, access information, and communicate via email or social media.
    - o **Pros:** Internet access in remote areas, supports various forms of communication.
    - o **Cons:** Expensive, potential latency, requires power.

Licensed Frequency Bands to Avoid
When setting up communication systems, especially in different countries, it's important to be aware

of licensed frequency bands. Using unauthorized frequencies can lead to interference with government, military, or commercial services and could result in hefty fines or legal action. Below is a list of licensed frequency bands to avoid in major countries:

United States:

- **Military and Government Bands:** 225-400 MHz (UHF), 1.240-1.300 GHz (L band).
- **Commercial Broadcast:** 470-512 MHz (UHF TV channels).
- **Public Safety Bands:** 806-824 MHz, 851-869 MHz (emergency services).

Canada:

- **Public Safety Bands:** 764-776 MHz, 794-806 MHz (emergency services).
- **Aeronautical Bands:** 108-137 MHz (VHF airband).
- **Commercial Maritime:** 156-162 MHz (VHF marine band).

Europe:

- **Military Bands:** 225-400 MHz (UHF), 1.240-1.300 GHz (L band).
- **Emergency Services:** 380-400 MHz (TETRA network).
- **Broadcast Bands:** 470-790 MHz (DVB-T TV broadcasting).

United Kingdom:

- **Emergency Services:** 380-400 MHz (Airwave network).
- **Aeronautical Bands:** 108-137 MHz (VHF airband).
- **Maritime Bands:** 156-162 MHz (VHF marine band).

Australia:

- **Military and Government Bands:** 225-400 MHz (UHF), 960-1215 MHz (radar).
- **Emergency Services:** 403-430 MHz (various services).
- **Maritime and Aeronautical:** 156-162 MHz (VHF marine), 118-137 MHz (VHF airband).

What Happens if You Use a Licensed Band?

Using a frequency that is reserved for government, military, or commercial purposes can result in significant legal consequences. In the best-case scenario, you might receive a warning or be asked to cease transmission. However, in more serious cases, fines can be substantial, and equipment might be confiscated. Interference with emergency services or aviation bands can lead to even more severe penalties, including criminal charges.

Advice for Legal Communication:

- **Research Local Laws:** Before setting up any communication system, research the local regulations in your area to ensure you're using approved frequencies.
- **Use License-Free Bands:** Many countries offer license-free bands for personal and community use, such as the ISM band (2.4 GHz) or certain UHF/VHF frequencies for walkie-talkies.
- **Get Licensed:** If you plan to use ham radio or other advanced communication methods, consider getting the appropriate license. This not only ensures you're operating legally but also gives you access to a wider range of frequencies and resources.

Establishing a Local Network: Mesh Networks and Alternatives

In a fully off-grid scenario, having a local communication network can be invaluable. Whether you're coordinating with neighbors, monitoring your property, or sharing resources, a local network ensures that everyone stays connected. But how do you set up a reliable, self-sustaining network in a remote area?

Consider this: In the event of a disaster, local networks can become lifelines, providing critical information when outside communication is impossible. For example, during the California wildfires, communities with established local networks were better able to coordinate evacuations and share resources, helping to save lives and property. Even in less extreme situations, a local network can streamline communication within a homestead or small community, making everyday tasks more efficient.

Mesh Networks in Off-Grid Living: Are They Worth It?

Many books on off-grid living advocate for setting up a mesh network, and while this can be an effective solution, it's not always the best fit for every off-grid situation. Let's explore why this might be the case.

A mesh network is an ideal solution for creating a local communication system in an off-grid environment. Unlike traditional Wi-Fi networks, which rely on a single router, a mesh network uses multiple nodes (routers or signal boosters) to provide seamless coverage across a wide area. This setup is particularly useful for large properties or homesteads with multiple buildings.

However, a mesh network typically requires an internet connection and a router to function as a traditional communication network, particularly for accessing the internet. In the context of off-grid living, where internet access may be limited or nonexistent, the utility of a mesh network might be reconsidered based on your specific goals and circumstances.

1. **Local Communication - Intranet Use:** Even without internet access, a mesh network can be used to create a local area network (LAN) or intranet. This can allow devices on the network to communicate with each other, share files, or even run local applications. This could be useful for a homestead or community where coordination and information sharing are important, even in the absence of a wider internet connection.

2. **Extending Communication Range - Local Device Connectivity:** A mesh network could extend the range of communication across a large off-grid property, allowing devices like smartphones, tablets, or computers to connect with each other without the need for cellular service or internet. This could be particularly useful for tasks like monitoring security cameras, managing solar power systems, or coordinating activities across a large homestead.

3. **Alternative Communication Methods - VOIP or Messaging Apps:** In an off-grid scenario, if you have a temporary or limited internet connection (e.g., through satellite internet), a mesh network could help distribute that connection across your property. This would allow for communication via VOIP (Voice Over Internet Protocol) or messaging apps even with a limited connection.

4. **Resilience and Redundancy - Emergency Use:** A mesh network can provide redundancy and resilience in communication during emergencies. Even if the main internet connection fails, the local network could still be used for critical communication and coordination among members of the household or community.

Is a Mesh Network Worth It?

While a traditional mesh network may not be essential for a basic off-grid lifestyle, it can be valuable in certain situations, particularly if you're managing a larger off-grid property or community where local communication and coordination are crucial. However, it's important to clarify the limitations and ensure that the primary goal isn't misunderstood as requiring internet access for functionality.

Alternative or Complementary Solutions to Mesh Networks

If the mesh network seems overly complex or not entirely necessary, consider these alternative or complementary projects:

1. **Local Intranet Setup:** A project that focuses on setting up a local intranet for sharing information, resources, and local applications across a property without needing internet access.

2. **Two-Way Radio Network:** Establishing a network of two-way radios (like walkie-talkies) across a property to maintain communication without relying on any internet or external infrastructure.

3. **DIY Signal Boosters:** Creating simple signal boosters for radios or even cellular devices to extend the range and improve the quality of communication without relying on complex infrastructure.

The value of including a mesh network project in your off-grid setup depends on your specific needs and context. If your circumstances benefit from local network capabilities and you have some technical know-how, it could be a worthwhile addition. Otherwise, you might focus on more universally applicable communication solutions that align more closely with the off-grid living ethos, ensuring practicality and accessibility for a wider range of scenarios.

DIY Project 36: Building a DIY Signal Booster

In off-grid living, reliable communication is vital, but sometimes the signal strength for your radios, cell phones, or other communication devices may be weak due to distance, obstructions, or environmental factors. Building a DIY signal booster is a practical and cost-effective way to enhance signal strength, ensuring you stay connected when it matters most. This project is simple to execute with readily available materials and can significantly improve the range and quality of your communication devices.

Cost	$$	Difficulty	★★★
Materials:			

- **Copper Wire (16-20 gauge):** Used to create the antenna that will capture and boost the signal.
- **Plastic or PVC Pipe (about 2-3 feet long):** Serves as the support structure for the antenna.
- **Coaxial Cable (RG6 or similar):** To connect the antenna to your device (e.g., a radio or a mobile phone signal booster).
- **Metal Reflector (such as a metal sheet or an aluminum pie plate):** Helps focus the signal and improve the booster's efficiency.
- **Electrical Tape:** For securing connections and insulating exposed wires.
- **Antenna Connector (specific to your device):** To connect the coaxial cable to your communication device.
- **Cable Ties or Zip Ties:** For securing the wire to the PVC pipe

Tools:

- **Wire Cutters/Strippers:** To cut and strip the copper wire and coaxial cable.
- **Drill:** For making holes in the PVC pipe to attach the wire and coaxial cable.
- **Soldering Iron and Solder (Optional):** For securing the connections between the wires and the coaxial cable if needed.
- **Screwdriver:** To secure the antenna connector to your device.

1	**Create the Antenna** - **Cut the Copper Wire:** Start by cutting a length of copper wire approximately 3 feet long. This will serve as the antenna element. - **Shape the Wire:** Bend the copper wire into a "V" shape or a simple loop, depending on the type of signal you want to boost (a loop for omnidirectional or a "V" shape for directional boosting). - **Attach the Wire to the PVC Pipe:** Drill small holes at the appropriate locations on the PVC pipe and thread the copper wire through these holes. Secure the wire to the pipe using electrical tape or zip ties, ensuring it remains in the desired shape.
2	**Attach the Coaxial Cable** - **Strip the Coaxial Cable:** Using wire strippers, carefully strip one end of the coaxial cable, exposing both the inner conductor and the outer shielding. - **Connect to the Antenna:** Attach the exposed inner conductor of the coaxial cable to one end of the copper wire (antenna) and the shielding to the other end. Solder these connections for better durability and signal transmission, if possible. Apply electrical tape to cover the connections, ensuring insulation and reducing the risk of short circuits.
3	**Add the Metal Reflector** - **Prepare the Reflector:** If using a metal sheet or an aluminum pie plate, cut or shape it to fit behind the antenna on the PVC pipe. The reflector should be positioned to direct the signal towards the antenna. - **Attach to the Pipe:** Secure the reflector to the PVC pipe using screws or tape, ensuring it is aligned with the antenna to focus the incoming signal.

4	**Connect to Your Device**
	• **Attach the Antenna Connector:** On the other end of the coaxial cable, attach the appropriate antenna connector that matches your communication device (e.g., a BNC connector for a radio or an SMA connector for a mobile phone booster).
	• **Test the Connection:** Plug the connector into your device and power it on. The signal booster should immediately begin improving signal strength.
5	**Fine-Tune the Setup**
	• **Adjust the Position:** Experiment with the placement and orientation of the antenna and reflector to achieve the best signal boost. The signal strength can vary depending on direction and height, so try different positions for optimal performance.
	• **Secure the Setup:** Once you've found the best position, secure the entire setup to ensure it remains stable. This could involve mounting the PVC pipe on a wall, post, or another elevated structure.

This DIY signal booster is a simple yet effective way to enhance your communication capabilities in an off-grid environment. Whether you're trying to improve radio reception or boost a weak cell phone signal, this project provides a practical solution using basic materials. By taking the time to build and fine-tune your signal booster, you can ensure that you're always within reach of essential communication channels, even in the most remote locations.

Practical Uses of the DIY Signal Booster in Off-Grid Living

A DIY signal booster can be a crucial tool in an off-grid environment where communication is vital, yet signal strength can be unreliable. Here are several practical scenarios where your homemade signal booster can make a significant difference:

Enhancing Emergency Communication

In an off-grid situation, being able to reach emergency services or communicate with nearby communities during a crisis is essential. A weak signal could mean the difference between getting timely help or facing severe consequences. The DIY signal booster can enhance your ability to:

- **Call for Help:** If you're in a remote area with a weak cell phone signal, the booster can help you connect with emergency services when you need them most. For example, in the event of a medical emergency, you can use the booster to strengthen your phone's signal and make that critical call.

- **Send SOS Messages:** If you're using a satellite phone or another communication device that requires a clear signal, the signal booster can ensure that your distress calls or SOS messages are transmitted clearly and received by the appropriate authorities.

Improving Communication with Nearby Neighbors or Community

Living off-grid often means you're part of a small, spread-out community or have a few neighbors nearby. Maintaining communication with them can be challenging if signals are weak. The signal booster can be used to:

- **Coordinate Activities:** Whether it's organizing a community gathering, coordinating shared resources like water or food supplies, or simply staying in touch, the booster can help keep everyone connected, even when distances are significant, and signals are weak.
- **Emergency Alerts:** In case of a local emergency, such as a wildfire or a severe storm, the booster ensures that you can quickly alert your neighbors, allowing for better coordination and faster response times.

Enhancing Radio Communication

For many off-grid residents, radios are a primary means of communication, whether it's a CB radio, ham radio, or two-way radio system. The signal booster can:

- **Extend Radio Range:** If you're part of a larger off-grid community that uses radios for communication, the booster can extend your range, allowing you to stay in touch with others over greater distances. This is particularly useful in mountainous or heavily forested areas where signals may be blocked or weakened.
- **Improve Reception:** Whether you're tuning in to weather reports, emergency broadcasts, or just chatting with others on a radio network, the booster can enhance the clarity and strength of incoming signals, ensuring you receive important information without interruption.

Enhancing Internet Access via Cellular Networks

If your off-grid location relies on a cellular network for internet access, signal strength can vary greatly depending on your location. The DIY signal booster can:

- **Strengthen Cellular Data Signal:** Use the booster to enhance the signal strength for your cellular data connection, allowing you to access the internet more reliably. This is useful for checking weather updates, receiving important emails, or even keeping up with the latest news when traditional forms of communication might be down.
- **Support Internet-Based Communication:** With a stronger signal, you can use VOIP (Voice Over Internet Protocol) services to make phone calls or use messaging apps that rely on data, keeping you connected even if traditional voice networks are down.

Supporting Off-Grid Surveillance Systems

If you've set up surveillance systems to monitor your property, particularly if they rely on internet connectivity for remote access, the signal booster can:

- **Improve Surveillance Reliability:** Boost the signal to ensure that cameras or sensors placed around your property are always connected and transmitting data properly. This ensures that you can monitor your surroundings in real-time, even in areas with traditionally poor reception.
- **Remote Monitoring:** If your surveillance system allows for remote monitoring via a mobile app or web portal, the signal booster ensures that you can access the system from afar, providing peace of mind when you're away from your homestead.

Facilitating Communication During Travel or Exploration

For those who enjoy exploring the wilderness or traveling to remote areas, having a reliable communication link is essential. The signal booster can be a portable solution to:

- **Maintain Contact While Hiking or Traveling:** When venturing into areas where cell or radio signals are weak, you can take the signal booster with you to maintain contact with your base or other travelers.
- **Emergency Preparedness on the Go:** In case of an emergency while on the move, a portable signal booster can be quickly set up to strengthen your communication devices, ensuring that you can reach out for help if needed.

In off-grid living, where conventional communication infrastructure is often unavailable or unreliable, the DIY signal booster becomes a vital tool. Whether you're enhancing emergency communication, staying in touch with neighbors, improving radio or internet connections, or ensuring the reliability of surveillance systems, this simple device can greatly enhance your ability to communicate and stay informed in an off-grid environment. By understanding and utilizing these practical applications, you can ensure that you remain connected and safe, no matter how far off the grid you choose to live.

The Power of Communication in Off-Grid Living

Communication is a vital part of any off-grid lifestyle, whether you're living in isolation by choice or due to circumstances beyond your control. By exploring and implementing the options outlined in this chapter — ranging from simple CB radio setups to more complex networks — you can ensure that you stay connected, informed, and prepared for whatever comes your way.

The goal of off-grid communication isn't just about maintaining a link to the outside world; it's about building a resilient, self-sufficient lifestyle that includes the ability to share information, coordinate with others, and call for help if needed. Whether you're using a refurbished smartphone for surveillance, setting up a local network to stay connected with neighbors, or relying on a CB radio during an emergency, these strategies will help you maintain the crucial connections that keep you safe and secure.

Chapter 10 - Survival Skills for Off-Grid Living: A Deeper Dive

Living off the grid is an exhilarating and empowering experience, but it also comes with its fair share of challenges. One of the most significant challenges is ensuring your safety and survival in unpredictable situations. Whether you're caught in a sudden storm, dealing with unexpected equipment failure, or facing a food shortage, the survival skills you develop will be your lifeline. In this expanded chapter, we'll take a closer look at some critical survival skills—each designed to equip you with the knowledge and confidence needed to thrive in the wilderness and off-grid environments. Through direct questions, real-life examples, and detailed techniques, you'll gain a comprehensive understanding of these vital survival skills.

Wilderness Survival Techniques

When you're living off-grid, especially in remote or wild areas, understanding how to survive in the wilderness is crucial. Even if you've established a comfortable homestead, emergencies like natural disasters, getting lost, or equipment failure can push you into situations where these skills are your lifeline. Let's explore the essential wilderness survival techniques you need to master.

How to Build a Shelter

Have you ever found yourself caught in a sudden downpour far from home, with no immediate shelter in sight? Imagine being miles from your off-grid cabin, and a storm rolls in. The temperature drops, the wind picks up, and you're suddenly exposed to the elements. In such a scenario, knowing how to quickly build an effective shelter could be the difference between discomfort and danger.

Types of Survival Shelters:

- **Debris Hut:** You're hiking through the woods when a cold front moves in unexpectedly. You're miles from your shelter, and hypothermia becomes a real threat.

  - **Construction:** Find a long, sturdy branch to serve as the ridgepole. Place it at an angle, resting one end on the ground and the other against a tree or large rock. Lean smaller branches along both sides of the ridgepole, forming an A-frame structure. Cover the frame by applying a substantial layer of leaves, grass and various debris.
  - **Problem-Solution:** The wind is strong, and you have limited materials. Use heavier branches and rocks to secure your structure and double the layer of debris for added insulation. Make sure the entrance is positioned so that it is not facing the wind to minimize exposure.
  - **Real-Life Example:** The debris hut is a technique that has been used by indigenous peoples and survival experts alike. During WWII, soldiers on long patrols would

construct similar shelters to protect themselves from the elements when far from their base camps.

- **Lean-To Shelter:** You're in an open area with little natural cover, and the wind is howling. You need a shelter that can withstand strong gusts.

  - **Construction:** Locate a large branch or fallen tree trunk to act as the main support. Position it horizontally between two trees or prop it up on one side. Lean smaller branches against the main support to form a wall. Cover the wall with leaves, grass, and other materials to insulate and protect against wind.
  - **Problem-Solution:** The wind is changing direction frequently. Build the lean-to with an angled roof to deflect wind from multiple directions. Add a reflective blanket on the inside to help retain body heat.
  - **Real-Life Example:** Lean-to shelters have been used by hunters and trappers in the northern forests of Canada for centuries. They provide quick, effective protection against the wind and can be enhanced with a fire in front to reflect heat.

- **Snow Cave:** It's the dead of winter, and you're caught in a snowstorm. The temperature is dropping rapidly, and there's no way to make it back to your cabin before nightfall.

  - **Construction:** Find a snowdrift deep enough to carve out a cave. Dig an entrance tunnel that slopes upwards into a domed chamber. Ensure the chamber is large enough to sit up in but small enough to retain body heat. Create a small air vent at the top of the cave to stop carbon dioxide from accumulating.
  - **Problem-Solution:** The snow is soft and prone to collapsing. Pack the walls and ceiling with snow to harden them and prevent collapse. If the snow is too powdery, consider finding a sheltered spot against a rock face where you can build a more stable structure.
  - **Real-Life Example:** Snow caves have saved countless lives in polar regions and mountainous areas. During the 1912 Terra Nova Expedition, members of Robert Falcon Scott's team used snow caves for temporary shelter during their ill-fated journey to the South Pole.

How to Start a Fire

Fire is important for keeping warm, cooking food, and calling for help. However, if your lighter stops working or your matches become wet, it can be a problem. Knowing how to create a fire in different situations is a key survival skill.

- **Friction-Based Methods - Bow Drill:** You're in a damp forest, and your usual fire-starting tools aren't working. You need to rely on the bow drill method, but everything around you is wet.
  - **Problem-Solution:** Use dry wood for the spindle and fireboard, and keep your materials as dry as possible by storing them under your clothing or in a dry bag. Consider placing a dry leaf or piece of bark underneath the fireboard to catch the ember.
  - **Real-Life Example:** The bow drill is one of the oldest methods of fire-starting, used by indigenous peoples across the globe. It's effective even in challenging conditions, provided you have the patience and technique.

- **Spark-Based Methods - Flint and Steel:** It's raining, and you're struggling to find dry tinder. Your flint and steel are your best bet, but can you get a fire going with wet materials?
  - **Problem-Solution:** Use char cloth or dry, fibrous material as tinder to catch the spark more easily. Even in wet conditions, you can often find dry material under rocks or logs. If necessary, use your knife to shave off the wet outer layers of wood to reach the dry core.
  - **Real-Life Example:** Flint and steel have been used for centuries as a reliable fire-starting method, particularly by explorers and pioneers who needed a durable and long-lasting fire source.

- **Chemical Methods - Battery and Steel Wool:** You're low on traditional fire-starting materials, but you have a 9-volt battery and some steel wool in your pack. Can you use them to start a fire?
  - **Problem-Solution:** Rubbing steel wool against the terminals of a 9-volt battery creates a short circuit, igniting the steel wool. Have tinder ready to catch the flame immediately after ignition. This method is particularly useful in cold or damp conditions where other methods may fail.
  - **Real-Life Example:** This method has been popularized in survival training and emergency preparedness courses due to its simplicity and effectiveness, especially in scenarios where conventional tools are not available.

Building the Fire

Starting a fire is only half the battle—building and maintaining it requires skill and attention. Have you ever struggled to keep a fire going, only to watch it sputter out just when you need it most?

- **Tinder:** Gather dry, fibrous materials like grass, bark shavings, or lint. This catches the initial spark or ember. Keep a small supply of dry tinder in a waterproof container to ensure you always have something to start with.
- **Kindling:** Use small twigs and sticks to build the fire up once the tinder is lit. Gradually increase the size of the sticks as the fire grows. If your kindling is damp, consider splitting it to expose the dry interior wood.
- **Fuel:** Larger logs and branches sustain the fire once it's established. Arrange these in a teepee or log cabin structure to allow airflow. Be mindful of the fire's needs—too much fuel too quickly can smother it, while too little can cause it to die out.

Real-Life Scenario: During a backcountry expedition, a group of hikers was caught in an unexpected snowstorm. Their only hope of warmth and survival was to start a fire. Using a combination of flint and steel and careful tinder management, they managed to ignite a small flame, which they nurtured into a lifesaving blaze. Their experience underscores the importance of practicing fire-starting techniques in controlled settings so that you're prepared when the stakes are high.

How to Find Food in the Wild

Imagine this: You've been living off-grid for months, relying on your garden and stored food. But then, disaster strikes—your crops fail, or a storm wipes out your food supply. What do you do? Foraging for food in the wilderness is a critical survival skill. Knowing how to identify edible plants, insects, and animals can sustain you when other food sources are unavailable.

Universal Edibility Test

The Universal Edibility Test is a method used to determine whether an unknown plant or part of a plant is safe to eat. This test is particularly useful in survival situations where you may need to rely on wild plants for food, and you aren't sure if a particular plant is edible. However, it's important to note that this test is not foolproof and can still pose risks, especially if a plant is highly toxic. It should be used with caution and only as a last resort when no other food sources are available.

Steps of the Universal Edibility Test

- **Separate the Plant - Identify and Separate:** If possible, separate the plant into its different parts (roots, stems, leaves, flowers, and fruits). Different parts of the same plant can have different levels of toxicity.
- **Perform a Contact Test:**
  - **Skin Test:** Rub a small part of the plant on your inner forearm or wrist and wait for 15 minutes. If you experience any irritation, itching, or burning, do not eat the plant.
  - **Lip Test:** If there is no reaction on your skin, place a small part of the plant (without swallowing) on your lips for 3 minutes. If you feel any burning, tingling, or other irritation, rinse your mouth thoroughly and do not proceed with testing that plant.

- **Taste Test:**
  - **Chew and Hold:** If there's no reaction on your lips, chew a small piece of the plant and hold it in your mouth for 15 minutes without swallowing. If there's no burning, bitterness, or other adverse reactions, you can proceed to the next step.
  - **Swallow a Small Amount:** If there is no reaction in your mouth after the taste test, swallow the small piece you've chewed and wait 8 hours. While you are waiting, avoid eating or drinking anything else. Keep an eye out for signs such as nausea, cramps, or diarrhea.

- **Wait and Observe: 8-Hour Observation:** If no symptoms occur after 8 hours, consume a slightly larger amount of the plant (about a quarter-sized portion). Wait another 8 hours to observe any reactions.

- **Gradual Increase: Increase Consumption:** If no adverse effects are observed after the second 8-hour period, the plant part may be safe to eat. However, continue to increase the amount you consume gradually, monitoring for any delayed reactions.

Important Notes

- **Avoid Plants with Known Toxic Characteristics:**
  - **Bitter Taste:** Most toxic plants have a very bitter taste.
  - **Almond-like Scent:** An almond scent in leaves or stems may indicate cyanide.
  - **Milky or Discolored Sap:** This often indicates toxicity.
  - **Umbrella-shaped Flowers:** Many plants with umbrella-shaped flowers are toxic.
  - **Three-leaved Growth Pattern:** Some plants, like poison ivy, have a distinct three-leaved growth pattern and should be avoided.

- **Cautions:** Even if a plant passes the Universal Edibility Test, it doesn't mean it's entirely safe, as some plants contain toxins that can build up in the body over time or in larger quantities. It's always better to avoid eating wild plants unless you're certain of their safety.
- **Use as a Last Resort:** The Universal Edibility Test should only be used when no other food sources are available, and you're in a survival situation.

While this test can help identify potentially edible plants, it's much safer to familiarize yourself with local edible plants and their look-alikes before you find yourself in a survival situation.

Foraging Basics
- **Edible Plants:** You're in an unfamiliar forest, and your food supplies are running low. You

need to forage, but how do you know what's safe to eat?

- o **Problem-Solution:** Learn to identify common edible plants in your area before you find yourself in a survival situation. For example, dandelions, cattails, and wild onions are widely available and nutritious. Always follow the "Universal Edibility Test" if you're unsure about a plant's safety. This involves testing a small part of the plant on your skin, lips, and mouth over several hours before consuming it.
- o **Real-Life Example:** Indigenous peoples have relied on foraging for centuries, passing down knowledge of edible plants through generations. Many of these plants are now recognized as superfoods, rich in nutrients and medicinal properties.

- **Insects:** You've been hiking for hours with no sign of food. The landscape is barren, but you notice an abundance of grasshoppers. Could these insects keep you going?
  - o **Problem-Solution:** Insects are a highly nutritious food source and often abundant. Grasshoppers, ants, and crickets are good options. Cook insects before eating to kill parasites and pathogens. Look for insects that are easy to catch and in plentiful supply, such as those found near water sources.
  - o **Real-Life Example:** In various cultures, insects have long been used as a common source of protein. In survival situations, they can be the difference between life and death, providing essential nutrients when other food sources are scarce.

- **Hunting and Trapping:** The winter months are harsh, and foraging becomes nearly impossible. How do you secure a reliable food source during these tough conditions?
  - o **Problem-Solution:** Small game like rabbits, squirrels, and birds can be caught using traps or hunting tools. Practice setting snares and traps beforehand so that you're prepared in a survival situation. Focus on setting multiple traps in different locations to increase your chances of success.
  - o **Real-Life Example:** Trapping has been a vital survival skill for centuries, especially in cold climates where food is scarce during winter. Trappers in the northern U.S. and Canada have used these techniques to provide food and furs for survival and trade.

Water Sources

Finding water is often more critical than finding food. Dehydration can kill in days, while hunger takes weeks to become life-threatening. Imagine being out in the wild with no clear water source in sight—what do you do?

- **Natural Water Sources:** Look for streams, rivers, and lakes. In areas with little surface water, search for animal tracks that lead to water or dig near green vegetation for underground moisture.

- **Problem-Solution:** If you're unable to find clear water, you can collect dew by laying out cloths overnight or dig a seep well near a dry riverbed. In desperate situations, building a solar still can extract moisture from the ground or plants.
- **Real-Life Scenario:** During the 1987 movie "The Survivors", a plane crash leaves a group stranded in the Andes without water. Using ingenuity and survival skills, they manage to find and purify water, illustrating how crucial water is to survival.

Purifying Water

Water might seem clear and safe, but it can still have dangerous germs in it. Drinking water that is not clean can make you very sick, and in a survival scenario, it could even be life-threatening. Have you thought about how you would handle a situation where your water source was no longer safe?

- **Boiling:** The safest way to ensure clean water is to boil it for at least one minute to eliminate bacteria and parasites. If you are at a high altitude, where water boils at a lower temperature, you should boil it for a longer time.
- **Problem-Solution:** What if you can't make a fire? In this case, a portable water filter is your next best option. Filters remove bacteria and protozoa, making water safe to drink.
- **Chemical Purification:** Water purification tablets or drops can kill bacteria and viruses. Use these as a last resort or when you need to purify large quantities of water quickly.

Real-Life Example: In 1993, a cryptosporidium outbreak in Milwaukee's water supply sickened over 400,000 people. This real-life example highlights the importance of always purifying your water, no matter how clean it appears.

First Aid and Emergency Medical Care

In an off-grid or wilderness setting, access to medical help may be limited or nonexistent. Have you ever thought about what you would do if you or a loved one were seriously injured, and help was hours—or even days—away? This section is designed to equip you with the knowledge and confidence to handle medical emergencies when professional help isn't an option.

Basic First Aid Techniques
- **Cuts and Wounds** You're cutting firewood when the axe slips, leaving you with a deep gash. The nearest medical facility is miles away—what do you do?
  - **Problem-Solution:** Rinse the wound with clean water to remove debris. Use antiseptic wipes or alcohol if available to disinfect the area. Cover the wound with a sterile bandage or clean cloth and apply pressure to stop the bleeding. If the cut is deep or won't stop bleeding, create a makeshift tourniquet above the injury to control the blood flow.
  - **Real-Life Example:** During the Alaskan Gold Rush, prospectors often found themselves far from medical care. Improvised first aid, such as using cloth bandages

and natural antiseptics, was crucial for survival in such remote conditions.

- **Burns:** You're cooking over an open flame when a pot of boiling water tips over, burning your arm. You're miles from a doctor—how do you treat the burn?
    - o **Problem-Solution:** To treat a burn, rinse it with cool water for at least 10 minutes right away. Do not use ice since it can harm the skin more. After cooling, cover the burn with a clean, non-stick bandage or cloth. If blisters appear, do not break them, as this can lead to infection.
    - o **Real-Life Example:** In the 1800s, settlers moving west often had to treat burns with limited resources. Many used cool river water and honey—a natural antibacterial agent—to dress burns when traditional medical supplies were unavailable.

- **Fractures:** You're hiking on uneven terrain when you slip, breaking your leg. You're alone, and the nearest help is far away. How do you immobilize the injury and get to safety?
    - o **Problem-Solution:** Splint the injured limb to prevent further damage. Use a rigid object (like a stick) and secure it with strips of cloth or bandages. Elevate the injured limb if possible to reduce swelling. In extreme cases, you may need to fashion a crutch from nearby branches or crawl to safety.
    - o **Real-Life Example:** During the Vietnam War, soldiers often had to treat fractures in the field using whatever materials were available. The improvisation of splints and slings with limited resources saved many lives.

- **Shock:** After a serious injury, you notice that the victim is pale, clammy, and breathing rapidly. They may be going into shock—how do you manage this?
    - o **Problem-Solution:** Lay the person down with their legs elevated to promote blood flow to vital organs. Keep them warm with blankets or clothing. Monitor their breathing and pulse, and if they become unconscious, ensure their airway is open. Avoid giving them anything to eat or drink until they recover from shock.
    - o **Real-Life Example:** Shock is a common response to traumatic injuries and was frequently encountered by soldiers during WWII. Quick action to manage shock often made the difference between life and death on the battlefield.

Advanced Emergency Medical Care
- **CPR (Cardiopulmonary Resuscitation):** You're working on your homestead when a family member collapses and stops breathing. You're far from any medical assistance—do you know how to perform CPR?
    - o **Problem-Solution:** Start with chest compressions by placing the heel of your hand on the center of the chest and pushing hard and fast at a rate of 100-120 compressions

per minute. If trained, give two breaths after every 30 compressions. If not trained, continue with compressions only. Ensure the airway is open before delivering breaths.

- o **Real-Life Example:** CPR has saved countless lives since its development in the 1960s. In remote locations, knowing how to perform CPR can buy precious time until professional help arrives or the victim regains consciousness.

- **Stopping Severe Bleeding:** A serious accident has caused a severe wound, and blood is gushing from the site. How do you stop the bleeding before it's too late?
  - o **Problem-Solution:** Use a clean cloth or bandage to press directly on the wound. If the bleeding doesn't stop, apply a tourniquet above the injury, tightening it until the bleeding slows or stops. Be aware of the risks of using a tourniquet and loosen it every 15-20 minutes if help is delayed.
  - o **Real-Life Example:** During hunting trips in remote areas, accidents with knives or arrows can cause severe bleeding. Experienced hunters often carry tourniquets and quick-clot agents in their first aid kits, knowing that these tools can make the difference between life and death.

- **Treating Hypothermia:** You've been exposed to freezing temperatures for hours, and you start to feel numbness in your extremities and severe shivering. You may be entering hypothermia—what's your next move?
  - o **Problem-Solution:** Go to a warm and dry area right away. Take off any wet clothes and put on a dry, warm layer instead. Gradually warm the core body temperature by wrapping in blankets, using warm (not hot) water bottles, and sipping warm fluids if the victim is conscious. Avoid direct heat, which can shock the body.
  - o **Real-Life Example:** Hypothermia is a real threat in cold climates. During Ernest Shackleton's Antarctic expedition, crew members used these techniques to stave off hypothermia during their harrowing survival journey.

- **Dehydration and Heat Exhaustion:** On a hot summer day, you've spent the whole afternoon working outdoors. Now, you begin to feel lightheaded, tired, and a bit sick to your stomach. You're at risk for heat exhaustion—how do you cool down quickly?
  - o **Problem-Solution:** Move to a shaded area and cool down with wet cloths or fanning. Sip water or an electrolyte solution slowly, avoiding large quantities at once, which can upset your stomach. If possible, immerse yourself in cool water to lower your body temperature quickly. Rest until your symptoms subside.
  - o **Real-Life Example:** Heat exhaustion is a common issue in desert regions or during heatwaves. During the 2011 Texas heatwave, many outdoor workers had to be treated for heat exhaustion and dehydration using similar methods.

First Aid Kits for Off-Grid Living

A well-stocked first aid kit is a must for any off-grid homestead. But have you ever considered what you would need in an emergency that lasts days—or even weeks—without outside help? Here's a basic list of items to include:

Basic Items:

- **Adhesive bandages (various sizes):** For small cuts and abrasions.
- **Sterile gauze pads and adhesive tape:** To cover bigger wounds and help stop bleeding.
- **Antiseptic wipes and creams:** Used to clean injuries and stop infections from happening.
- **Scissors, tweezers, and safety pins:** Essential tools for a variety of first aid tasks.
- **Disposable gloves:** To protect against bloodborne pathogens.
- **Oral rehydration salts:** To treat dehydration from heat, illness, or injury.

Advanced Items:

- **CPR face shield or mask:** To provide rescue breaths safely.
- **Splinting materials (SAM splints, padded aluminum):** For stabilizing fractures.
- **Tourniquet:** For controlling severe bleeding when direct pressure isn't enough.
- **Trauma shears:** For cutting through clothing and bandages quickly.
- **Burn gel or dressing:** To soothe and protect burn injuries.
- **Suture kit (only if trained to use):** For closing deep cuts when medical help is far away.

Medications:

- **Pain relievers (ibuprofen, acetaminophen):** For managing pain and inflammation.
- **Antihistamines (for allergic reactions):** To treat allergic reactions from stings, bites, or plants.
- **Anti-diarrheal medication:** To control diarrhea and prevent dehydration.
- **Antibiotic ointment:** Used to stop infections in small cuts and scratches.
- **Prescription medications (in an extended supply):** Ensure you have enough for extended periods without access to a pharmacy.

Emergency Items:

- **Emergency blanket:** For warmth in cases of shock or hypothermia.
- **Snake bite kit (if applicable to your region):** To treat bites from venomous snakes.
- **Cold packs:** For reducing swelling from injuries.
- **Blood-clotting agent:** For rapid control of severe bleeding.

Real-Life Scenario: During a two-week trek through the Appalachian Trail, a hiker sustained a serious ankle injury. The group's well-prepared first aid kit included splinting materials and pain relievers, allowing them to stabilize the injury and manage pain until they could reach help. This example underscores the importance of having a comprehensive first aid kit tailored to your environment and activities.

Navigation and Orientation

When living off-grid, especially in remote areas, the ability to navigate effectively can mean the difference between life and death. Have you ever wondered what you would do if you got lost in the wilderness with no GPS or cell service to guide you? Whether you're exploring your surroundings, looking for resources, or trying to find your way back to safety, strong navigation skills are essential.

Using a Compass and Map Reading

- **Understanding a Compass:** You're deep in the forest, far from any recognizable landmarks. Your GPS device has lost signal, and you need to find your way back to camp. How do you navigate without electronic assistance?
    - o **Problem-Solution:** Familiarize with the parts of a compass — baseplate, direction of travel arrow, rotating bezel and magnetic needle. Keep the compass level in your hand, aim the direction of travel arrow at where you want to go, and turn the bezel until the needle lines up with the orienting arrow. Check the bearing at the index line and follow that direction.
    - o **Real-Life Example:** In 1996, a group of hikers in the Grand Canyon lost their way after their GPS device malfunctioned. Using basic map and compass skills, they were able to reorient themselves and find their way back to safety, proving the importance of traditional navigation skills.

- **Reading a Map:** You have a topographic map but aren't sure how to read it. The terrain is complex, and you need to understand the landscape to navigate effectively.
    - o **Problem-Solution:** Learn to read topographic maps by understanding contour lines, symbols, and scales. Contour lines represent elevation; closer lines indicate steeper terrain. Orient the map by matching landmarks on the map to those in the environment and use your compass to help with orientation.
    - o **Real-Life Example:** During the Vietnam War, soldiers relied heavily on topographic maps for navigation through dense jungle terrain. Accurate map reading often made the difference between reaching their objectives safely or becoming disoriented and lost.

- **Navigating with a Map and Compass:** You're tasked with leading a group through unfamiliar terrain, but the path isn't clearly marked. How do you ensure you stay on course?
    - o **Problem-Solution:** Plot your route on the map by marking start and end points, then

take bearings and measure distances. Follow these bearings with your compass as you navigate. Use pacing techniques to estimate how far you've traveled and compare this with your map readings.

- o **Real-Life Example:** During the 1930s, early explorers of Antarctica used basic map and compass techniques to navigate the frozen landscape, often covering vast distances with only these tools to guide them.

DIY Project 37: Homemade Compass

A compass is an essential tool for navigation, especially when you're off-grid or exploring the wilderness. While modern GPS devices are handy, they rely on battery power and can fail in remote areas. Knowing how to make a simple compass using basic materials can be a lifesaver in such situations. This project will guide you through the steps to create a functional, homemade compass using readily available items.

Cost	$	Difficulty	★

Materials:

- **Needle or Small Metal Object:** A sewing needle, paperclip, or even a small nail can work.
- **Magnet:** A refrigerator magnet, a small bar magnet, or any other magnet you have on hand.
- **Cork or a Piece of Foam:** To float the needle. A cork from a wine bottle or a small piece of styrofoam works well.
- **Bowl of Water:** This will allow the needle to float freely.
- **Non-metallic Knife or Scissors:** To cut the cork or foam.
- **Optional: A Marking Pen** to label the compass points on the cork or foam.

Tools:

- **Magnet:** Used to magnetize the needle. This could be a refrigerator magnet, a small bar magnet, or any strong magnet available.
- **Non-metallic Knife or Scissors:** To cut a slice from the cork if you're using a wine bottle cork. This ensures the cork is thin enough to float properly.
- **Tweezers (Optional):** If you need precision when placing the needle on the cork, tweezers can help ensure the needle is positioned correctly without disturbing the setup.
- **Shallow Bowl or Dish:** To hold the water in which the cork and needle will float. This bowl should be non-metallic to avoid any interference with the needle's alignment.

1	**Magnetize the Needle** The key to making a compass is to magnetize the needle or metal object so that it aligns with the Earth's magnetic field. **Method 1: Using a Magnet** - **Stroke the Needle:** Hold the needle and stroke it with the magnet, always in the same direction, about 30 to 50 times. This process magnetizes the needle, causing it to become a mini-magnet itself. - **Test Magnetization:** If the needle attracts small metal objects like paperclips, it's magnetized and ready to use. **Method 2: Using Silk or Hair (If you don't have a magnet)** - **Rub the Needle:** Rub the needle with silk, a piece of cloth, or even your hair. This won't magnetize it as strongly as a magnet, but it can give it a weak magnetic charge that might be sufficient for a basic compass.
2	**Prepare the Floating Platform** The needle needs to float freely on the surface of water, so you'll need to prepare a platform to keep it afloat. - Cut the Cork: If you're using a cork, slice off a thin disk, about 1/4 inch thick, so it can easily float on water. - Cut the Foam: If using foam, cut a small piece large enough to support the needle without sinking. - Place the Needle: Carefully insert the needle horizontally through the center of the cork or foam piece. If the cork is too hard, you can carefully balance the needle on top of it.
3	**Assemble the Compass** - Fill the Bowl with Water: Pour water into a shallow bowl or dish. The water should be deep enough for the cork or foam to float freely without touching the bottom. - Float the Needle: Carefully set the cork or foam, with the needle attached, on the water's surface. Make sure the needle lies as flat as you can, allowing it to spin easily.

	• Watch the Needle Align: After a few moments, the needle should slowly align itself with the Earth's magnetic field, pointing roughly north-south.
4	**Mark the Directions (Optional)** • Label the Cork or Foam: If you want to make the compass more permanent, use a marking pen to label one end of the needle as "N" for north and the opposite end as "S" for south. • Check Accuracy: To verify your compass, use a known directional reference, like the position of the sun at a specific time of day, or compare it with a standard compass.

Additional Tips:

- **Storing the Compass:** Keep the magnetized needle away from other metal objects when not in use, as it could lose its magnetism over time. If it does, simply remagnetize it using the steps above.
- **Practice:** Try making the compass a few times in different conditions to ensure you're comfortable using this technique in an emergency.

Creating a homemade compass is a simple yet crucial skill for anyone living off the grid or spending time in the wilderness. This project not only equips you with a basic navigation tool but also enhances your understanding of magnetic fields and the Earth's natural forces. Whether you're exploring new terrain or simply practicing your survival skills, this DIY compass is an invaluable addition to your off-grid toolkit.

Natural Navigation Techniques

When you're without a map or compass, natural navigation can help you find your way. Imagine being lost in the wilderness with nothing but the sun and stars to guide you—would you know what to do?

- **Using the Sun:** It's late afternoon, and you're unsure which direction you're heading, and unfortunately your compass is broken and you need to find your bearings.
  - **Problem-Solution:** Use the position of the sun to determine cardinal directions. The sun rises in the east and sets in the west. In the Northern Hemisphere, if you face the sun at noon, north will be to your left, and south to your right. In the Southern Hemisphere, it's the opposite. For more precision, use the shadow stick method— place a stick in the ground, mark the tip of the shadow, and after 15 minutes, mark the new tip position. Draw a line between the two marks to determine the east-west line.

- o **Real-Life Example:** Ancient mariners and explorers relied on the sun for navigation long before the invention of compasses. Their ability to determine direction using natural indicators was key to successful long-distance travel.

- **Using the Stars:** Night has fallen, and you've lost the trail. The sky is clear, but you have no idea which way to go. Can the stars help you find your direction?
  - o **Problem-Solution:** In the Northern Hemisphere, you can find the North Star, also known as Polaris, by first spotting the Big Dipper and then tracing the outer edge of its "bowl" upward. The North Star always points to true north. In the Southern Hemisphere, use the Southern Cross constellation to find the south by drawing an imaginary line through its long axis.
  - o **Real-Life Example:** Throughout history, sailors and explorers have used the stars to navigate the open seas. The North Star was crucial in guiding ships across the Atlantic during the Age of Exploration.

- **Using Nature:** You're deep in a dense forest with no clear path. The landscape all looks the same—how do you navigate using nature's clues?
  - o **Problem-Solution:** Moss often grows on the northern side of trees in the Northern Hemisphere and the southern side in the Southern Hemisphere, but this is not always reliable. Instead, look for other natural indicators like the direction of river flow, the shape of sand dunes (which usually point downwind), or the growth of tree branches (which often lean towards the sun).
  - o **Real-Life Example:** Indigenous peoples around the world have used natural navigation techniques for millennia. For example, Polynesian navigators read the patterns of waves and the flight paths of birds to guide them across vast ocean distances without modern tools.

Emergency Navigation Without Tools

If you're completely without navigation tools, you can still find your way by observing your environment. Have you ever been lost in the wilderness with no map, compass or GPS? Here's how you can rely on your senses and surroundings to find your way.

- **Stick to Known Landmarks:** You've lost your way during a day hike. The sun is setting, and you have no navigation tools. How do you find your way back?
  - o **Problem-Solution:** Try to retrace your steps by looking for recognizable landmarks or terrain features you passed earlier. If you can't retrace your steps, follow linear features like rivers, ridgelines, or trails, which often lead to human settlements or safer areas.
  - o **Real-Life Example:** In 2003, a hiker in the Utah desert became disoriented after

taking a wrong turn. By following a dry riverbed, he eventually found his way to a road, where he was rescued. His story highlights the importance of sticking to natural landmarks and linear features in survival situations.

- **Using Your Senses:** You're in an unfamiliar forest, and visibility is low due to fog. Your navigation tools are lost—how do you find your way?
  - o **Problem-Solution:** Use your senses to navigate—listen for sounds like running water, bird calls, or distant traffic, and follow them if they lead towards safety. Pay attention to temperature changes, which can indicate proximity to water or open areas. If you can smell smoke or other strong scents, they might lead you to a campsite or human habitation.
  - o **Real-Life Example:** During WWII, downed pilots often had to rely on their senses to navigate through dense jungles. By listening for aircraft, water, or human activity, they were able to find their way to safety, despite the lack of traditional navigation tools.

Foraging for Wild Edibles

Foraging for food is a valuable skill that can supplement your diet, especially in a survival situation. But have you ever thought about what you would do if your food stores ran out? Would you know how to identify safe, nutritious food in the wild? This section will help you develop the confidence to forage effectively and safely.

Identifying and Harvesting Edible Plants

- **Common Edible Plants:** You've run out of food while exploring a remote area. The landscape is teeming with plant life, but you're unsure which plants are safe to eat.
  - o **Problem-Solution:** Learn to identify common edible plants in your area before you find yourself in a survival situation. Dandelions, cattails, and wild onions are widely available and nutritious. Dandelion leaves can be eaten raw or cooked, while cattail roots and shoots provide starchy carbohydrates. Wild onions add flavor and nutrients to meals. Always follow the "Universal Edibility Test" if you're unsure about a plant's safety.
  - o **Real-Life Example:** Native Americans and early settlers relied on wild plants like cattails and dandelions as staple foods during lean times. Their knowledge of local flora was essential for survival in the North American wilderness.

- **Safety Tips for Foraging:** You've found a patch of berries, but you're unsure if they're safe to eat. How can you avoid poisoning yourself in a survival situation?
  - o **Problem-Solution:** Always avoid plants with milky sap, bitter taste, or bright, glossy

leaves, as these characteristics are common in poisonous plants. When in doubt, use the Universal Edibility Test. Test the plant by rubbing a small part on your skin, waiting for a reaction, then testing on your lips and mouth. If there's no adverse reaction, consume a small amount and wait several hours before eating more.

- o **Real-Life Example:** In 1846, the Donner Party, stranded in the Sierra Nevada, relied on foraged plants and roots to survive. Unfortunately, some members consumed toxic plants, leading to illness and death. This tragic event underscores the importance of proper plant identification.

- **Sustainable Harvesting:** You've discovered a rich foraging spot, but you're concerned about depleting the resources. How can you forage sustainably to ensure food sources remain available?
    - o **Problem-Solution:** Only take what you need, and never harvest more than 10% of a plant population. Leave some behind to ensure regrowth and sustainability. Rotate your foraging areas to avoid overharvesting a single spot.
    - o **Real-Life Example:** Many indigenous cultures practice sustainable harvesting techniques, taking only what they need and leaving enough for the ecosystem to recover. These practices have allowed them to maintain a balanced relationship with their environment for generations.

Foraging for Mushrooms

Mushrooms can be a nutritious addition to your diet, but they require careful identification. Have you ever wondered if the mushrooms growing in your yard are safe to eat? Here's how to identify and harvest edible mushrooms safely.

- **Common Edible Mushrooms:** You're in a forest with a variety of mushrooms growing at your feet. Some look delicious, but you know that others could be deadly. How do you identify which ones are safe to eat?
    - o **Problem-Solution:** Discover how to recognize popular edible mushrooms such as morels, chanterelles, and oyster mushrooms. Morels have a distinctive honeycomb appearance, chanterelles are bright yellow or orange with wavy edges, and oyster mushrooms are fan-shaped and grow on decaying wood. Always avoid mushrooms with white gills, a skirt or ring on the stem, and a bulbous base, as these characteristics are common in poisonous varieties.
    - o **Real-Life Example:** In 1978, a group of foragers in Oregon mistakenly consumed Amanita mushrooms, thinking they were safe. The resulting poisoning was severe, leading to several deaths. This tragic case illustrates the critical importance of correct mushroom identification.

- **Mushroom Foraging Tips:** You've found what you believe to be an edible mushroom, but you're not 100% sure. How can you confirm its identity before eating?
  - **Problem-Solution:** Take a spore print by placing the mushroom cap on a piece of paper and covering it overnight. The color of the spore print can help confirm the species. If you're still unsure, consult a detailed field guide or an experienced forager before consuming the mushroom.
  - **Real-Life Example:** The spore print method has been used by mycologists (mushroom scientists) for decades to differentiate between similar-looking species. t's a straightforward yet powerful method that helps ensure safe foraging.

- **Cook Before Eating:** You've identified an edible mushroom, but you're unsure if it's safe to eat raw. Should you cook it, and if so, how?
  - **Problem-Solution:** Always cook mushrooms before consuming them. Cooking destroys toxins that may be present in certain varieties, even those considered edible. Sautéing, boiling, or roasting are all effective methods of preparing mushrooms safely.
  - **Real-Life Example:** Even commonly foraged mushrooms like morels contain small amounts of hydrazine toxins, which are neutralized by cooking. This practice has been followed by foragers for centuries to ensure that the mushrooms they consume are safe.

Foraging for Berries and Fruits

Wild berries and fruits are another excellent food source. Have you ever come across a patch of berries while hiking and wondered if they're safe to eat? This section will guide you in identifying and harvesting edible wild berries and fruits.

- **Edible Wild Berries:** You've come across a dense thicket of berries. Some look familiar, but others don't. How do you know which ones are safe to eat?
  - **Problem-Solution:** Learn to identify common edible berries like blackberries, raspberries, blueberries, and elderberries. Blackberries and raspberries grow on bramble thickets and are safe to eat raw. Blueberries are small, round, and sweet, often found in forested areas. Elderberries grow in clusters and are safe to eat when cooked. Avoid berries that you cannot positively identify, as some, like nightshade berries, can be deadly.
  - **Real-Life Example:** During WWII, British soldiers were trained to forage for wild berries like blackberries and elderberries to supplement their rations. These berries provided essential vitamins and nutrients, helping to prevent scurvy and other deficiencies.

- **Foraging Tips:** You've found a patch of ripe berries, but you're not the only one interested in them. Birds and animals are competing for the same food source—how do you ensure you get your share?

- o **Problem-Solution:** Harvest berries early in the morning before birds and animals have had their fill. Look for hidden clusters that animals may have overlooked. When harvesting, be mindful of the environment—leave some berries for wildlife and future growth.
- o **Real-Life Example:** Foragers have long known that early morning is the best time to gather berries, as animals are less active, and the berries are at their freshest. This practice ensures a more abundant and sustainable harvest.

- **Safety Considerations:** You're in a new area with different plant life, and you come across a bush laden with berries. They look delicious, but you're not sure if they're safe. What do you do?
  - o **Problem-Solution:** Avoid unknown berries. If you cannot positively identify a berry, do not eat it. Some berries, such as those from the yew tree or deadly nightshade, can be extremely toxic and difficult to distinguish from edible varieties. When in doubt, it's better to go hungry than to risk poisoning.
  - o **Real-Life Example:** In 1992, a group of hikers in the Pacific Northwest mistakenly consumed poisonous berries, thinking they were edible. The resulting illness was severe, requiring hospitalization. This incident highlights the importance of caution when foraging in unfamiliar areas.

Mastering Survival Skills for Off-Grid Living

Living off-grid is about more than just independence—it's about developing the skills to thrive in any situation, no matter how unpredictable. The survival skills covered in this chapter are your lifeline when the unexpected happens, whether it's a sudden storm, a critical equipment failure, or a food shortage. By mastering these techniques, you ensure that you're not just prepared but empowered to face whatever challenges off-grid living throws your way.

From building emergency shelters and starting fires in adverse conditions to foraging for food and finding water in the wild, these skills form the foundation of your self-reliance. They're not just about surviving—they're about thriving, even when the odds are against you. With practical knowledge and regular practice, these skills will give you the confidence to handle the toughest situations with ease.

Remember, survival is as much about mindset as it is about technique. Preparation and practice are key. Make these skills a regular part of your off-grid life, so when the time comes, you're ready to act swiftly and effectively. By doing so, you'll not only safeguard your well-being but also deepen your connection to the environment and the true essence of off-grid living. In mastering these survival skills, you're ensuring that your off-grid journey is not just possible but profoundly rewarding.

Chapter 11 - Forced Off-Grid Living: Preparing for the Unexpected

In an ideal world, the decision to live off the grid would be a deliberate choice, made after careful consideration and ample preparation. However, life often throws us into situations where we must adapt quickly, whether we're ready or not. Emergencies such as natural disasters, economic downturns, pandemics, or societal breakdowns can force us into off-grid living with little to no warning. In these scenarios, your survival depends on how well you've prepared in advance.

This Chapter is dedicated to helping you prepare for the possibility of forced off-grid living, where the shift from a connected, convenience-driven lifestyle to one of self-sufficiency happens abruptly. We'll explore the essentials of building a bug-out bag that can sustain you in the immediate aftermath of a crisis, how to quickly prepare your current home for off-grid living, and strategies for surviving and thriving in the days, weeks, and months that follow.

By the end of this Chapter, you will have a comprehensive plan that ensures you and your loved ones can navigate a sudden transition to off-grid living with resilience and confidence. You'll learn not only how to meet your basic needs but also how to adapt to a new way of life that prioritizes self-reliance, safety, and sustainability.

Understanding Forced Off-Grid Scenarios

Before diving into the practical aspects of preparation, it's crucial to understand the types of scenarios that could force you into off-grid living. Recognizing potential threats and understanding their impact will help you better prepare for them, allowing you to take swift and effective action when necessary.

Common Scenarios Leading to Forced Off-Grid Living

When considering the possibility of being forced off the grid, it's essential to think about the various situations that could disrupt your normal way of life. Here are some common scenarios:

Natural Disasters

Natural disasters are perhaps the most common cause of sudden off-grid living. Hurricanes, earthquakes, wildfires, and floods can all devastate infrastructure, cutting off access to electricity, water, and other vital utilities. In severe cases, you might be forced to evacuate your home entirely. Even if your home remains intact, prolonged power outages and disruptions to supply chains can push you into an off-grid situation where you must rely on your own resources to survive.

Practical Suggestion: Always have a disaster preparedness plan tailored to the types of natural disasters most likely to occur in your area. The plan must outline escape paths, a specific spot for family members to gather, and a way to communicate. Also, have an emergency kit at home with important items such as canned food, water, first aid materials and a portable charger.

Economic Collapse

An economic collapse can lead to widespread unemployment, loss of income, and the breakdown of essential services. In such a scenario, even if your home remains intact, you may be unable to afford utilities, food, or other necessities, forcing you to live off the grid by necessity rather than choice. The collapse of a national or global economy can also result in the devaluation of currency, leading to hyperinflation and shortages of goods.

Practical Suggestion: Diversify your assets by investing in tangible items that hold value, such as precious metals, land, and tools. Build a pantry stocked with non-perishable foods, seeds for planting, and other essentials that can last for months. Consider learning bartering skills, as trading goods and services may become necessary in a post-collapse economy.

Pandemics

The COVID-19 pandemic was a stark reminder of how quickly a global health crisis can disrupt everyday life. Lockdowns, supply chain disruptions, and social distancing measures can make it difficult to access basic necessities. In a more severe pandemic, where infrastructure collapses or access to services is severely restricted, you may need to rely on self-sufficiency to avoid exposure and ensure your family's survival.

Practical Suggestion: Prepare a dedicated quarantine area in your home where sick individuals can be isolated from the rest of the household. Stockpile medical supplies, including masks, gloves, disinfectants, and over-the-counter medications. Learn basic medical skills, such as wound care and how to administer first aid, in case professional healthcare is unavailable.

Societal Collapse

Civil unrest, political instability, or large-scale social disruptions can lead to the breakdown of law and order, making it unsafe to rely on external systems for your survival. In such cases, being able to live off the grid provides not only independence but also security from the chaos that can arise in urban areas.

Practical Suggestion: Strengthen the security of your home by installing reinforced doors and windows, establishing a perimeter defense, and creating a safe room where you can retreat in case of an attack. Form alliances with trusted neighbors to create a community defense plan, and consider learning self-defense skills.

Power Grid Failures

The modern power grid faces many risks, such as cyberattacks, physical assaults and natural disasters. A prolonged power grid failure can lead to a cascade of other issues, such as water shortages, food supply disruptions, and communication breakdowns. In such a scenario, you may need to quickly transition to off-grid living to maintain access to basic necessities.

In 2021, a harsh winter storm hit Texas, causing major power outages. This left millions of people without electricity, heat, or running water for several days. The sudden loss of these essential services forced many residents into a state of emergency, where they had to rely on makeshift solutions for warmth, food, and water. This event highlights the importance of being prepared for forced off-grid living, as even areas that typically enjoy stable infrastructure can be vulnerable to unexpected crises.

Practical Suggestion: Invest in alternative energy sources, such as solar panels, wind turbines, or portable generators, to ensure you have a reliable power supply during a grid failure. Store fuel safely and in sufficient quantities to last for at least a few weeks. Additionally, consider purchasing a solar-powered or hand-crank emergency radio to stay informed about the situation.

Assessing Your Vulnerability

Understanding the scenarios that could lead to forced off-grid living is just the first step. Next, you need to assess your own vulnerability to these threats. Assessing your vulnerability involves evaluating both your personal circumstances and your environment. By identifying your specific risks, you can better tailor your preparations to ensure you're ready for whatever may come.

In 2012, Hurricane Sandy brought significant destruction to the East Coast of the United States. New York City, one of the most developed and populated areas in the world, was severely impacted, with millions of people losing power, water, and heat. Those who had prepared for such an event—by having generators, water storage, and non-perishable food—were able to weather the storm much more comfortably than those who were caught unprepared.

Questions to Consider:

1. **Location:** Do you live in a place that often faces natural disasters like floods, earthquakes or wildfires? Is your home in a crowded city that might get chaotic during an emergency?
   - **Practical Suggestion:** Research the history of natural disasters in your area and understand the local geography. Consider relocating if you live in a high-risk area, or at least ensure that your home is fortified against potential threats. Keep an evacuation plan ready, including multiple routes out of the city or town where you live.

2. **Infrastructure Dependence:** How reliant are you on public utilities for electricity, water, heating, and communication? Do you have any alternative systems in place?
   - **Practical Suggestion:** Conduct a thorough audit of your home's reliance on public utilities. Invest in alternatives such as solar panels, rainwater harvesting systems, and wood-burning stoves. Additionally, ensure that you have backup communication

methods, such as a satellite phone or ham radio, in case traditional networks fail.

3. **Financial Stability:** How secure is your income? Do you have savings or investments that could be affected by an economic collapse?
   o **Practical Suggestion:** Diversify your income streams to include passive income, such as rental properties or dividends, which may be more resilient in an economic downturn. Build an emergency fund that can cover at least six months of living expenses and consider converting part of your savings into tangible assets that retain value in a crisis.

4. **Health and Safety:** Do you or your family members have medical conditions that require regular treatment or medication? How would you manage these needs if access to healthcare was disrupted?
   o **Practical Suggestion:** Stockpile necessary medications and medical supplies, including those for chronic conditions like diabetes or asthma. Learn about natural alternatives and remedies that can be used if pharmaceuticals become scarce. Ensure that you have the knowledge and tools to manage minor medical issues at home and have a plan for accessing healthcare in a prolonged crisis.

5. **Community and Security:** How secure is your community? Are there risks of civil unrest or crime that could threaten your safety during a societal collapse?
   o **Practical Suggestion:** Get to know your neighbors and build strong relationships within your community. Consider joining or forming a neighborhood watch group to increase collective security. Develop a communication plan with trusted neighbors to share information and resources in an emergency.

Building a Comprehensive Bug-Out Bag

In any emergency where you might need to evacuate quickly, having a well-prepared bug-out bag is essential. Your bug-out bag should contain everything you need to survive for at least 72 hours while you figure out your next steps. This chapter will guide you through building a comprehensive bug-out bag tailored to your specific needs and the scenarios you're most likely to encounter.

The Essentials of a Bug-Out Bag

When disaster strikes, your bug-out bag becomes your lifeline. It's not just a collection of items—it's a carefully curated kit designed to keep you alive, healthy, and secure in the first critical hours and days following an emergency. But how do you ensure that your bug-out bag is equipped to handle the specific challenges you might face? Below a list of core components is depicted:

- **Water:** is your top priority in every survival situation. At a minimum, your bug-out bag should contain at least one liter of water per person, per day, for three days. This means your bag should have at least three liters of water per person. However, since water is heavy and bulky, it's also important to include water purification tools such as a portable filter (e.g., LifeStraw), purification tablets, and a metal container for boiling water.
  - o **Practical Suggestion:** Consider adding a collapsible water container, which can hold additional water when you find a source, and a lightweight water bladder that can be carried in your bag. These tools will allow you to increase your water-carrying capacity as needed.

- **Food:** Your bug-out bag should contain enough food to last for 72 hours. Choose foods that are high in calories and can be stored for a long time without spoiling, and that don't need much cooking. Some great choices are energy bars, trail mix, jerky, dried fruits,and meals that can be freeze-dried and just need water to prepare. If you think you will need to warm up food or water, bring along a light stove and some fuel.
  - o **Practical Suggestion:** Add a multi-tool with a can opener and a small camping pot to your bag. This will allow you to prepare meals or boil water on the go. Also, include some comfort food or small treats to boost morale during stressful situations.

- **Shelter:** Keeping yourself safe from the weather is very important. Make sure to pack a lightweight tent, tarp, or bivy sack in your emergency bag so you can set up a quick shelter when needed. You'll also need an emergency blanket or sleeping bag to retain body heat at night.
  - o **Practical Suggestion:** Consider packing a lightweight, durable tarp that can be used in various configurations depending on the environment. Paracord is also essential for securing your shelter and has multiple other uses.

- **Clothing:** Pack weather-appropriate clothing, including a moisture-wicking base layer, insulating layers, and waterproof outerwear. Don't forget extra socks and a hat, which are vital for preventing hypothermia in cold weather.
  - o **Practical Suggestion:** Choose clothing made from merino wool, which is naturally moisture-wicking, odor-resistant, and provides excellent insulation even when wet. Pack a bandana or multi-functional scarf, which can be used as a face covering, sun protection, or even as a makeshift sling.

- **Fire-Starting Tools:** Fire is important for keeping warm, cooking food, and calling for help. Bring several tools to start a fire, like waterproof matches, a ferrocerium rod and a lighter.

Also, pack a small bag of tinder, such as cotton balls soaked in petroleum jelly, to make starting a fire easier and faster.

- **Practical Suggestion:** Include a magnesium fire starter in your kit, as it works even in wet conditions. Practice using all your fire-starting tools before you need them in an emergency.

- **First Aid Kit:** Your bug-out bag should include a comprehensive first aid kit with supplies to treat wounds, prevent infection, and manage pain. Important items to have are bandages, gauze, antiseptic wipes, tweezers, medical tape and pain relievers that you can buy without a prescription. If you or someone in your family needs prescription medicine, make sure to include some in your kit.
  - **Practical Suggestion:** Consider adding a tourniquet, burn cream, and a small guidebook on emergency first aid. If you wear glasses, pack an extra pair, as well as any other personal medical items like inhalers or EpiPens.

- **Navigation Tools:** If you need to travel on foot, reliable navigation tools are critical. Make sure to carry a map of your location, a compass, and a GPS device if you have one. It can also help to bring a whistle to signal for help and a mirror to reflect sunlight.
  - **Practical Suggestion:** Invest in a quality multi-function compass that includes a signal mirror and a small magnifying glass. This tool can help you navigate, signal for help, and even start a fire in an emergency.

- **Security Items:** In a situation where law and order are not guaranteed, personal security becomes a concern. Consider packing a multi-tool or a small, sturdy knife for self-defense and general tasks. Pepper spray can also be an effective non-lethal deterrent. If you're trained and legally permitted, a firearm may be included as well, along with extra ammunition.
  - **Practical Suggestion:** If you decide to carry a firearm, make sure it's stored safely and that you have sufficient training to use it responsibly. Consider less-lethal options like pepper spray or a tactical flashlight that can temporarily blind an attacker.

- **Multipurpose Tools and Supplies:** Pack a quality multi-tool (e.g., Leatherman), duct tape, zip ties, and a small roll of wire. Also, include a flashlight with extra batteries, a solar charger for electronics, and a small notebook and pen for communication or leaving notes.
  - **Practical Suggestion:** A solar-powered flashlight with a hand-crank backup is a great addition to your kit, as it ensures you'll have light even if batteries run out. A small spool of fishing line and hooks can also be useful for catching food or repairing gear.

Real-Life Example: During the 2018 California wildfires, thousands of residents had to evacuate with little notice. Those who had prepared bug-out bags were able to leave quickly and had the essentials needed to survive the first few days of displacement. In contrast, those who had to gather supplies last minute faced significant challenges, including shortages of food and water, exposure to the elements, and a lack of essential medications.

Personalizing Your Bug-Out Bag for Specific Emergencies

While there are standard items that every bug-out bag should contain, it's important to tailor your bag to the specific types of emergencies you're most likely to face. This customization ensures that you're not only prepared for the generic aspects of a disaster but also for the unique challenges that come with your particular situation.

Customizing for Natural Disasters

- **Earthquakes:** If you live in an earthquake-prone area, ensure your bug-out bag includes sturdy footwear, gloves, and dust masks to protect against debris. Pack a crowbar or similar tool to help you navigate through or out of collapsed structures.
  - **Practical Suggestion:** Add a pair of safety goggles to your bag to protect your eyes from dust and debris. A headlamp with an adjustable beam can also be invaluable if you need to navigate in the dark or through rubble.

- **Hurricanes:** In hurricane zones, waterproof your supplies by sealing them in ziplock bags. Include a rain poncho and additional waterproof gear to stay dry during heavy rainfall. A small portable pump might be useful if you need to deal with minor flooding.
  - **Practical Suggestion:** Consider adding a personal flotation device (PFD) to your kit if you live in a flood-prone area. Also, pack a few chemical light sticks, which are waterproof and can provide light in wet conditions.

- **Wildfires:** For those in wildfire-prone areas, pack N95 masks to protect against smoke inhalation and goggles to shield your eyes from ash. Consider including a fireproof document bag for important papers and a headlamp with extra batteries for navigating in low-visibility conditions.
  - **Practical Suggestion:** Include a lightweight fire-resistant blanket that can be used to protect yourself from radiant heat. A small shovel can also be useful for creating a firebreak if you're caught in an advancing wildfire.

Customizing for Health Needs

- **Medical Conditions:** If you or a family member has a medical condition, your bug-out bag should include extra medication, medical supplies, and documentation of the condition, including prescriptions and a list of allergies. If someone relies on a medical device, pack spare batteries or a manual alternative if possible.

- o **Practical Suggestion:** Consider packing a small, insulated cooler with ice packs for medications that need to be kept cold. A pill organizer can help you keep track of daily medications during a chaotic situation.

- **Infants and Children:** For families with young children, pack baby formula, diapers, wipes, and a small comfort item like a toy or blanket. Include snacks that are suitable for children and additional clothing layers.
  - o **Practical Suggestion:** If you have an infant, pack a baby carrier that allows you to keep your hands free. Also, consider including a few small, quiet toys to help keep children calm and entertained.

- **Elderly:** For elderly family members, consider mobility aids like a cane or walker, hearing aids with extra batteries, and easily digestible food options. Make sure the first aid kit includes items like blood pressure monitors or glucose meters if needed.
  - o **Practical Suggestion:** Pack a lightweight, foldable chair or stool for elderly family members who may need to rest frequently. Also, ensure that their bug-out bag is not too heavy, as it should be manageable for them to carry.

Real-Life Example: During the 2011 Tōhoku earthquake and tsunami in Japan, many people were forced to evacuate with little more than the clothes on their backs. Those who had prepared bug-out bags with essential supplies tailored to their needs, such as prescription medications and emergency documents, were able to manage the immediate aftermath much more effectively than those who had to leave unprepared.

Being forced into off-grid living by an emergency is a scenario that can be both terrifying and overwhelming. With proper preparation, you can handle this change with strength and assurance. Building a comprehensive bug-out bag, tailored to the specific risks you face, is one of the most important steps you can take to ensure your survival in the critical first 72 hours of a crisis. By thinking ahead, planning for the worst, and customizing your emergency kit to meet your unique needs, you'll be ready to face whatever challenges come your way. Remember, preparedness is about more than just having supplies—it's about having the knowledge, skills, and mindset to protect yourself and your loved ones when the unexpected happens.

Rapidly Preparing Your Home for Forced Off-Grid Living

When a crisis hits and evacuation is not an option, your home becomes your fortress—a place where you must secure the essentials for survival without relying on modern utilities. While many homes are not designed to function off the grid, with the right strategies and preparations, you can quickly transform your home into a sustainable environment that supports you and your family through the emergency. This chapter will guide you through the critical steps of securing water, power, and food supplies, ensuring that you are ready to face the challenges of living off the grid.

Securing Emergency Water Supplies

Water is the foundation of life, and in a forced off-grid situation, securing a reliable and safe water supply is your top priority. Without access to municipal water systems, you must immediately establish alternative sources and methods to ensure that your household has enough water for drinking, cooking, hygiene, and sanitation.

Strategies for Securing Water

- **Emergency Water Storage:** If you have advance warning of an impending crisis, your first step should be to store as much water as possible. Fill every available container—bathtubs, sinks, pots, bottles, and large storage containers such as water bricks or 55-gallon drums. These can be critical for sustaining your household until a more permanent solution is established.
  - **Practical Suggestion:** Make use of any spare containers you have around the house, such as food-grade plastic buckets or jugs, and keep a siphon pump handy for accessing water from deeper containers like barrels. If you're filling bathtubs, consider using a bathtub water bladder, such as a WaterBOB, which can store up to 100 gallons of water in a clean, enclosed environment.

- **Rainwater Harvesting:** Rainwater harvesting is one of the most practical and sustainable methods of securing water in an off-grid situation. Even a simple system using tarps, gutters, and barrels can collect significant amounts of water during a rainstorm. Set up collection points around your home where water runoff is likely, and ensure that you have clean, food-grade containers to store the harvested water.
  - **Practical Suggestion:** If you live in an area with frequent rain, consider installing a more permanent rainwater harvesting system with gutters, downspouts, and large storage tanks. Attach a first flush diverter to your system to ensure that the initial runoff, which may contain debris, is separated from the water you store. Always have a method to filter or purify the water before drinking, such as a Berkey water filter or DIY sand filter.

- **Alternative Sources:** If there are natural water sources near your home, such as rivers, lakes, or streams, these can be invaluable during a crisis. However, water from these sources must be treated before it is safe to drink. Portable water filters, such as the LifeStraw or Sawyer Mini, can remove harmful bacteria and parasites, while boiling water can eliminate viruses. Keep purification tablets on hand as a quick solution for making water safe.
  - **Practical Suggestion:** Identify and map out nearby water sources before a crisis

occurs. Practice using your water filtration and purification methods to ensure that you know how to operate them effectively. If you live in a cold climate, remember that accessing frozen water sources may require tools like an ice auger or a sturdy shovel.

Real-Life Example: During the Flint, Michigan water crisis, residents found their municipal water supply contaminated with lead. Those who had the foresight to store water or had already installed rainwater collection systems were in a better position to handle the crisis. Others had to rely on bottled water distributed by aid organizations, highlighting the importance of being prepared to secure your own water supply in an emergency.

Emergency Power Solutions

A sudden and prolonged loss of electricity is one of the most daunting challenges in a forced off-grid situation. Without power, you may lose the ability to heat or cool your home, refrigerate food, and communicate with the outside world. Securing alternative power sources quickly is essential for maintaining a semblance of normalcy and ensuring the safety and comfort of your household.

Setting Up Emergency Power

- **Generators:** Generators are a reliable source of backup power during an emergency. If you own a generator, ensure it's well-maintained and ready to use at a moment's notice. Regularly check that it has enough fuel, and store additional fuel in a safe location away from living areas to minimize the risk of fire or carbon monoxide poisoning.
  - **Practical Suggestion:** Think about a generator that can use both gasoline and propane, allowing you to choose the fuel that works best for you. Additionally, install a transfer switch to connect your generator directly to your home's electrical panel, allowing you to power essential circuits without running extension cords through the house.

- **Solar Power:** Solar energy is a sustainable and increasingly accessible option for generating electricity off the grid. Portable solar panels and solar chargers can provide enough power to run small devices like phones, radios, and lights. For larger needs, consider investing in a home solar power system with battery storage to keep critical appliances running even when the grid is down.
  - **Practical Suggestion:** Start by investing in portable solar chargers that can power small electronics and batteries. For a more robust setup, look into solar generators with built-in inverters and battery storage. These systems can be expanded over time as you add more solar panels and batteries to increase capacity.

- **Battery Banks:** A deep-cycle battery bank can store electricity for use during power outages, ensuring that you have a reserve of power when the sun isn't shining or your generator isn't running. These batteries can be charged via solar panels, wind turbines, or a generator and can provide power to essential systems in your home.

- o **Practical Suggestion:** Opt for lithium-ion batteries, which offer higher energy density and longer life compared to traditional lead-acid batteries. Set up an inverter to convert stored DC power to AC, allowing you to run household appliances. Frequently inspect and care for your battery bank to make sure it is completely charged and prepared for use.

Real-Life Example: In the aftermath of Hurricane Maria in 2017, Puerto Rico experienced a total collapse of its power grid, leaving residents without electricity for months. Those who had prepared with solar panels and battery storage were able to maintain critical power for lights, refrigeration, and communication. This disaster underscores the importance of having reliable alternative power solutions in place before a crisis occurs.

Rapid Food Production and Storage Solutions

When forced to live off the grid, food security becomes a primary concern. With supply chains disrupted and grocery stores potentially inaccessible, you must be able to produce and store your own food. While establishing a long-term food supply takes time, there are immediate steps you can take to ensure that your family has enough to eat during the initial phase of the crisis.

Strategies for Securing Food

- **Stockpiling Non-Perishables:** As soon as you become aware of an impending crisis, start stockpiling non-perishable food items. Start by prioritizing items like canned foods, dried beans, rice, pasta, and freeze-dried meals. It's also important to have a manual can opener and essential cooking tools that work over an open flame or with a portable stove.
  - o **Practical Suggestion:** Create a pantry inventory and rotate your stock regularly to ensure that nothing expires. Store food in a cool, dry place, and consider vacuum-sealing items like grains and beans to extend their shelf life. Include comfort foods and snacks to help maintain morale during a prolonged emergency.

- **Gardening in a Crisis:** If you have some time before the crisis fully impacts your area, consider planting fast-growing vegetables such as radishes, lettuce, spinach, and herbs. These crops can be harvested within a few weeks, providing fresh produce when other food sources are scarce. Raised beds, container gardens, and vertical gardening can maximize space and yield.
  - o **Practical Suggestion:** Keep a stash of heirloom seeds that can be planted in an emergency. Focus on plants that are hardy, easy to grow, and have multiple uses (e.g., herbs that can be used for both cooking and medicine). If you don't have a garden, consider growing microgreens indoors, which can be harvested within days.

- **Foraging and Hunting:** In rural areas, gathering wild food and hunting can help increase your food resources. It's important to recognize local edible plants like dandelions, wild garlic, and various berries. Make sure to have simple hunting tools or traps ready and get some practice with them before an emergency happens.
    - o **Practical Suggestion:** Invest in a good field guide to edible wild plants specific to your region, and practice foraging regularly to build your knowledge and confidence. Keep a slingshot, bow, or small caliber rifle for hunting small game, and learn basic trapping techniques to increase your chances of success.

Real-Life Example: During the Great Depression, many American families relied on victory gardens, foraging, and hunting to supplement their diets as food prices soared and jobs disappeared. Urban and rural communities alike turned every available space into gardens, producing vegetables, fruits, and herbs to sustain themselves. This period in history underscores the importance of being able to produce and secure your own food when traditional supply chains fail.

In a forced off-grid situation, the ability to quickly and effectively prepare your home for self-sufficiency can make the difference between mere survival and maintaining a decent quality of life. By securing emergency water supplies, setting up alternative power sources, and establishing food production and storage solutions, you can ensure that your household remains safe, comfortable, and well-nourished during a crisis. The strategies outlined in this chapter are not just about survival—they are about resilience, adaptability, and the ability to thrive in even the most challenging circumstances.

Preparation is key. The time to act is now, before a crisis hits. By taking these steps today, you will be ready to face whatever challenges the future may bring, with confidence and peace of mind knowing that you have the knowledge and resources to protect your loved ones.

Psychological and Emotional Preparedness

When faced with the reality of forced off-grid living, the challenges go beyond securing food, water, and shelter. The sudden shift away from the comforts of modern life, combined with the stress of an ongoing crisis, can have a profound impact on your mental and emotional well-being. It's essential to prepare yourself mentally for these challenges just as thoroughly as you prepare your physical environment. This chapter will guide you through the strategies needed to maintain psychological resilience, manage stress, and ensure that you and your loved ones can stay mentally strong in the face of adversity.

Coping with the Shock of Sudden Change

One of the most significant challenges in a forced off-grid situation is coping with the abrupt and drastic change in your daily life. The routines and conveniences you've come to rely on are suddenly unavailable, replaced by uncertainty and the need for constant vigilance. How do you adapt to this new reality without being overwhelmed by fear and anxiety?

Strategies for Mental Resilience

Acceptance: The first step in coping with sudden change is accepting the situation as it is. This doesn't mean giving up hope, but rather recognizing that your previous way of life has been disrupted and that you must adapt to survive. Accepting reality can help you focus on what you can control and make the most of your current situation. Have you practiced mindfulness or meditation techniques that can help you stay grounded during a crisis? These practices can help you remain calm and clear-headed, allowing you to make better decisions under pressure.

Routine: In an off-grid emergency, establishing a new daily routine is crucial. Routine provides structure, which can be comforting in a chaotic environment. Setting daily goals, such as gathering water, preparing food, or maintaining your shelter, can give you a sense of purpose and help reduce anxiety. Do you have a plan for how you'll structure your days in an off-grid emergency? By creating a new routine, you can regain a sense of normalcy, even in the midst of a crisis.

Support Systems: Even in isolation, maintaining connections with others is vital for your mental health. Whether it's family, friends, or neighbors, having a support system can help you share the emotional burden of a crisis. Use any available means to stay in touch, whether it's through ham radio, satellite phones, or even handwritten notes. Have you identified ways to stay connected during a crisis? Sharing your experiences and offering mutual support can help you feel less alone and more capable of handling the challenges ahead.

During the Blitz in World War II, Londoners faced the constant threat of bombing raids. Despite the fear and destruction, many people found ways to cope through community support, routine, and resilience. They established air raid shelters, shared resources, and maintained a spirit of defiance against the enemy. This sense of community and routine was crucial in helping them endure the prolonged crisis, demonstrating the importance of mental resilience and support systems in difficult times.

Maintaining Morale and Motivation

In a prolonged off-grid situation, maintaining morale becomes increasingly important. The longer the crisis lasts, the more challenging it can be to stay motivated and focused. Without a strong sense of purpose and the ability to find joy in small things, you risk succumbing to despair or complacency. How do you keep your spirits up and ensure that you don't lose hope?

Strategies for Maintaining Morale

Focus on Small Wins: During a crisis, it can be hard not to feel swamped by everything happening around you. To help with this, try to concentrate on little successes, like getting clean water, fixing a tool, or making a good meal. These small accomplishments, even if they seem trivial, can lift your spirits and show that you are making progress. Have you thought about small goals you can achieve and celebrate to stay motivated? By noticing and valuing these small victories, you can create positive energy and keep a hopeful mindset.

Stay Informed: Knowledge is power, especially in a crisis. Staying informed about the situation can help you feel more in control and reduce anxiety. Listen to emergency broadcasts, read updates if available, and keep track of any changes in the situation. Being informed allows you to make better decisions and stay ahead of potential threats. Is there a dependable method for getting information during an off-grid emergency? A hand-crank or solar-powered radio can be extremely helpful for keeping in touch with the outside world.

Creativity and Entertainment: Finding ways to bring creativity and entertainment into your daily life can provide a much-needed mental break from the stress of survival. Whether it's drawing, writing, playing music, or reading, these activities can help you relax and recharge. Have you packed a few small items, like a book or a deck of cards, to help you pass the time and lift your spirits? Taking part in creative activities can create a feeling of normalcy and support your emotional health.

During the long Arctic expeditions of the 19th century, explorers faced months of isolation, extreme weather, and limited resources. To maintain morale, they established routines, held regular social events, and even put on plays and musical performances. These efforts to maintain a sense of normalcy and camaraderie were crucial in helping them survive in one of the harshest environments on earth. This historical example underscores the importance of maintaining morale and finding joy in small things, even in the most challenging situations.

Long-Term Survival Strategies

While the initial focus in a forced off-grid situation is on immediate survival, it's equally important to think about the long-term. If the crisis extends for weeks, months, or even longer, you'll need to shift from short-term survival strategies to sustainable living. This chapter will guide you through the process of transitioning to long-term off-grid living, ensuring that you're prepared for whatever the future holds.

Establishing Long-Term Food Security

After securing your immediate food needs, it's time to consider how you'll sustain yourself over the long term. Establishing a reliable food supply is critical for long-term survival. This may involve expanding your food production efforts, improving your food storage methods, and finding new ways to gather or hunt food.

Here there are some long-term food strategies you can adopt.

- **Gardening:** Start or expand your garden to include a wider variety of crops, focusing on those that store well or can be preserved. Perennial plants like asparagus, fruit trees, and berry bushes can provide food year after year with minimal maintenance. Have you planned for a diverse garden that can sustain you over the long term? Consider growing crops that are well-suited to your climate and that can be easily stored, such as root vegetables, beans, and grains. These crops can be dried, canned, or stored in a root cellar for use throughout the year.

- **Livestock:** If you have the resources and space, consider raising small livestock like chickens, rabbits, or goats. These animals can provide a steady supply of meat, eggs, milk, and other products, helping to diversify your diet and increase your food security. Have you considered the care and feeding requirements of livestock in an off-grid situation, and do you have the necessary supplies? Raising livestock requires a commitment of time and resources, but it can be highly rewarding and provide a reliable source of nutrition.

- **Foraging and Hunting:** Keep adding wild foods and game to your meals. Learn the seasonal patterns of local plants and animals to maximize your foraging and hunting efforts. Have you expanded your knowledge of local wildlife and edible plants to ensure a sustainable food supply? Foraging for wild berries, nuts, and greens can provide variety to your diet, while hunting or trapping small game can add valuable protein.

During World War II, the British government encouraged citizens to grow their own food through the "Dig for Victory" campaign. Many people turned their lawns, parks, and even bomb craters into vegetable gardens. This effort helped alleviate food shortages and increased self-sufficiency, demonstrating the power of community-based food production in times of crisis. The success of this campaign highlights the importance of establishing a reliable and sustainable food supply in a long-term off-grid situation.

Improving Shelter and Security

As you transition to long-term off-grid living, it's important to ensure that your shelter is both comfortable and secure. As time goes on, your needs might shift, so it's important to adjust your living space to fit those changes. This may involve making repairs, improving insulation, and enhancing your security measures to protect against potential threats.

Shelter Improvements

- **Weatherproofing:** Ensure that your shelter is well-insulated and protected from the elements. This may involve adding extra insulation, sealing gaps, and reinforcing windows and doors. Have you conducted an assessment of your shelter's vulnerabilities and made the necessary improvements? Proper insulation and weatherproofing can make a significant difference in your comfort and energy efficiency, especially in extreme weather conditions.

- **Security Enhancements:** As time goes on, the risk of crime or looting may increase, especially in a prolonged crisis. Consider reinforcing doors and windows, setting up perimeter alarms, and establishing a watch schedule if you're living in a group. Have you thought about ways to make your shelter more secure in a long-term off-grid scenario? Security measures might also include creating escape routes, installing motion-sensor lights, and building hidden storage areas for valuables and supplies.

- **Comfort and Livability:** Over time, small comforts can make a big difference in your mental and physical well-being. Consider adding features like a wood stove for heating and cooking, comfortable bedding, and a designated space for relaxation or entertainment. Have you identified ways to improve the comfort and livability of your shelter as you settle into long-term off-grid living? Creating a space for socializing, hobbies, or even just relaxing can help maintain morale and provide a sense of normalcy in an otherwise challenging environment.

In the aftermath of Hurricane Katrina, many people who returned to their homes found that they needed to make significant repairs to make their homes livable again. Those who had prepared for long-term off-grid living were better able to rebuild and secure their homes, allowing them to stay safe and comfortable even as recovery efforts continued for months. This experience demonstrates the importance of being prepared to adapt your shelter to changing conditions and ensuring that it remains a safe and comfortable place to live in the long term.

Establishing a Sustainable Community

In a long-term off-grid situation, forming or joining a community can greatly enhance your chances of survival. A community provides not only physical security but also emotional support, shared resources, and collective knowledge. But how do you establish a sustainable community in a post-crisis world?

Building a Community

- **Shared Resources:** Pooling resources like food, tools, and knowledge can create a more sustainable living environment for everyone. Establishing shared gardens, kitchens, and workshops can increase efficiency and reduce individual burdens. Have you identified others in your area who might be interested in forming a community, and have you discussed how you'll share resources? By working together, you can create a more resilient community that can withstand the challenges of long-term off-grid living.

- **Skill Sharing:** Everyone has unique skills that can benefit the community, whether it's gardening, carpentry, first aid, or cooking. Encourage skill sharing and cross-training to ensure that everyone can contribute and that critical skills are not concentrated in just one or two individuals. Have you considered how you can contribute to a community and what skills you might need to learn? Sharing skills and knowledge can also foster a sense of unity and purpose within the community.

- **Governance and Decision-Making:** Establishing a system for making decisions, resolving conflicts, and ensuring that everyone's needs are met is essential for a sustainable community. This could involve regular meetings, a council or leadership group, or a consensus-based decision-making process. Have you thought about how your community will handle leadership and governance in a long-term off-grid situation? Effective governance can help prevent disputes and ensure that the community functions smoothly and harmoniously.

The kibbutzim in Israel are an example of successful communal living, where shared resources, collective decision-making, and mutual support have allowed these communities to thrive for decades. Originally established in the early 20th century, these agricultural communes continue to be a model of sustainable, self-sufficient living in a challenging environment. The success of the kibbutzim highlights the importance of community in long-term off-grid living and demonstrates how collective effort and shared values can lead to a resilient and thriving community.

Embracing Preparedness for Unexpected Off-Grid Living

In an ideal world, the decision to live off the grid would be a carefully planned choice. However, life's unpredictability often means we may be thrust into off-grid living due to emergencies like natural disasters, economic crises, or societal disruptions. When that time comes, your survival will hinge on how well you've prepared.

This chapter has provided you with the tools and knowledge to prepare for the possibility of being forced into off-grid living with little to no warning. From building a comprehensive bug-out bag to rapidly preparing your home for self-sufficiency, the strategies discussed are designed to ensure that you and your loved ones can navigate this sudden transition with resilience and confidence.

Understanding the scenarios that could lead to forced off-grid living is the first step. Natural disasters, economic collapse, pandemics, societal breakdowns, and power grid failures can all dramatically change the way you live, often with little warning. By assessing your vulnerability to these threats and taking proactive measures now, you'll be better equipped to handle whatever comes your way.

In the event of a sudden crisis, your ability to quickly secure essentials—water, food, shelter, and power—will be crucial. Establishing a bug-out bag tailored to your specific needs and the potential emergencies you might face ensures that you're prepared for the first critical days of a crisis. Rapidly converting your home into a sustainable, off-grid living environment will help you maintain a decent quality of life even when modern conveniences are stripped away.

Long-term survival requires a shift in focus from immediate needs to sustainable living. This means improving your shelter, establishing food security, and perhaps most importantly, building a community. A supportive community can provide shared resources, skills, and emotional support, making it easier to thrive in a prolonged off-grid situation.

Being mentally and emotionally ready is just as crucial as being physically fit. Coping with the shock of sudden change, maintaining morale, and adapting to a new routine are essential for long-term resilience. Remember, survival isn't just about getting through the day—it's about finding ways to live a fulfilling life despite the challenges.

Forced off-grid living may not be something you can predict, but with the right preparation, it's something you can face with confidence. The key is to start preparing now. By taking the steps outlined in this chapter—and throughout this book—you'll be ready to protect and provide for yourself and your loved ones, no matter what the future holds. In doing so, you're not just preparing to survive; you're preparing to thrive in any situation life throws your way.

Embracing Your Off-Grid Journey and Preparing for the Unexpected

As we conclude this book, it's important to pause and reflect on the unique journey you've embarked upon. While many people actively choose to transition to an off-grid lifestyle, for others, this path may be thrust upon them due to unforeseen circumstances like natural disasters, economic collapse, or societal disruptions. Whether by choice or necessity, off-grid living requires more than just practical skills—it demands resilience, adaptability, and a commitment to self-sufficiency.

This book has provided you with the foundational knowledge to survive, thrive, and grow in an off-grid environment, regardless of how you arrived at this point. Let's revisit some of the key lessons that have shaped your journey and explore how you can continue expanding your skills with the bonus materials included in this book.

Reflecting on Your Journey: Key Lessons and Projects

Throughout this book, you've learned how to master various aspects of off-grid living. Each chapter has provided you with practical skills, valuable insights, and hands-on projects that are essential to building a successful, self-reliant life off the grid. Here's a comprehensive recap of your journey:

1. Setting Up an Off-Grid Base Camp: Shelter, Heating, and Hygiene

- **Off-Grid Shelter and Heating:** You've explored how to establish a reliable shelter suited to various climates. From insulating your home to building wood-fired heating systems, you've gained essential knowledge to maintain a safe and warm living environment in any condition.
- **Maintaining Hygiene:** In the absence of modern plumbing, maintaining hygiene becomes critical. You've built composting toilets, created greywater systems, and learned how to manage sanitation without conventional infrastructure — all while minimizing environmental impact.

2. Water Collection, Purification, and Storage

- **Water Solutions**: Water is the most critical resource in off-grid living. From rainwater harvesting to solar distillation, you've learned how to collect, purify, and store water safely. These methods ensure that your household will always have access to clean, drinkable water, even when cut off from traditional supply systems.

3. Food Production, Preservation, and Consumption

- **Off-Grid Food Production and Preservation:** Growing your own food is one of the cornerstones of self-reliance. You've developed skills in sustainable gardening, raising livestock, and even foraging. Alongside that, you've learned how to preserve your harvest through canning, drying, and fermenting—ensuring a year-round supply of nutritious food.
- **Cooking Off the Grid:** Cooking without the convenience of modern appliances requires creativity. You've learned various off-grid cooking methods such as wood-fired stoves, solar ovens, and rocket stoves, all designed to keep you well-fed in any situation.

4. Off-Grid Power Solutions, Security, and Communication

- **Harnessing Energy:** Power is often one of the most challenging aspects of off-grid living. You've mastered the fundamentals of setting up solar panels, calculating energy needs, and using battery storage to create a sustainable energy system. You also explored wind turbines and other alternative energy sources, giving you flexibility in your power options.
- **Security and Communication:** Staying safe and connected in a remote environment is crucial. You've learned how to secure your property through perimeter defenses, self-defense strategies, and by maintaining communication channels through low-tech solutions like radios and high-tech options like satellite communication systems.

5. Survival Skills for Off-Grid Living

- **Critical Survival Skills:** From building shelters in the wilderness to starting fires without matches, you've honed essential survival techniques that will keep you safe in any environment. These skills extend beyond off-grid homesteading and are critical in survival situations when immediate help is unavailable.

6. Forced Off-Grid Living – Preparing for the Unexpected

- **Adapting to Sudden Off-Grid Scenarios:** This journey hasn't just been about voluntary off-grid living. You've also explored the realities of being forced off the grid due to disasters or societal collapse. You learned how to rapidly transition to off-grid living in emergencies, secure your water and food supplies, generate power, and protect your loved ones when the unexpected happens.

Expanding Your Knowledge: Go Further with the Bonus Materials

This book has given you the tools to begin your off-grid lifestyle, but the journey doesn't end here. Included with this book are bonus resources designed to help you expand your knowledge and deepen your skills even further. By utilizing these additional materials, you can continue to refine your skills, experiment with new techniques, and push the boundaries of what's possible in off-grid living.

<u>Discover your bonuses in the next Chapter!</u>

Continuing the Journey: Learning, Adapting, and Thriving

Off-grid living is not a static goal—it's a dynamic and ongoing adventure. Whether you came to this lifestyle by choice or were forced into it by circumstances, the skills you've learned here will serve you for life. However, living off the grid requires continuous learning and adaptation.

- **Stay Curious and Open to Innovation:** Off-grid technologies and methods are constantly evolving. Stay informed about the latest innovations in sustainable living, and don't hesitate to integrate new techniques into your life. Whether it's experimenting with new gardening methods or upgrading your solar power system, always be ready to adapt and evolve.
- **Review Your Progress and Set New Goals:** Reflect on your journey and consider the progress you have made. What skills have you mastered? What challenges remain? Setting new goals for your off-grid life—whether it's achieving complete energy independence or expanding your food production—will keep you motivated and moving forward.
- **Embrace Resilience and Self-Reliance:** Off-grid living is as much about mindset as it is about practical skills. The ability to stay resilient in the face of challenges and adapt when things don't go according to plan is essential to long-term success.

The Off-Grid Life: An Ongoing Adventure

Living off the grid is not a destination—it's a continuous journey filled with challenges, growth, and endless possibilities. Every day brings new opportunities to learn, adapt, and become more self-sufficient. The skills you've developed through this book, combined with the bonus materials, provide a solid foundation to continue building a life of independence, freedom, and sustainability.

Remember, the off-grid lifestyle is not just about survival—it's about thriving. It's about living in harmony with nature, reducing your environmental impact, and embracing the freedom that comes from self-reliance.

As you move forward, keep exploring, keep building, and most importantly, keep growing. This journey is yours to shape, and with every new step, you get closer to mastering the art of off-grid living. Embrace the challenges, celebrate the successes, and continue to push the boundaries of what's possible.

Your adventure is just beginning — embrace it fully.

Talon

Bonus Section: Take Your Off-Grid Journey Even Further

These exclusive bonuses are crafted to complement the concepts you've learned throughout the book, providing you with practical tools to expand your self-sufficiency and resilience. Whether you're fine-tuning your emergency preparedness, optimizing your gardening techniques, or ensuring your home is sustainably built, these resources are here to guide you every step of the way.

Share Your Opinion

Before continuing, if you've found this book helpful on your journey to off-grid living, I would greatly appreciate it if you could **take a moment to share your thoughts**.

Your feedback is invaluable and helps others who are exploring self-reliance to find the guidance they need. By leaving a review you're not only supporting this work but also contributing to a community of individuals seeking greater independence and resilience. Your opinion truly makes a difference.
Thank you!

Access your Bonus Page

To access these invaluable resources, simply scan the QR-Code to visit the link provided below. You will be redirected to a dedicated landing page where you can download all the bonuses at your convenience.

GET YOUR BONUSES!

SCAN ME

These bonuses are more than just add-ons; they are integral components designed to complement the content of this book, helping you to continue your journey toward complete self-reliance.

Here's What You Can Expect:

1. **Book 1: Food Security and Self-Sufficiency**: This bonus book dives deep into strategies for ensuring year-round food security and self-sufficiency. From innovative growing techniques to sustainable ecosystem design, this resource will empower you to establish a resilient food system that stands the test of time. You'll gain insights into how to secure your food supply, regardless of the challenges you face, ensuring that you and your loved ones are always well-fed.

2. **Book 2: Expert Gardening Techniques for Off-Grid Living**: Go beyond the basics with this comprehensive guide to advanced off-grid gardening. Learn how to regenerate and maintain soil health, explore companion planting and crop rotation, and master the art of seed saving. This book is your key to creating a productive, resilient garden that can sustain you and your family year-round.

3. **Book 3: Off-Grid Health and Wellness** This guide covers everything you need to know about maintaining health and wellness in an off-grid environment. From herbal medicine to mental and emotional well-being, this book equips you with the knowledge to care for your body and mind using the resources available in your environment. It's an essential resource for anyone looking to live well naturally, even without modern conveniences.

4. **Book 4: Sustainable Building Techniques**: Learn how to construct eco-friendly, resilient homes using sustainable building techniques. This book explores methods like earthbag construction, straw bale homes, and cob and adobe building, providing you with the tools to create structures that are both environmentally friendly and durable. Whether you're building a retreat in nature or simply want to reduce your environmental impact, this book is your guide to sustainable living.

5. **Book 5: Urban Off-Grid Living**: Achieving off-grid living in an urban setting is not only possible but also highly rewarding. This guide offers practical techniques for maximizing small spaces, implementing alternative energy systems, and reducing your reliance on public utilities—all within the confines of a bustling city. Whether you're in a high-rise or a suburban neighborhood, this book will help you navigate the complexities of urban life while embracing off-grid principles.

6. **Emergency Preparedness Plans**: These templates are designed to ensure you're ready for any situation. With a family or community emergency plan and a disaster scenario checklist, you'll have the tools you need to organize, prepare, and protect your loved ones during unexpected events. These plans will help you navigate crises with confidence, ensuring that you're never caught off guard.

7. **Skill Evaluations - Comprehensive Assessment for Off-Grid Living:** To thrive in an off-grid lifestyle, it's essential to possess a diverse set of skills. These evaluations will test your knowledge and abilities across various critical areas, such as survival techniques, basic chemistry, electrical work, and food preservation. By identifying your strengths and areas for

improvement, these assessments will help you gauge your readiness and plan your next steps on the path to self-sufficiency.

8. **Seasonal Planting and Harvesting Calendars:** These detailed guides are practical tools designed to maximize the productivity of your garden. Tailored to various regions, these calendars provide insights into the best planting and harvesting times, along with companion planting schedules. Understanding your specific climate zone and the relationships between plants will allow you to create a thriving, sustainable garden that provides fresh produce throughout the year.

9. **Stay Connected:** By accessing the bonus page, you'll ensure that you stay updated with future projects, new resource and valuable updates — **free and forever**! Discover how on the bonus page.

So, take the next step — explore your bonuses, apply what you've learned, and continue to build a life of true freedom and resilience. The world of off-grid living is vast, and with these resources in hand, you're well on your way to mastering it.

Appendix – List of Projects

Project Name	Costs Estimation	Difficulty Rate	Page Number
DIY Project 1: Portable Shelter Construction	$$	★★	12
DIY Project 2: Natural Insulation Solutions	$$	★★	17
DIY Project 3: Building Your Rocket Mass Heater	$$	★★★	21
DIY Project 4: Rainwater Harvesting System	$$	★★★	28
DIY Project 5: Building a DIY Water Filtration System	$	★	34
DIY Project 6: Solar Water Disinfection (SODIS)	$	★	36
DIY Project 7 - Distillation: Removing Contaminants and Pathogens	$$	★★★	38
DIY Project 8: Hand-Dug Well	$$$$	★★★★★	41
DIY Project 9: Building a Greywater Recycling System	$$	★★★	45
DIY Project 10: Raised Bed Garden Construction	$$	★★	52
DIY Project 11: Build a Chicken Coop	$$	★★★	55
DIY Project 12: Solar Dehydrator	$$	★★	62
DIY Project 13: Zeer Pot Refrigerator	$	★	68

DIY Project 14: Solar Oven Construction	$	★★	78
DIY Project 15: Tin Can Rocket Stove	$	★★	83
DIY Project 16: Gallon Drum Smoker Construction	$	★★★	85
DIY Project 17: Build a Composting Toilet	$$	★★	95
DIY Project 18: Build a DIY Compost BinDIY Project 21: Making Homemade Soap	$	★	98
DIY Project 19: Turn Metal Cans into a Herb Planter	$	★	100
DIY Project 20: Make a Mini Tool Organizer	$	★	101
DIY Project 21: Making Homemade Soap	$	★	104
DIY Project 22: Making Homemade Toothpaste	$	★	108
DIY Project 23: Natural Deodorants	$	★	110
DIY Project 24: Creating Homemade Wet Wipes	$	★	111
DIY Project 25: No-Water Shaving Cream	$	★	113
DIY Project 26: Building a Hand-Powered Washing Machine	$	★★	114
DIY Project 27: Building a DIY Clothes Wringer	$$	★★★	115
DIY Project 28: Outdoor Shower	$$	★★★	117

Construction			
DIY Project 29: Make Your Own Natural Cleaning Products	$	★	121
DIY Project 30: Build Your Own Solar Power Generator	$$$$	★★★★	126
DIY Project 31: DIY Wind Turbine	$$$	★★★	129
DIY Project 32: Battery Bank Setup	$$$	★★★	131
DIY Project 33: Perimeter Security System	$$$	★★★	134
DIY Project 34: Safe Gun Storage	$$$	★★★	137
DIY Project 35: Panic Room Construction	$$$$$	★★★★★	139
DIY Project 36: Building a DIY Signal Booster	$$	★★★	148
DIY Project 37: Homemade Compass	$	★	165

About the Author

Talon Waverly is a seasoned expert in off-grid living, survival skills and holistic health, with a passion for helping others achieve self-reliance and resilience in an ever-changing world. With a diverse background that spans military service, wilderness survival training and a deep commitment to sustainable living, Talon brings a wealth of knowledge to his writing.

Having spent years honing his skills in some of the world's most challenging environments, Talon has a unique perspective on what it takes to thrive independently, whether in the wilderness or an urban setting.

In addition to his expertise in off-grid living, Talon is also deeply invested in fitness and wellness. He believes that true self-reliance extends beyond survival skills to include physical health, mental resilience and a deep connection with nature.

When he's not writing, Talon spends his time exploring the great outdoors, testing new survival techniques, and staying fit through a variety of outdoor activities. His personal journey of self-reliance continues to inspire his work, making his books a trusted resource for anyone looking to live a life of true independence and resilience.

Made in the USA
Columbia, SC
16 December 2024

49455752R00115